TOM SPRING

Bare-knuckle Champion
of All England

TOM SPRING

Bare-knuckle Champion
of All England

JON HURLEY

First published 2002
This edition first published 2007

STADIA is an imprint of
Tempus Publishing Limited
The Mill, Brimscombe Port,
Stroud, Gloucestershire, GL5 2QG
www.tempus-publishing.com

© Jon Hurley, 2002, 2007

British Library Cataloguing in Publication Data.
A catalogue record for this book is available from the British Library.

ISBN 978 07524 2940 3

Typesetting and origination by Tempus Publishing Limited
Printed and bound in Great Britain

Contents

They don't look at fighters to have brains. They don't look at fighters to be businessmen, or humans, or intelligent. Fighters are just brutes. You have to be a little crazy to be a fighter.

Muhammad Ali,
World Heavyweight Champion

'A FATAL OCCURRENCE AT EPSOM DOWNS'

After the races, on Friday, a boxing match took place, and such was the eagerness to witness it, that horsemen and pedestrians rapidly flocked to the scene, but in such confusion, that many persons were knocked down and trampled on by the horses; one lady had her jaw broken by a horse treading on her, a countryman received a severe fracture of his arm, and a boy was so dreadfully injured that his life is despaired of. A coachman residing near Kew Bridge was so dreadfully kicked by a horse, that he was 'completely stove in'. He was conveyed instantly to the Magpie, in Epsom, where he died in about an hour after. A groom residing at Banstead was thrown from his horse, in consequence of a cart running foul of him; the shaft of the cart entered the horse's chest, and the animal died almost instantly; the rider had his skull fractured, and now lies without hope of recovery.

Hereford Journal, 16 June 1824

The Church on the Side of the Hill

A few days before the 'Fatal Occurrence', Tom Spring had successfully defended his title against Jack Langan, the Irish Champion. Spring was now the undisputed bare-knuckle champion of Britain and, since Britain dominated bare-knuckle fighting, could lay claim to being the first bare-knuckle champion of the world.

★★★★★★★★

Tom Spring was born Thomas Winter on 22 February 1795 at Witchend, in the village of Fownhope in Herefordshire. The countryside was lying under swirling water at the time, as the banks of the Wye had overflowed, with the river running twenty feet higher than usual. The Winters were hard-working butchers, neither particularly rich nor living on the breadline, and Tom was the youngest of five children: three boys and two girls.

Young Tom's relations and connections in the neighbourhood were respectable; indeed, his mother was better connected than his father, Joseph. On 13 February 1778, she inherited a 'Tenement at Witchend with the garden and Orchard adjoining thereto' from her father John Davies, who had been a victualler in Fownhope. Tom's father, on the other hand, was rather feckless and always short of money. After receiving small amounts from various local charities – as is shown in records such as '1819 Whitsunday: 1/6 to Joseph Winter from the Anna Lechmere benefaction', Joseph eventually mortgaged the house and lost it.

In the early nineteenth century Fownhope ('The church on the side of the hill') was a thriving hamlet with a population of 789 (curiously, this number included anyone living on a boat moored on an inland waterway in the area). The fields around the village were planted with cider apple trees and were romantically named: Slipper's Thorn, Ragged Cot, Sweet Apple Tree, Strip under Wood, Little Boar Meadow, Rainbow Acre, Locken Stock, Upper Warlocks, Thistle Croft and Cuckoo Pen.

A fifth of Fownhope's male population at this time were uneducated farm labourers who lived in places with musical names like Bagpiper's Tump and Fiddler's Green. This was a time when a whole family would work in a muddy field for a combined salary of thirteen shillings a week. It was also a time of immense brutality, when life was short and cheap, and when even women might engage in the odd bare-knuckle fight to earn an extra few pounds, often cheered on by their husbands.

On Sundays in Fownhope, everyone would turn up for church clutching Bibles and wearing their best clothes. The better off joined their smooth hands in prayer, thanking the Lord for their good fortune. The Winters, several of whom were churchwardens, would fervently thumb their Bibles on the hard benches behind the comfortable box pews which were reserved for the gentry. Now, in the quiet graveyard, Tom's relatives lie peacefully under heavy bramble and ivy-wrapped monuments, their names etched on crumbling plaques which cling like limpets to the sunny south side of the church. Outside the church gate are the remains of the village stocks. The last man to be publicly humiliated there was a Winter, who sat there from dawn until dusk, his head, hands and feet secured. It could have been worse – in nearby Ross-on-Wye, women were still flogged and a fellow called Gammond was the last man in England to be hanged for rape.

The Winters lived by the ferry crossing, a few hundred yards down the road from the Green Man public house. Established in 1485, during the reign of Henry VII, this old black-and-white pub still provides sustenance and succour. In Tom Winter's time, it was the theatre, the opera house and the library; there, visitors could enjoy penny readings, philosophical and religious discourses, concerts by strolling players and even handbell ringing. Coaches hauled by sweating, wall-eyed horses

Fownhope. A wood engraving by Mary C Soulsby.

halted outside the inn on their way to Wales. Occasionally, a van with barred windows would pull up. Miscreants in halters were led into the tavern to be tried by a magistrate, who had no doubt already enjoyed a good lunch.

Occasionally, the hard-pressed women of Fownhope, who largely had to make do with whatever life had to offer them, were allowed out with their children to joyously kick their legs in the air at the open-air dances behind the pub, while local fiddlers sawed energetically and tapped their hobnailed boots. The men would make their way to the Green Man after a long day's work in King Connop's limekilns. Their faces yellowed by the glow of the fire, they smoked, swore and sluiced the dust from their throats with good locally-brewed ale and freshly-pressed cider. Noisily they caroused, their songs raucously invading the dark lanes until Miss Connop, the lime king's daughter, pinched the candles and ushered them out into the muddy street.

* * * * * * * *

Fownhope was a contented and fairly self-sufficient place. Craftsmen created rustic masterpieces from iron and wood while the unskilled herded pigs on unfenced common or earned a living sharpening saws. The postman would walk to Hereford and back. Only the gentry actually walked for pleasure, ambling along woodland paths identifying moths and birdsong, usually led by some wildflower-fancying vicar. Outside the blacksmith's forge, dray horses waited sleepy in their halters. Behind his curved window, the saddler worked with needle and hemp, beeswax and leather. Shops sold bacon, broom handles, bootlaces and brown Spanish wine.

Animals feathered and furred festered in the sun outside the butcher's. The tannery's fumes mingled with the fragrance of baking bread and the whiff of malt from Mr Purchas' brewery. A woman in a bib sequinned with fish scales sat on a wall selling slices of the salmon which her husband had netted while the mist was still on the river. Girls spread washed sheets along laundry walls. Lads mended holes in the road. Fownhope in Tom Winter's day was poor – there were plenty of rows over money – but life was colourful as well as hard.

The *Hereford Journal* was read in half-literate households in the village. Buried in its flyblown print were patriotic stories from the Empire, reports of accidents involving children and deep wells, and drunken draymen rolling under the wheels of their carts clutching their crushed heads. Advertisements expounded on Welch's Female Pills, Dr Bateman's Pectoral Drops and Pike's ointment for cutaneous eruptions. Sport concerned horses and hounds. Occasionally, however, a report of a bare-knuckle fight would creep in, and there were a few seasoned fighters in the area – men like Welsh, who later killed himself swallowing half a pint of gin for a bet, Thomas Smith, George Henley and John 'the Hammer' Hollands. These were experienced men who had fought in alehouses, fairs and boxing booths for several years. Tom's eventual meeting with Hollands would have a profound effect on his future.

Young Thomas Winter trotted to school twice a week at the Old Malt House and gazed idly at boys playing on Whiterdine Meadow and at the calm Wye beyond, glimpsing barges pushing water like broken glass before them on their way to Ross or Hereford. Tom's schooling was paid for by the Reverend Richard Gwatkin. He had died in 1789, and had left provision to fund a schoolmaster, who would teach reading, writing and arithmetic for a stipend of £3 19s. Young Winter was soon numerate and he could write as well as most doctors.

2

Boxing in his Blood

Both Tom Winter's father and his grandfather – the latter another Joseph, married to another 'unknown' Mary – were devotees of the art of boxing, so it wasn't long before young Tom was pounding the bag of sand his father hung from the bough at the back of the cottage. A beanpole of a boy, Tom was light on his feet and learned to move sweetly to avoid his father's heavy blows. He was an attractive lad, upright, elegant and polite with good manners and respect for his elders. One day when his parents were away, the recruiting sergeant travelled up from Hereford looking for drummer boys for Wellington's war against Napoleon. He was wearing a uniform with shiny buttons, which must have looked exotic in Fownhope. He teased young Tom with tales of adventures and wages. All Tom would have to do was to keep time and his nose clean. Tom signed up, but his father returned to beat up the recruiting officer and redden Tom's ear.

With a father like that, pugilism was always going to be an option. Bare-knuckle fighting was exciting and well paid. It was said that its popularity 'extended from labourer to lord, and in many instances both social extremes were to be found at the same match.' According to Pierce Egan, the great sporting author, boxing 'engendered a noble spirit into the Mind of Man, encouraged him to act nobly on all occasions, to curb the passions – and put a stop to the assassin-like conduct of introducing the knife.'

★ ★ ★ ★ ★ ★ ★

RULES

TO BE OBSERVED IN ALL BATTLES ON THE STAGE

I. THAT a fquare of a Yard be chalked in the middle of the Stage; and on every frefh fet-to after a fall, or being parted from the rails, each Second is to bring his Man to the fide of the fquare, and place him oppofite to the other, and till they are fairly fet-to at the Lines, it fhall not be lawful for one to ftrike at the other.

II. That, in order to prevent any Difputes, the time a Man lies after a fall, if the Second does not bring his Man to the fide of the fquare, within the fpace of half a minute, he fhall be deemed a beaten Man.

III. That in every main Battle, no perfon whatever fhall be upon the Stage, except the Principals and their Seconds; the fame rule to be obferved in bye-battles, except that in the latter, Mr. Broughton is allowed to be upon the Stage to keep decorum, and to affift Gentlemen in getting to their places, provided always he does not interfere in the Battle; and whoever pretends to infringe thefe Rules to be turned immediately out of the houfe. Every body is to quit the Stage as foon as the Champions are ftripped, before the fet-to.

IV. That no Champion be deemed beaten, unlefs he fails coming up to the line in the limited time, or that his own Second declares him beaten. No Second is to be allowed to afk his man's Adverfary any queftions, or advife him to give out.

V. That in bye-battles, the winning man to have two-thirds of the Money given, which fhall be publicly divided upon the Stage, notwithftanding any private agreements to the contrary.

VI. That to prevent Difputes, in every main Battle the Principals fhall, on coming on the Stage, choofe from among the gentlemen prefent two Umpires, who fhall abfolutely decide all Difputes that may arife about the Battle; and if the two Umpires cannot agree, the faid Umpires to choofe a third, who is to determine it.

VII. That no perfon is to hit his Adverfary when he is down, or feize him by the ham, the breeches, or any part below the waift: a man on his knees to be reckoned down.

As agreed by feveral Gentlemen at Broughton's Amphitheatre,

Broughton's Rules.

Jack Broughton wrote the first rules of boxing in 1743 and used a character called Buckhorse to promote his boxing theatre. It was said that Buckhorse's 'ruling passions were love and boxing, in both of which he was equally formidable and neither nymph nor bruiser could withstand the violence of his attack, for it was generally allowed he conquered both by the strength of his members, and the rigour of his parts.' Broughton lived to be eighty-five and was buried in Westminster Abbey.

Cross Buttock and Suit in Chancery.

Joseph Winter taught his son well. Tom gradually became a clever boxer who had a classic stance – left hand extended, chin protected, left foot forward, perfectly balanced and weight evenly distributed. Add a cool head, a big heart and amazing recuperative powers and the young Marcher boy had the makings of a formidable fighter. Tom was not a big hitter, but he was economical. He jabbed and hooked, using his long reach to pepper his opponent and his nimble feet to dance or slide away from the counter. He was patient, measured and brave, and was certainly an unusual talent at a time when fighters spilt their blood for spectators who demanded violence, noise and spectacle in the same way as the Romans had centuries earlier.

Young Winter soon mastered Mendoza's first principle, the ability to 'change from a right- to a left-handed position, to advance or retreat, striking or parrying, and to throw the body either backward or forward, without difficulty or embarrassment'. He practised the 'Suit in Chancery' and the 'Cross Buttock', for bare-knuckle prizefighting was as much wrestling as boxing. To execute the Suit in Chancery 'the fighter grabbed his opponent in a headlock, held him till his eyes bulged then rapped him with the free hand until he was senseless'. Vincent Dowling, editor of *Fistiana*, a key work of the time, describes the Cross Buttock as follows:

> You get your arm firmly over your adversary's neck, grasping his loose arm with the other hand – then shifting yourself to his front, get his crutch upon your hip or buttock, and give him a cant over your shoulder. If well done his heels will go up in the air, he goes over with tremendous violence, you fall on his abdomen. The chances are that he is either insensible or so shaken by the fall that he loses all power of resisting your future attacks.

While still a teenager, Tom developed a sound defence and he could hook, duck and weave like the mercurial Jem Belcher, the great Bristol fighter. Unfortunately, he also shared a flaw with the brilliant West Country middleweight – weak hands. Like Belcher, Winter's hands would be the bane of his professional career.

3

The Duke and the Butcher's Boy

Tom Winter followed his father into the butchering business, becoming a delivery boy. He loaded the gig and drove to outlying houses to deliver meat, game and eggs, pursued by a halo of flies. Tom was kept fit running up and down the sloping fields and dodging through orchards with his butcher's basket on his arm. His routine took him to the beautiful Jacobean mansion at Fownhope Court, as well as Capler Farm, with its ancient cruck-trussed beams, Nash Farm, which still stands on a hill above the village, and across the river by ferry to Holme Lacy. This great house, owned by the 11th Duke of Norfolk, a wealthy aristocrat famous for his love of good food, sat on a knoll above the Wye. It was the largest house in Herefordshire.

Hom Lacy, as it was known in the nineteenth century, was situated only a mile or two from Fownhope, but the only way the modest and hard-working Winters could hope to gain admission was via an open window or through the tradesmen's entrance. Standing four-square, its elephant-grey walls blotched with ivy still stand. From its highest point it was possible to see the Black Mountains in Wales, Clee Hill in Shropshire, and the Malvern Hills in Worcestershire. The Scudamores held the property for five centuries and John, 1st Viscount Scudamore bred the famous Red Streak cider apple there. Another Scudamore was immortalised in Spenser's *Faerie Queene.*

The Duke was 'fond of collecting the most heterogeneous assemblies of guests to partake of his sumptuous venison and turtle feasts.'

Holme Lacy House.

Holme Lacy was indeed a honey pot. Guests trailed in from London and elsewhere, a continuous gaggle of sycophantic rhymesters and wordsmiths who included the poets John Gay and Alexander Pope. The latter, arriving after 'walking along the gravel terraces and amongst the magnificent majestic yews, absorbing the splendour of the setting and the natural picturesque qualities of the Wye Valley', scribbled an ode to John Kyrle, transforming an anonymous, long-dead bachelor into the enduring legend, 'The Man of Ross'.

★ ★ ★ ★ ★ ★ ★ ★

To keep his guests amused, the Duke would encourage the playing of sports and sparring matches in the grounds. It was said that on a fine sunny day, when the lawns were crowded with distinguished visitors, the scene resembled a painting by the French artist Jean Antoine Watteau. His Grace, an avuncular figure with humorous eyes, a whisky-tinted nose and a penchant for decorative apparel, seldom visited his Herefordshire estate. When he did, it amused him to take two of the prettiest maids and button them 'close packed and smiling' into one of his capacious waistcoats. The Duke's pealing laughter, it was said, 'echoed along the corridors'. One night while 'over fatigued' after a riotous dinner the Duke stumbled into the fountain on the eastern side of the house and was nearly drowned. Next morning, the Duke had the offending fountain filled in.

On hearing of young Winter's enthusiasm for boxing his Grace invited him to join the troupe of boxers who entertained his guests by sparring on the front lawns. The Duke's interest was not unusual for men of his class. Boxing in the eighteenth and nineteenth centuries was the horse racing of today, supported by everyone from pearly kings to Arab princes. As the Duke waddled off with a wave of his stick, one can imagine young Tom galloping down the drive and hollering for the ferryman to take him back to tell his father. Joseph Winter would have heard gossip about the goings on behind the high hedges at Holme Lacy. Here was a wonderful opportunity for young Tom to enter the secret world of bare-knuckle fighting, to compete with the best boxers around, and earn a little money at the same time.

In the run-up to his boxing debut, young Tom kept busy in the butcher's, plucking fowl, boning joints, making pies and building up muscle carrying carcasses from the abattoir. As a boxing butcher he was in good company. Jem Belcher, John Gully, Bill Neat, Peter 'Young Rumpsteak' Crawley, Sam Davis, Sam Martin, Josh Hudson, Cy Davis, George Nicholls, and Jack Payne all worked in the meat trade.

Joseph would have made his own body rubs from the herbs that grew in hedge, pasture or bog, blending a paste from comfrey, ground madder roots, feverfew and oil of mint and briskly rubbing the pungent concoction into his son's body. Breeches would have been made for his debut, stockings gartered with spotted blue ribbons, light, spiked pigskin shoes from the Fownhope cobbler.

Father and son would have heard the buzz of voices as they crossed the river to Holme Lacy. Standing empty, the newly erected ring awaited the gladiators. The Duke's private guests would have assembled, some fashionably 'effecting to look like ruffians' in their 'slouched hats, jockey boots, leather breeches, and unpowdered hair'. Some were blue-blooded, others 'bucks without blood', while alongside them would be a sprinkling of local farmers intent on seizing the rare opportunity to hobnob with the great and the good. With their hats tilted, their fobs Silvo'd and their kerchiefs neatly tied they unashamedly 'aped the dress of people of rank'.

Boxers from Wales and Gloucestershire, Worcester and Staffordshire toed the white line, touched knuckles and bobbed around as if they had thorns in their bare feet. To the swish of feet on grass and the echo of fist on bone, poor, half-naked men landed punches on each other, their craniums colliding and their noses leaking blood as they milled away with both hands. Their fight over, the boxers cautiously helped each other from the ring as if they had become suddenly old, and trudged back to the stables with bloodstained towels around their necks. Oozing sweat and liniment, they ate their fill of the victuals laid on by the Duke. Such a meal was a godsend to a poor man. After the tables were cleared, more young men entered the ring, grimaced, wagged their heads from side to side and stamped their feet like impatient cobs. There is no telling who Tom actually boxed against that day. His opponent may have been a bear of a man with a stubbled chin and tangled black hair from his navel to his neck, or a lightweight with a choirboy's consumptive pallor. The sparring was generally a rough and tumble: lusty thumping and not a lot of skill.

When he saw young Winter box for the first time, the Duke was ecstatic. He 'hobbled across the lawn as fast as his age and gout would permit and swore there never was a Greek demigod to compare with young Tom Winter.' Outside the ring Tom was modest and unassuming. Inside the roped square he was tough and resilient but always a good sportsman. He quickly became the main attraction, fought all-comers and was never beaten.

The soft emerald lawns overlooked verdant meadows dotted with old hardwoods. 'Few trees,' according to a contemporary account, 'came close in straightness and height to the great oaks of Holme Lacy. It would be a brave rook that would fly o'er the top of them.' One evening, the boxing over, Tom Winter was carrying his kit back to the ferryboat when, according to legend, he was hailed by the Duke who was 'beginning to grow feeble and sat in his easy-chair on the lawn.' Laying his hand on the young boxer's arm, his Grace nodded towards the noble oaks. 'Winter,' he said, 'I would sacrifice a few of those sticks to possess such limbs as yours, and be able to do what you can do.'

4

Cribb Visits Mordiford

Winter continued to gain in weight, height, strength and experience and was now an accomplished fighter. He was developing all the time, but lost his mentor and trainer when his father was sent to prison for non-payment of a debt. A public notice in the *Hereford Journal* read:

> I, Joseph Winter, late of the parish of Fownhope, butcher, now con-
> fined in prison for the county of Hereford, and not being charged
> in custody on the first day of May, 1811, with any debt or debts, sum
> or sums of money exceeding in the whole the sum of 40 pounds,
> do hereby give this public notice, that I intend to take the benefit of
> an act passed for the relief of certain insolvent debtors in England,
> and I hereby give notice that a true and perfect schedule, contain-
> ing discovery of all my real and personal estate, is now ready to be
> given to any creditor applying for same, to the keeper or gaoler,
> or the deputy of the said prison, witness my hand the tenth day of
> September 1811.
>
> Joseph Winter, *witness*, John Preece, *gaoler*.

Joseph wriggled and lied and robbed Peter to pay Paul the way all conmen do and was eventually allowed out of prison, but his calm and brilliant son had lost faith in him. Young Tom butchered on until his next break in 1814 when a local promoter somehow persuaded Tom Cribb, the legendary Bare-knuckle Champion of All England, to stop off at Mordiford while on a nationwide sparring tour. This man was more

Mordiford.

famous than Wellington. It was akin to Don King convincing Mike Tyson he should box for nothing at the Fownhope Women's Institute at ten in the morning after a cup of Earl Grey and an arrowroot biscuit.

Mordiford was an unlikely place for a man such as Cribb to visit. Maybe the old champion liked scenery. Certainly, it is a delightful spot, sitting prettily astride the swirling meeting of the majestic Wye and the smaller Lugg, which the poet Drayton termed as 'the more lovelie' of the two. Close to the spot where Cribb performed, the visitor has to cross 'a massive stone bridge which adds greatly to the picturesque scenery of this parish'. Maybe the old champion had already heard from the London swells about the tall young lad from Fownhope. His career over, perhaps he was looking for a boxer to manage. There were plenty of pretenders eager to swap their stunted lives for the glamour, fame and money which they imagined would be their lot in bare-knuckle fighting, the cruellest of sports if they only knew it.

* * * * * * * *

Both sides of the Lugg were crowded when Cribb and his entourage arrived. Spectators lined the ancient bridge like starlings to see the gnarled legend toying with his faithful sparring partners.

Unlike bare-knuckle boxing, gentle sparring with mufflers (gloves) was not illegal. The old pros reserved real punches for the swaggering Johnny Raws, hulking farm labourers or even wealthy landowners who fancied their chances. Tom Winter lived just down the road from Mordiford. Was it fate that he should be matched with John 'The Hammer' Hollands? There was a suggestion of a little needle between the two. Something about a girl. Perhaps the older man was jealous of young Winter's calm superiority and unblemished looks.

Hollands knew how to frustrate a youngster like Winter. 'The Hammer' was a crowd-pleaser, who could be relied upon to give value. Spring was obviously nervous but must have been confident his smoothly honed skills would see him through when the command went to start fighting. He was class, the best young fighter around. Each sure of his advantage, the two men climbed into a roped square erected within the shadow of the red-bricked old rectory, with the spire of Hereford Cathedral visible in the distance.

What happened next merits a mention in Herefordshire folklore. Hollands tore into Winter like a freshly castrated bull with sea salt in the wound. Winter backpedalled, picking off his belligerent opponent with ease and leaving Hollands to swat nothing more substantial that balmy Herefordshire air. Cribb was watching. What he saw was a young novice clinically dismantling a stronger, heavier, more experienced man by superior boxing. After a desperate battle lasting one hour and twenty minutes, Hollands was prevailed upon to resign the match. In defeating Hollands, a game man, Spring garnered plaudits 'not only for the courage he displayed, but his science as a boxer'. Cribb was so impressed he convinced Winter there was a future in London for a young man with his obvious talent for boxing and his quiet and courteous demeanour.

* * * * * * * *

Winter didn't accept Cribb's offer immediately, and two years later he was back at Mordiford fighting George Henley, a local celebrity who 'fancied he could do a little in the milling way'. The match was made at three guineas-a-side and Winter prevailed after eleven rounds, giving Henley a boxing lesson in the process. The Fownhope lad was content to mark time in the butcher's shop and continue to show off his pugilistic talents at the kind of local fairs and feasts which were common at the time. One historian feverishly describes them as 'heavy drinking, wild dancing, singing, shouting and the loosening of sexual inhibitions' descending into something akin to the Roman Saturnalia. This was all too frenetic for the docile tribe from which Tom Winter sprung. His people would have been just as happy playing skittles in the Green Man or grabbing a well-oiled pig by the tail while the old ones sat by as spectators with their bottles.

5

Young Tom Heads for London

Tom Winter was now over twelve stone and had reached his full height at just under six feet. Having licked everyone in Herefordshire and the surrounding counties, he was ready to move on, and old enough now to make the decision. He packed a few things, hugged his mother and quit tiny Fownhope, with its communal warmth and familiar ghosts, to take a coach to London. The journey was long and it gave Tom plenty of time to reflect on things to come. It was a time of flux across the land, a time of great mobility, when a peasant could become a gentleman in a generation and when revolution seemed a hair's breadth away. There was a danger Tom might sink into 'obscurity and darkness' like so many an innocent who left home seeking betterment in the seething metropolis, abandoning themselves 'to low profligacy and vice'.

Winter, shy and gauche, made his way to the Union Arms in Panton Street and crept under the wing of the most famous boxer in the land. Cribb replaced the errant Joseph Winter in Tom's affections and soon began to refer to Tom as his 'boy'. Tom returned the compliment, calling Cribb his 'old Dad'. Cribb was the most respected boxer in the land and he had many influential friends. For the young Winter it was a shrewd move.

★ ★ ★ ★ ★ ★ ★ ★

Tom Cribb.

And what of Cribb? Who was this burly stranger who persuaded the Fownhope lad to swap his cosy village life in Herefordshire for the unpredictability of teeming London? Tom Cribb was a good man. He understood what it was like to leave the rustic hearth behind. He too had left home, at thirteen years of age, to take the well-worn road to London, where he worked as a docker and coalheaver. He survived hunger, poverty and at least two serious accidents, once when, laden with a 500lb crate of oranges, he fell between two barges and on another occasion when he was so badly injured internally that 'he spat blood for days'.

Now a scarred thirty-year-old with his best days as a pugilist behind him, Cribb eked out a living boxing exhibition matches and being the smiling 'mine host' behind the bar of his pub. Although a blood-spattered hero of many gory battles, it was his two fights with Tom Molyneaux, 'the ebony imposter', that made his name. Molyneaux – raw, good-looking and massively built – had everything a fighter needed except self control. He preferred the soft option in all things and the story is that he worked as a flunkey for a Mr Pinkney, then the United States ambassador in London. Molyneaux loved women and food and hated training.

The amiable black's first battle with Cribb attracted a Burke's Peerage of racist gentry who backed the round-shouldered Bristolian to send the American home in bits. Those attending included the Duke of Beaufort, Lord Gwydyr, Earl Grosvenor, the Duke of St Albans, Lord Barrymore, the Earl of Sefton, Sir Clement Briggs, Sir Henry Smythe, Lord Stradbroke and Sir Bellingham Graham. The Prince of Wales, in bed with a fierce hangover, sent his apologies and instructed an aide, Jack Ratford, to bring back a full report of the fight.

Molyneaux was described in the intemperate language of the time as 'as ugly as they make them, with an animal face with huge pro-truding lips, expanded nostrils, low forehead, and ape-shaped skull covered with a thick woolly thatch. His aspect was ferocious and savage although there were times when his features were lit with comic good humour.' Cribb on the other hand was 'a fine stalwart specimen of sturdy English manhood, broad, solid, thickset with great shoulder blades and a back like a wall. There was about him... a calm imperturbability; an air of dogged resolution which contrasted favourably with Molyneaux's ferocious expression.' Both men were within a pound of each other, with Cribb slightly the heavier at 14st 3lb. Compared with today's giants of the ring, Molyneaux was a small, compact man of just over 5ft 8in. Cribb was a couple of inches taller. Pierce Egan, describing a late round in the fight, wrote:

> If anything could reflect credit upon the skill and bottom of Cribb
> it was never more manifested than in this contest, in viewing what

a determined and resolute hero he had to vanquish. Molyneaux in spite of every disadvantage, with a courage and ferocity unequalled, rising superior to exhaustion, and fatigue, rallied his adversary with as much resolution as at the commencement of the fight, his nob defying all the milling it had received, that punishment seemed to have no effect upon it and contending nobly with Cribb right and left, knocking him away by his hits and gallantly concluded the round by closing and throwing the champion.

The fight was declared 'the greatest ever, with thousands pending'. Cribb owed his victory to his cornermen, seasoned old fighters Joe Ward and John Gully. With Cribb in serious trouble, his head unclear and unable to get his wind, Ward rushed over to Molyneaux's corner and accused the American of having stones in his hands while Gully slapped, punched and poured cold water over Cribb. By the time the furore was settled and the curses exchanged, Cribb had recovered. The referee, Sir Thomas Apreece, ignoring complaints from Molyneaux's corner, allowed Cribb to plod, gouge and elbow his way to victory in the pouring rain. Convinced that he was cheated of victory, Molyneaux demanded an early opportunity for revenge.

In a diplomatic letter despatched from St Martins Street, Leicester Square, dated 21 December 1810 and addressed to Mr Thomas Cribb, the American blamed the English weather for his unfair defeat. He tactfully hoped that there should be a return, and that 'being of a different colour would not operate to his prejudice'. Some hope.

Knowing he had been lucky to win, Cribb was determined to get himself in condition for the return. He put himself in the hands of a Captain Barclay who had his own reasons to get even with Molyneaux – the American had broken the captain's rib while they were sparring in Jackson's gym. Ignoring the earnest advice given in *Fistiana* – 'each day rise with the sun, eat a dry biscuit, wash, trot (the extreme pace of toe and heel), eat boiled mutton, spar and go to bed with the sun' – Barclay, an eccentric soldier and famous long-distance walker, devised a sadistic regime to shift the lard off Cribb. The menus Barclay offered were miserably devoid of vegetables, eggs, butter and cheese. Even a cheering shot of 'ardent spirits' was out of the question, although an occasional beaker of mature home-brewed beer was allowed. 'Sexual intercourse!' Barclay bristled, 'must vanish and be no more heard of …'. He even examined

Cribb's excrement, sniffing and intoning, 'one stool per day; if that be in form, or shape, and of a yellow tinge, will have no occasion for physic.' *Blackwood's Magazine* ran a cod article on the subject:

> In the morning, at four of the clock, a serving-man doth enter my chamber, bringing me a cup containing half one quart of pig's urine, which I do drink...At breakfast I doe commonly eat 12 goose's eggs, dressed in whale's oil wherefrom I experience much good effects. For dinner I doe chiefly prefer a roasted cat, wherof the hair has first been burned by the fire. If it be stuffed with salted herrings which are a good and pleasant fish, it will be better. Cow's tripes with cabbage is likewise a dish which I much esteem... I drink each two or three goblets of cordial spirit, whereof I prefer gin, as being of a diuretic nature, and salutiferous to the kidneys. My supper consisteth of a mess of potage, made with the fat of pork, and the whale's oil aforesaid; after which I doe drink another cup of pig's urine which helpeth digestion and maketh me sleep sound.

Joking aside, Barclay's methods worked brilliantly. Cribb, 'who from his mode of living in London and the confinement of a crowded city, had become corpulent, big-bellied, full of gross humours and short breathed', was turned into a sleek, well-oiled Centurion tank. The coalheaver lost over two-and-a-half stone and was fitter for fighting than he had ever been.

* * * * * * * *

The return fight was a promoter's dream. Black against white, great British hero versus muscle-bound Colonial upstart. Cribb knew he had let down his fans and his backers, and was fired up and determined. The venue was Thistleton Gap in Leicestershire, the date 28 September 1811. Over 20,000 vociferous spectators, Cribb supporters to a man, attended. The fight was a brutal, heart-stopping and sadly brief battle between two men who knew only one way to fight, teeth bared and throwing bombs.

With his squashed nose, and steady eyes, the heavily-muscled Bristolian was like a thirteen-and-a-half-stone hungry bulldog eyeing a juicy ribeye. Molyneaux had sneered at his trainer Tom Richmond's attempts to get him even half prepared and had not altered his training routine for the return. For breakfast he devoured a whole boiled fowl, a large sugar-dusted apple pie and a tankard of porter. Now, as he looked across the ring and saw the new slimline Cribb, Molyneaux must have felt a twinge of regret. Even so, when he shrugged off his silk shirt, ringsiders gasped. The American was like Charles Atlas on steroids. But faced with an opponent oozing confidence, Molyneaux knew his only chance of victory was to walk across the ring and knock the last of Cribb's teeth down his neck.

Cribb, roared on by his fans, ruined the plot by bursting from his corner like a mastiff after a fleeing postman. Cornering the backpedalling black, he floored Molyneaux with a swing that started in the high street. When the American scrambled to his feet he threw everything he could lay his hands on at Cribb. Blinking, the champion backed away under the wuthering, blasting out his short-armed counters as he slowly retreated.

Weathering Cribb's opening onslaught, Molyneaux dug deep and gradually got on top, battering Cribb mercilessly. He punched the Bristolian in the eyes and rattled his ribcage with heavy swings. But Cribb was up for this one. Although smashed from pillar to post and bleeding like a stuck pig, he snorted with indignation, gritted his gapped teeth and belaboured the black man's flaccid belly with wicked hooks, his coalheaver's arms going like the pistons in one of Brunel's steam ships. Very soon the American was leaning on Cribb like a dirty dancer. The boiled chicken he'd had for breakfast was climbing his gullet but the black man kept swinging. One of his unorthodox piledrivers landed and caused an egg-sized bruise to erupt over one of Cribb's eyes. As the champion groped for his corner the cunning Gully, who had learned his corner craft with Tom Belcher, Joe Ward and Harry Lee, grabbed a razor, sliced the swelling, squeezed the gore, mopped it off Cribb's hairy chest and pushed his man back into the fray.

With a grunt, Cribb hitched up his breeches and marched up to his tormentor and smashed him around the ring. The rejuvenated Bristolian, the slash over his eye like a second gaping mouth, his muscles bulging, waded through Molyneaux's dozy swings and planted a tree-felling blow onto the American's jaw which broke it like a china plate and slit a jugular. Another mighty clout powdered two of the Negro's ribs. When Molyneaux staggered up to scratch he was bleeding like a traffic accident and gasping for breath.

Cribb versus Molyneaux.

Instead of finishing off his damaged opponent, the champion, determined the crowd should 'should fully witness his superiority in giving away his chance', stubbily danced around the ring, torturing his victim 'when he ought to have been proclaimed the conqueror'. The humiliation of the battered American was made to last another two rounds before Cribb measured him to apply a spectacular coup de grâce. Before he could land the punch, the terribly injured American collapsed in a tangle at his conqueror's flat feet. It had been a disastrous fight for Tom Richmond, to whom Molyneaux owed money, and for whom he had placed a substantial bet in an effort to wipe the slate clean. 'Gentleman' John Jackson, who sat ringside, lived up to his sobriquet by organising a whip-round amongst his wealthy friends, slyly shoving fifty notes into Molyneaux's blood-stained mitt. Richmond, normally 'intellectual, witty and well informed', was stunned to silence.

The roar of the crowd fell on the grinning Cribb like snowflakes on a medieval gargoyle. He had fought the fight of his life and defended his title against the 'dusky foreigner'. Gully joined in the fun by grabbing his sweaty, bloodstained chum and dancing a wild 'Scotch Reel' with him. It must have looked a ghoulish sight next to the badly injured Molyneaux, bent double in agony and with a pool of blood forming around his feet in his corner.

Even the normally fair-minded Egan saw the result as a modern tabloid editor would. An English victory, the great journalist pronounced, was essential 'to protect the honour of his country, and the reputation of British boxing.' As for poor Molyneaux, 'illiterate and ostentatious, but good tempered, liberal and generous to a fault', he was in a semi-coma for weeks after the fight. Little wonder that the Primitive Methodists fulminated against the evil of prizefighting.

After the fight Cribb was quoted as saying that 'nothing would ever tempt him to fight again.' Captain Barclay collected the incredible sum of £10,000 in bets while Cribb picked up a measly £400. After a lifetime of taking and giving pain, the tough but ageing Bristolian was ready to be put out to grass. He was now a national hero, as famous and revered as Nelson. He headed for London in a gaily decorated baroville-and-four with his friend, the rotund and smiling Gully. They cantered through Stamford, cheered by vast crowds, stopping only to call on the injured Molyneaux.

On his arrival in London on 30 September 1811, Cribb was received with rapturous acclaim. The champion was invited to the Castle Tavern to be crowned, and everyone of any reputation or influence in the fight game was present. Peer, poet and peasant were jostling to touch the hem of the mighty coalman. A massive silver cup was carried into the bar by Cribb's seconds, John Gully and Joe Ward. John Emery, the Master of Ceremonies, hauled the fidgeting and grinning Cribb in front of the crowd like a schoolboy on presentation day. The Fancy and the Corinthians applauded, as did the boxing reporters. The essayists were represented by William Hazlitt, the versifiers by Byron, 'not a bad boxer when I could keep my temper – which was difficult' and Thomas Moore. The latter immortalised Cribb by making him the hero of his satirical poem 'A Memorial to Congress'. Emery embarrassed Cribb by blathering on about the old champion's 'valour and integrity, and his several combats' but in particular his last fight with Molyneaux when he 'gave proof that the hand of the foreigner when lifted against a son of Britannia must not only possess the strength of a lion but be aided by the heart of one also.'

Everyone clapped and shouted, and the Castle Tavern shook when Cribb lifted the huge trophy and no doubt put the lid on his head for a pencil sketch. The cup was inscribed with a line from *Macbeth*:

'And damn'd be him who first cries "Hold, Enough".' It was a fitting end to a brilliant career.

Molyneaux fought again in order to clear his debts, without any lasting success. He died of liver failure, penniless, and in Galway of all places. He had gone there in the forlorn hope of linking up with some black soldiers he met who were serving in the British Army. At this sad juncture, he was only thirty-four years of age.

Cribb returned to the coal business, but this time as owner rather than heaver. For a while he ticked delivery dockets, looking a little uncomfortable in a jacket and tie until the business failed. With the help of a few admirers he 'underwent the usual metamorphosis from pugilist to publican', taking over the King's Arms, at the corner of Duke Street and King's Street, St James. The old champion's move into the booze business prompted the ditty:

> Black Diamonds adieu – Tom's now took to the bar,
> The Fancy to serve with new charms,
> For a chop or a glass – to mill or to spar,
> They'll be at home to a peg at the 'Arms'.

6
Cribb's Pub

Young Tom Winter helped Cribb in the pub and trained between times. After his native Herefordshire, London must have seemed dark and dreary. Winter jogged along the lanes and the commons keeping fit and waiting for his first fight. As he galloped back through the dark narrow streets to his tiny room above Cribb's parlour London revealed itself. George Borrow describes the scene in *Lavengro:*

> Our ears were greeted by a confused hubbub of human voices, squealing of rats, barking of dogs, and the cries of various other animals. Here we beheld a kind of cock-pit, around which a great many people gathered, and in which we saw a dog destroy a great many rats in a very small period; and when the dog had destroyed the rats, we saw a fight between a dog and a bear, then a fight between two dogs.

George Cruikshank painted an even worse picture in 1818:

> ... in returning home between eight and nine o'clock down Ludgate Hill, and seeing a number of persons looking up the Old Bailey, I looked that way myself, and saw several human beings hanging on the gibbet opposite Newgate prison. To my horror two of these were women; upon enquiring what these women had been hung for, I was informed that it was for passing forged one-pound notes.

* * * * * * * *

Cribb's pub.

Patiently, Tom Winter waited to make an impact on the London fight scene. For an aspiring pugilist, London was the place to be. The capital boasted more fighters than anywhere else. Thirty-six men plied their brutal trade in the metropolis between 1780 and 1824. They often trained in the back rooms of pubs where their minders and managers might meet a wealthy backer. Of course there were risks. Gamblers gathered around boxers like bluebottles around carrion and their influence on a fight was often malign. On one occasion a surgeon was not allowed to bleed a badly injured fighter in the ring because the bets were laid on whether the wretched man would live or die. Gentlemen with nothing else to do except enjoy themselves offered their country seats as fight venues to the slab-shouldered working men who broke noses and necks for money.

Backers came from many walks of life but it did no harm if they were titled. Lord Barclay Allardice, who was chief backer and trainer to Cribb, also supported John Gully. The Lords Pomfret, Camelford, Fife, Thurlow, Milsington, Albemarle, Eardley, Craven, Somerville, Brook and the Barrymores also supported fighters, as did Sir John Seebright, MP, the Duke of Hamilton, and Sir Charles Lennox, later the 3rd Duke of Richmond. Lord Yarmouth, one of Jackson's patrons, was a close friend of the Prince Regent as well as being the model for 'Steyne' in *Vanity Fair*. He lived in 13 Piccadilly Terrace, a house owned by the Duchess of Devonshire before Lord Byron moved there in 1815.

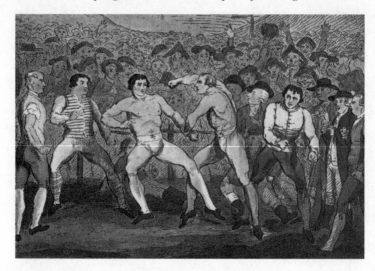

'Gentleman' John Jackson holding and hitting.

The Duke of Clarence, who sired ten illegitimate children by the actress Mrs Jordan, was a backer, as were 'commoners' like Mr Bullock, backer of Bill Richmond, and Harvey Aston, who introduced 'Gentleman' John Jackson to boxing. Laurence Sant, a wealthy Wandsworth brewer, backed several fighters, but most notably Tom Winter. Fletcher Reid supported the Belcher brothers and Gully. A few of the gentlemen supporters were quite mad, either from drink and drugs or the debilitating effects of syphilis, and several died horrible deaths.

Richard 'Hellgate' Barrymore, a sadistic bully who backed the fighter Bill Hooper, loved to have the boxer on his arm like a organ-grinder's monkey when he played billiards in his club, visited the races, travelled in his chaise or turned up at an election meeting. His manic life came to a fitting end when a loaded gun he kept by him in his curricle went off and blew his head off when he hit a bump on the road from Brighton. Handsome young boxers up from the country were often stalked by wealthy men, colourful characters on the lookout for the next up-and-coming man.

****

With the advent of the turnpikes, the newly privatised roads gave access to the countryside, where most of the major fights were held. Although *The Times* allocated a few column inches to the barbarous sport of boxing, bare-knuckle bouts were hastily arranged and illegal, the promoters being constantly harassed by magistrates. But boxing had a surreptitious life of its own and it grew organically. Like horse racing it attracted all society, from the sly pickpocket and the brash bookie with his bulging moneybag, to the extravagant lord with his huge entourage of friends, his splendid barouches, and his hampers of fine foods and wines.

Bare-knuckle fights, often fantastically well supported, were inflicted on unsuspecting communities. The first the locals knew of an impending battle was when 'a crowd of vagabonds, the parties, and their seconds, bottle holders forcibly took possession of a field, common or racecourse in defiance of the exertions of the magistrate and peace officers.' The 'vagabonds' were assisted by 'principal ringleaders who considered themselves respectable'. Although prizefighting could be readily restrained under the law, either as a breach of the peace or as an unlawful assembly, many matches were 'winked at', that is, sanctioned and protected by influential patrons. Others were allowed to go on because the crowds were too large for the inadequate resources of the local constabulary to deal with. Bare-knuckle fighting often ended in accidental deaths or, at the very least, serious injury, and was therefore viewed with a great deal of criticism. One contemporaneous observer commented: 'the established order, and good decorum of society, have been of late much disturbed and nearly set in defiance by the prevalence of boxing matches.' Many thought boxing was evil because, they said, it was difficult for 'Good-nature, Compassion and Tenderness' to regain 'Possession, if the Mind be first tinctured with Inhumanity and Blood.'

Bare-knuckle fighting sorely needed a gifted boxer who relied on speed of thought and movement to outwit the slugger. Tom Winter was that man. There were too many tearaways like Jack Scroggins, who tore from their corner, 'closed' on their man, and attached themselves by fair means or foul, pinning the wretch in a perspiring embrace before wrestling him to the ground. Men like that seem to enjoy shedding blood and teeth. But clever boxers could handle such ruffians. 'Hitting under the ear' was a good way to stop them. The tiny

Mendoza invented another ploy. He stood his ground, watched hawk-eyed as his foe charged towards him, then planted a punch as hard as he could deliver to the man's kidneys. It was guaranteed to 'occasion an instant discharge of urine', put the recipient of the blow 'in the greatest torture' and render him 'for some time a cripple'. As no gloves were allowed in the professional ring the force of the blow was magnified several times. Bare hands colliding with a shaven, rocklike cranium often caused broken fingers and wrist fractures.

* * * * * * * *

Under Cribb's tutelage, Tom Winter trained hard and obediently trudged off to bed every night, no doubt thinking of home as he watched the moon over London through a tiny widow. A regular stream of country lads like him arrived in London with nothing but a handkerchief for luggage after establishing a local reputation knocking over drunks at country fairs. They soon found out that conquering the capital was a daunting prospect. But in spite of its every disadvantage, including the notorious decisions that worked against outsiders, London proved an attractive lure for aspiring pugilists. The lucky ones scratched out a living but the majority either returned home chastened or fell into bad company and died in the gutter. Tom Winter was a very lucky young man to have the inestimable Cribb as his adviser and guardian.

7

Cribb Introduces Spring to the Fancy

The sports-mad Fancy, who slavishly supported the big fight around the country and took a great interest in the fighters, were often wealthy and uneducated young men with sunny dispositions and a wish to die tragically. They were attracted to the reckless and nomadic life of the fighter. They rubbed shoulders with the uncultured peasant who gambled sixpence on two cockroaches racing along a pub beam. Not that the Fancy had a levelling disposition, by any means. The nobs might be howling and dropping their twenties with just as much enthusiasm as the weaver alongside staked his bob but the two never communicated. When the riot of pleasure was over and the two men separated the Lord hailed his barouche and clattered off to his country seat while the weaver slipped through an opening in the sooty bricks of some slab-sided building in an unlit alley.

Cribb was eager to show off his exciting new find to his noble and influential friends, among whom was 'Gentleman' John Jackson, a builder's son and former pugilist who ran the Fives Court in Little St Martin's Street, a venue known as 'the temple to pugilism'. Unlike Winter, Jackson always had an eye for social advancement. He was a handsome, well built figure, a dapper dresser. When he strode down Holborn Hill he stood out head and shoulders above his fellows:

He wore a scarlet coat, worked in gold at the button holes, ruffles, frill of fine lace, a small white stock, and a looped hat with a broad black band, buff knee breeches and long silk stockings, pumps and

paste buckles; his waistcoat was pale blue satin, sprigged with white.
It was impossible to look upon his fine ample chest, his noble
shoulders, his waist, if anything too small, his large but not too large
hips, his limbs, his balustrade calf and beautifully turned ankle, his
firm foot, and peculiarly small hand, without thinking that Nature
had sent him to earth as a model. He was the envy of all men and
the admiration of women.

The personable Jackson was taken up by the gentry, significantly by
Lord Byron, who had the pugilist's 'graven image' hung among the
fine portraits in Newstead Abbey, the poet's family home. Byron had
something of a fixation for the swashbuckling Jackson, who could
sign his name with an 84lb weight dangling from his little finger!
Jackson was a brave and resourceful fighter in his time. When he
fought George 'The Brewer' Ingeston, Jackson fell and broke both his
ankles. Undeterred, he offered to continue the fight strapped to a chair.
He won the English title in 1795, the year Tom Winter was born, beating Daniel Mendoza in ten-and-a-half minutes at Hornchurch when
'the Jew appeared overpowered by the Christian'. Jackson flouted the
rules by grabbing the Jew by his lanky hair and, while pulling it from
its roots, smashing Mendoza in the face. Jackson retired as undefeated
champion in 1803 to develop a boxing school at 13 Bond Street. Here
'the bucks and dandies, shaved, shampoo'd, powdered, and pomatuned,
flocked to spar, fence and wrestle.' Jackson's boxing school attracted
London's fashionable elite. Noblemen of the highest rank assembled
there, keen to put the gloves on and swap blows with Jackson, who
stood steely-eyed in front of these 'bottomless' gentlemen, defying
them to hit him. When they swung with all the ferocity and skill of
a dowager handbagging a mugger, Jackson simply leaned back and
clipped their noble chins. Clever and articulate, Jackson had a reputation as a fair-minded man who put boxers first, helping many an old
toothless pug down on his luck.

When the Pugilistic Club, 'a fair ring and no favour and may the
best man win', was formed in 1814 to bring discipline and control to
bare-knuckle fighting, Jackson was the obvious choice for secretary and
chief. He attended many a fight with his friend Byron, who shared an
enthusiasm for boxing with Homer, Hazlitt, Cobbett, Shaw, Hemingway,
Borrow, Mailer and many another famous scribbler. Born with the

Achilles tendons of both feet so contracted he could only walk on the balls of the toes, the poet looked up to the handsome and beautifully proportioned Jackson. He was a game little bantam whose 'strength of arm made him formidable in spite of his lameness'. Wearing 'mufflers' – old-fashioned leather boxing gloves – and embroidered pantaloons to hide his affliction, Byron, who was cruelly reviled as a 'a lame beast' by his mother, liked nothing better than to spar with Jackson before rushing off a couplet or an ode to Napoleon. Jackson taught him to move nimbly on his deformed feet and punch his weight. When a Cambridge master who had seen Byron in Jackson's company remonstrated with the young poet Byron replied that Jackson's manners were 'infinitely superior to those fellows of the college whom I have met at the high table'. An engaging and compulsive man, Byron was not just another foppish aristo affecting the ways of the pugilist but a useful boxer who sparred on the morning his mother died to keep up his spirits. He loved the 'flash' language heard in inns like the Castle Tavern where fighters and the demi monde met. In an addendum to the 11th Canto of *Don Juan,* he referred to Jackson as 'My friend and corporeal master and pastor', and he remembered him in 'Hints from Horace':

The interior of the Fives Court with Randall and Turner sparring.

And men unpractised in exchanging knocks
Must go to Jackson ere they dare to box.

Byron had an amused respect for Jackson's good friend Tom Cribb
and he visited Cribb's pub on several occasions to eat, drink, and
simply enjoy the robust company of real men, a refreshing change
from the watery-eyed sops he so often encountered in his role as
'great poet'. Cribb's reputation as 'the best man in England' attracted
the right sort of customer to his pub. As a guest of Jackson, or 'the
emperor of Pugilism' as Byron called him, the grizzled old Bristol
bruiser broke bread and quaffed the house red with the well-bred
poet. Byron wrote after the event:

> I drank more than I like, and have brought away some three bottles
> of very fair claret – for I have no headache. We had Tom (Cribb), up
> after for dinner; very facetious, though somewhat prolix. He don't
> like his situation – wants to fight again ... pray Pollux, (or Castor,
> if he was the miller) he may. Tom has been a sailor – coal heaver
> – and some other genteel profession before he took to the cestus.
> Tom has been in action at sea, and is now only three and thirty!
> Has a wife and mistress conversations well. Tom is an old friend of
> mine; I have seen some of his best battles in my nonage. He is now
> a publican, and, I fear, a sinner for Mrs Crib (*sic*) lives on alimony
> and —'s daughter lives with the champion.

Cribb tried to pass off his mistress as his missus to Byron but the
poet wrote, 'Talking of her, he said, she was the truest of women
– from which I immediately inferred she could not be his wife, and
so it turned out'. Tom bored on rather in praise of his jilted wife's
virtue, causing Byron to write. 'I listened with great credence and
patience, and stuffed my handkerchief into my mouth when I found
yawning irresistible.'

In this atmosphere of success, fame and self-regard, young Tom
Winter, the polite young boxer from Hereford, was rather overshad-
owed. Did the great poet shake his hand as the Fownhope lad cleared
the bones off the table and replenished the beakers of claret? Not
according to the poet's voluminous letters. Perhaps Tom was too limited, too lacking in social graces, or not famous or beautiful enough to

Lord Byron sparring with Jackson.

become one of Byron's muses, in spite of the latter's liking for 'animal energy of all kinds'. The cocksure little poet was less interested in the plain-born Herefordshire lad polishing glasses and sweeping the bar-room floor than he was in his drinking companions, the gnarled champion Cribb and the sophisticated Jackson, who was of particular interest to Cribb since he controlled the Fives Court, the most famous fighting club in town.

8

From Winter to Spring

When Cribb took Winter to the Fives Court everyone was eager to see the lad the old champion had enticed up from Herefordshire and Cribb was anxious to give his boy 'an opportunity of showing off his points and perfections in the fistic art'. The Fives Court was ideal, a relatively bloodless showcase for any raw novice eager to show his mettle. It also introduced new talent to potential backers.

As usual, the place was stuffed with its motley quota of gamblers and book-keepers, nobles and ne'er-do-wells. They all shared an interest in male company and combat. The place rocked with excitement as fight fans stamped their feet, smoked their pipes, cast experienced eyes over the programme, discussed with colleagues the form and placed a bob or two on their fancies. Jackson, like most promoters, had his favourite fighters and woe betide anyone who crossed him.

While every pub in the country had a small fives court out the back next to the gents, the large London version could accommodate up to 1,000 spectators and players. It was an important venue for the fives player but it became famous through boxing and was used for sparring exhibitions and benefits from 1802 until 1826. At the rear of the main hall was a small dressing room where the boxers stripped. Into this private space, with its proximity to the well-muscled young warriors, crowded dozens of noblemen whose generous contributions added greatly to the evening's takings. The building itself was a cold and dusty rectangle with steep walls and dark, damp corners where on fight nights pickpockets and other dodgy characters conspired to relieve the unsuspecting of their 'blunt'. Matches were made and bills advertising fighters and the cost of admission – 'two bobs', 'half a bull' or 'three bobs and a bender' – were pinned to walls, window shutters and inn noticeboards all over the town. A boxing ring was erected to allow those standing on the uncarpeted floor a better view of the action. Cribb knew young Tom Winter would soon prove good enough to be offered a paid assignment against one of the many old pros who hung around the Fives desperate for work.

Then as now, the backer, or promoter, played an essential part in building the image of a good novice, sponsoring their man against all-comers either for monetary gain or just for the sport. Backers were always on the lookout for a game lad they could call their own, one who would set their friends' wigs wobbling and their beringed fingers drumming impatiently on the card tables. Tom Winter would prove to be the latest and most exciting thing to happen in the drab hall for a long time. And he had the burly Cribb alongside him to make sure none of the gentleman took too keen an interest, for it was well known that certain promising young fighters were ruined by their gentlemen backers dressing them up in flashy clothes and leading them around town like pit bull terriers to impress and intimidate their rivals.

Tom was stripped, weighed, measured and inspected like a good fat bullock back in Hereford Market. As he stood on the elevated, deal-floored ring he was overlooked by the nobles who eyed him from the comfort of their cosy 'lounge'. The MC for the evening, old 'Paddington' Jones, who had fought more battles than any other fighter, growled above the din. 'Name, boy?' When he heard 'Winter, sir', Jones, who 'like Homer gave every Hero some favourite cognomen,' snapped back, 'Let it be Spring!' When the bell went, the newly minted Spring, boxing in gloves, moved smooth as silk into his elegant stride, chin protected, feet dancing, long reach snapping out stinging punches. The Marquis of Worcester, who was among the aristocrats filling the small windows that overlooked the ring, lisped, 'My lords, here is a young fellow come up amongst us, a pal of Tom Cribb's who will be a teaser among the big one day.' The Marquis proved a good judge.

* * * * * * * *

Tom 'Paddington' Jones.

Jackson, who had trained Jem Belcher, Tom Owen, Bill Richmond, Andrew Gamble, Dutch Sam and Dick Humphries, also recognised Spring's talent and kept an affectionate eye on the Hereford man's progress, playing no small part in Tom's quest for the title. One night Spring sparred with a new beefy import from Ireland, Dan Donnelly. Tom's footwork and adroit moves kept the big, heavy-hitting Irish lad off balance and by the end of the exhibition both novices would have relished a real fight, if only they could find a backer. Donnelly later said he could have taken Spring but Dan, 'whose reputation was far bigger than his actions merited', was prone to exaggeration. Spring was delighted to be able to spar with the most prominent fighters of the day. One veteran from whom he learned a great deal was the inimitable George Head, a skilful fighter who was reputed to be able to down sixteen glasses of 'blue ruin' without losing his cool fighting demeanour. Cribb recruited Head to fine-tune Spring.

The regular programmes at the Fives Court kept boxers fed and fit while they waited for their backers to come up with an offer to box at a famous outdoor venue like Moulsey Hurst, Epsom Downs or Wimbledon Common, where an attractive match drew huge crowds and could mean a payday of £200 or more for a top fighter. Spring was impatient. In bed at night he listened to the noises of London and the chanting of the boxers, trainers and hangers-on as they caroused below. Above the bar perched Billy, Cribb's terrier and the most famous rat catcher of them all. In his prime Billy could break the necks of up to fifty rats in a minute while salivating gamblers placed their bets. The ratpit and the cockpit drew the Fancy in droves, according to Egan:

> ... dustmen, lamp-lighters, stagecoachmen, bakers, farmers, barristers, swells, butchers, dogfanciers, grooms, donkey-boys, weavers, snobs, market-men, watermen, honourables, springs of the nobility, MPs, mailguards, awaddies etc., all in one rude contact, jostling and pushing against each other when the doors were opened to procure a front seat.

* * * * * * * *

Before he could 'drop his blunt', though, Spring had to earn it. There was plenty of manual work in London for a strong, clean-living young man, especially for a lad who could boast the great Tom Cribb as a friend. Winter could earn a bob or two portering, building or navvying. However there was a easier source of income open to young men blessed with fine figures: modelling. It was Bill 'Lily White' Richmond, landlord of the Horse and Dolphin which stood next door to the Fives Court, who initiated the fashion for upper-body nudity by casting off his shirt at the Fives to reveal an impressively honed body, described as 'a study for the sculptor'. When Dutch Sam disrobed, the 'symmetry' of the 'parts being expressed were much admired' by the sculptor John Rossi. Soon the creative fraternity were turning up at the Fives Court in droves clutching their charcoal and sketching pad. Their number included Benjamin Haydon and Joseph Farrington, the president of the Royal Academy. When Tom Spring threw off his chemise he too was quickly snapped up as a model. The modest fee was useful. In the meantime he polished his more physical skills by sparring with tough, experienced fighters and training hard under the alert eye of Tom Cribb, waiting for the chance to prove himself in the ring. Spring had added grit and variation to his jab-and-run routine. He was young, strong, and optimistic with nothing to lose.

Satisfied that his boy was ready to fight professionally Cribb sent a note to the *Sporting Magazine*.

> To All England. The Championship
> Tom Crib (*sic*) having been called to the bar, which now completely occupies his time, has in consequence, entirely resigned the whole of his practice in the ring to Tom Spring, his adopted boy: therefore, wishing to tread in the steps of his 'father', and not to lead a dull inglorious life! And anxious seeking the path of glory informs all those heroes whom it may concern that for three months he is open to all England, for 100 to 200 guineas a side.

It was a very confident call and one can only assume backers who had seen Spring spar were very impressed.

9

Spring's First
Professional Contest

As a 'trial horse' for his young protégé, Cribb chose a fighter called
Stringer, an 'ugly-looking customer' from Rawcliffe in Yorkshire, who
trained under the aegis of Bill Richmond. The stake of £40 was up for
grabs, as well as a purse given by the Pugilistic Club, which counted
Lord Byron and the Dukes of Clarence and Queensbury among the
nobles on its committee. Stringer was no pushover. He was an experienced fighter, a rugged, mature man who had been through the mill
and, although a veteran, he could still give a good account of himself
– Richmond did not waste his time on no-hopers.

Though lacking in facial beauty, Stringer was a fine physiological
specimen. Like Spring, as a young man he modelled for students of the
Royal Academy. He was 'athletic and big but by no means fresh and his
cut of countenance was rough and weather-beaten'. As a benchmark
against which to measure Spring's potential, Stringer was an ideal
opponent. Indeed, the burly Yorkshireman, who had no intention of
playing the sacrificial lamb, was a slight favourite to win.

Spring was unblemished, twenty-two years of age but as tall as
Stringer and in better physical condition. At barely thirteen stones
he was conceding half a stone to the experienced northerner. When
he stripped, one ringsider thought Spring 'resembled the great Jem
Belcher but on a larger scale'.

The fight took place at Moulsey Hurst in Surrey, on 9 September 1817.
It was a popular venue for boxing, and half the matches made in the
London area from 1805 to 1824 were staged there. The site was originally

famous for golf and cricket, witnessing the first ever recorded instance of lbw (against the Hon. J. Tufton playing for England against Surrey in August 1795) and the first game of golf on English soil in 1758.

Fight day would have been a colourful sight at Moulsey. From all corners of the country crowds poured into the 'Pugilistic Waterloo'. As every vehicle that could be pulled by a human or animal arrived packed with cheering fans, tents mushroomed in the soft mud. Horses whinnied and whips cracked. Fight days meant good business for local inns and taverns, and tradesmen of every hue turned up to ply their business and relieve the boxing fans of their cash – whether hard-earned or inherited.

Although Tom Spring was an untested Johnny Raw from the sticks, the fact that he was 'Cribb's boy' attracted a large crowd. Cribb was familiar with Moulsey, having beaten Bob Gregson there for the title in 1808. But the boxer turned publican was not in Spring's corner for the lad's debut; instead, he trusted that task to one of the best and wisest cornermen around, Tom Owen, 'The Sage of the East', assisted by Gilbert 'The Waterman' Parish. In Stringer's corner stood the formidable pairing of Bill Richmond and Tom Shelton.

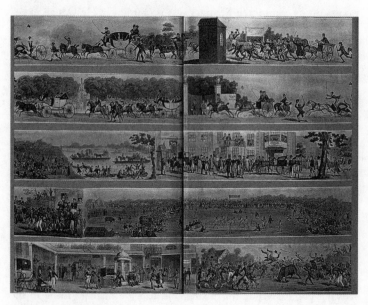

The Road to Moulsey Hurst.

Tom Shelton.

As the men squared up, Spring was valued at two to one, while Stringer held steady at seven to four. In the opening round, Stringer, who had the look of a good fighter, sent Spring sprawling but the youngster hauled the older man down with him. Concentrating on boxing, Spring confused the big Yorkshireman with his technical finesse.

He impressed ringsiders with the way he moved the big man about and made him miss with his crude swings. Jabbing and teasing like a boy opening his first oyster, the Fownhope novice threw calculated shots with both hands, and gradually assumed control. As early as the end of the third round, Spring was favourite to dispose of the Yorkshire veteran.

In the fourth, Stringer, urged on by his corner, charged at Spring to try to unsettle him. The tussle ended with the youngster sprawled on the grass. Spring survived the crisis, however, and, showing great determination, went out to punish Stringer in the next round. Head down, the Yorkshire charged in flinging crude punches which Spring easily avoided, and the newcomer clobbered Stringer to the floor. The contest was now one-sided until the sixth, when Stringer got a second wind and grimly closed on Spring. The two men 'hammered at each other like a couple of blacksmiths'. Spring gradually regained the upper hand, hunting Stringer down implacably. Then, in a move that would be mirrored and echoed in his later fights, when Spring had Stringer at his mercy, on the ropes and incapable of defending himself, the Fownhope lad stepped back and allowed his foe to squirm free and collect his senses.

The crowd enjoyed this unusual show of sportsmanship and there was 'great applause from all parts of the ring'. Stringer repaid the raw young Herefordian by attacking him like a madman in the seventh. Spring calmly nailed the Tyke with a 'tremendous nobber'. Stringer went down bloodied, muddied and as helpless as a kitten. In modern times the fight would have been stopped right there. But even though he was completely outclassed Stringer gamely plodded forward, his mouth open, and for the next few rounds he was mercilessly battered by the younger, fitter, more accomplished Spring.

Stringer rumbled forward in the next round, eating lefts and rights, blood pouring from both eyes. It was a gory baptism for Spring who, try as he might, could not find the one clean, direct shot to the point of Stringer's grizzled chin that would finally separate him from what little sense he still possessed. Spring was winning but his good looks had taken a beating and, although he had plenty of energy left, it was dispiriting to know that no matter how many times he hit the tough Stringer, he could not stop him inflicting damage with his lumpen swings.

The fight went on into the sixteenth round, with the two exchanging a hailstorm of blows. Once more Spring out-toughed the Yorkshire hard man and finally decked him with an accumulation of punches, but again infuriated his corner by letting Stringer get away when he had him trapped and at his mercy. The two men battled away into the twenty-first round, when Richmond, a stylish fighter in his own right, got sick of trying to tell Stringer how to fight and said 'go on, then, fight your own way.' It didn't make any difference. Stringer was soon crawling around the ground, bloody and bemused. The Yorkshireman was now down so often it looked as if he were having a love affair with the grass. Spring waded into Stringer, pulverising him until he dropped. The crowd was now baying for the fight to be stopped.

The last round of the fight was described as 'one of the severest ever seen'. Spring's backers were rubbing their hands with glee at the way their young novice blasted Stringer to destruction in the twenty-ninth. The final spectacle came through Spring, in the jargon of the period, 'catching Yorky's nob, and instantly flooring him on his back!'

Spring left the ring victorious to collect the special prize donated by the Pugilistic Club, while Stringer, dazed and bruised, was hauled from the ring by his seconds. It was a tough initiation for the boy but Spring justified Cribb's confidence in him. He proved he had the guts, resilience, heart and skill to make it in a very tough game, and his sportsmanship endeared him to the crowd. It was a fine start but what was worrying was Spring's lack of a decent punch. It would mean this fine, upright decent young man would have to take more punishment than he should.

* * * * * * * *

Stringer boasted at the post-fight interview that he felt 'as hearty as a buck' in the later rounds. It was Spring, though, who got the rave reviews. 'From the exhibition of Spring in this battle,' Downes Miles wrote, 'he bids fair to put all the "big ones" on the alert.' Spring's generous behaviour when he had his opponent in trouble was 'manly and humane and ought not to be forgotten'.

10

A Dangerous Opponent

Although he had fought only one low-key fight, Spring, keen to work his way swiftly up the rankings, 'without hesitation challenged Ned Painter for 100 guineas-a-side.' This was a bold, if not foolhardy move. It was considered by the Fancy and the bare-knuckle cognoscenti that the fight had come a little too early for Spring, and doubts were cast on Cribb's managerial skills. Spring was being thrust into a potentially dangerous battle against one of the top bare-knuckle warriors in the land.

Painter, who was born in Stretford, Manchester, in 1784, was only 5ft 9in tall but he was stoutly built, weighed thirteen stones and was a tough and experienced thirty-four-year-old with a terrific punch. He had started out as a brewer's assistant, but after clobbering Wilkins, a fellow worker and 'a man of heavy build' in the yard of the Swan Inn, Manchester – and revealing in the process 'unusual powers as a boxer' – he was snapped up by Bob Gregson.

After beating a series of moderate fighters Painter was matched with the rugged 'Chelsea Gardener', Tom Oliver, on Tuesday 17 May 1814 at Shepperton Range, Middlesex, for a purse of £50, donated by the Pugilistic Club. Painter landed a stunning blow in the second round which all but disabled Oliver, who later compared the blow to a light-ning bolt. After smelling salts, a face slapping and a dousing with cold water, the bemused Oliver fought on in a dream until the fight was stopped in the eighth when his second 'threw in the hat'. On 14 and 15 June 1814, Painter had the honour of being invited by 'Gentleman' John Jackson to spar at Lord Lowther's house in Pall Mall with Cribb, Jackson and others in front of the Emperor of Russia, the King of Prussia, the Prince Royal of Russia and the celebrated General Blücher.

Painter resumed his sporadic career with losses against John Shaw, the lifeguardsman and later war hero, at Hounslow Heath, Middlesex, on 18 April 1815 and two years later on 23 July against Harry 'The Black' Sutton at Moulsey Hurst. Unhappy with this result, Painter accepted a rematch in Bungay, Suffolk, on 7 August 1818, which attracted an excited crowd of 15,000 spectators. After another rugged encounter, the determined Painter prevailed, winning in fifteen rounds.

* * * * * * * *

Before the fight, Tom Spring was persuaded by Bill Scroggins to take Painter on in a five-mile dash for ten guineas. Spring had done no special training for the race, which was held on 7 November 1817, starting 'from the four mile stone on the Essex road'. Spring sprinted ahead and led for two miles with Painter jogging ominously at his elbow. Every time Tom increased his pace, Painter did the same. As they approached the halfway point, Painter shot past the youngster to touch the marker handkerchief and doubled back on the trot, completing the return two-and-a-half miles comfortably while the exhausted Spring was left for dead.

Painter, 'one of the gamest pugilists to have pulled off his shirt', decided it was time he took on the cocky Herefordshire boy and gave him a more painful lesson in the boxing ring. That he would do so was in little doubt: in fact, Spring was so little fancied that backers could not be found to sponsor the fight. The money was eventually stumped up by a gentleman who felt it charitable to save everyone the disappointment of cancellation. In the event, the fight – the first big promotion of the year, with the great Jack Randall topping the bill against Abe Belasco – was a sell-out. Henry Downes Miles observed:

> The sun had scarcely shed his beams over the metropolis on Wednesday morning, 1 April 1818, when the roads leading to Mickleham Downs, near Leatherhead, in Surrey were thronged with vehicles of every description ... The situation of the ring was truly picturesque and delightful, commanding an uninterrupted view of diversified scenery for sixty miles. Some fir trees contiguous to it had an animated appearance from the numerous spectators

Ned Painter.

mounted on its boughs. Wagons were arranged around the ring for
the yeomanry and the shopkeepers and artisans.

The poor, who had an insatiable appetite for prizefighting in spite
of the difficulties presented by the lack of cash and transport, lolled
on the grass after their long walk, hungrily awaiting the impending
action. Painter was a hot favourite but there were those who, taken by
Spring's youth, science and strength and emboldened by the chance
of long odds, put their money on Spring to cause an upset. Still, the
lion's share of the spectators, warmed by the sun, fully expected the
reliable and experienced Painter to take care of the youngster from
Herefordshire.

Just after one o'clock the two men made their way to the ring.
Spring, with Cribb and Byrne in his corner, looked out on the massive
crowd that occupied every vantage point. Seconded by Tom Belcher

and Harry Harmer, Painter warmly shook Spring's hand and made the young man feel at ease during the preliminaries, which lasted a full half-hour.

Cribb advised Spring to stay away from his rushing opponent in the early rounds then step up the pace and pick his man off as he tired. Tom was in great shape for a long fight if necessary. The veteran's strategy worked. The fight began sensationally. After three minutes of sizing each other up, Spring made to drop his hands. Painter fell for the ruse and as he advanced Spring lashed out, striking the older man on the throat. Painter fell backwards, violently hitting his head and shoulder on one of the rough-hewn ring posts with an impact that reverberated around the ground. Painter was in terrible pain and the timekeepers thought the fight was over. Even 'Gentleman' John Jackson who officiated 'deemed it next to an impossibility the fight would continue'. Painter seemed utterly insensible as his cornerman dragged him deadweight to the side of the ring. Jack Randall and Abe Belasco began to warm up.

The fight should have been stopped there and then, but Painter's seconds somehow got him up to scratch. He sported a huge lump on his head and the skin on his shoulder was cut. Though dazed, he fought like a cornered rat but Spring was treating him like a punchbag and had him down again and again. The crowd, thinking Painter was finished, cheered. But his seconds, using every trick of their art, had him upright again, bleary, unsteady but ready to fight to the death. He survived another round. Spring was picking his punches and enjoying himself so much that 'he laughed and gave Painter a nobber, and got away dextrously.' Painter wearily plonked himself on Harmer's knee and asked, 'What is it?' He had fought the first two rounds without knowing it. In the fourth, as Painter's head cleared, he attacked more but Spring grabbed his hand. It was a trick taught to him by Tom Owen and known as 'Owen's stop'.

Much to Cribb's chagrin, Painter, having marshalled his wits, began to score heavily, even though the Fownhope lad was visibly the stronger of the two. By the eighth round Painter had completely recovered. He caught Spring with several 'facers' and did the same in the next round. Now it was Spring's turn to wobble and only his fitness and youth kept him upright.

Spring survived the crisis and, boxing beautifully, had Painter in trouble in the tenth but he could not finish him off. Still the crowd yelled their approval as he sidestepped Painter's punches and planted both fists in the former brewer's face. By the eleventh they were cheering the gentlemanly conduct exhibited by Spring who received 'thunders of applause' as he let Painter down gracefully when he could have punched him senseless. Painter was still hanging on in the sixteenth, connecting with a severe body blow that made Spring grunt, but by the eighteenth the older man looked in distress as Spring maintained a barrage of blows to his head.

Spring was now winning every round, as Painter went down without landing a punch. It was time to terminate the unequal contest but still Painter was allowed to fumble and stumble for another thirteen one-sided rounds before a halt was mercifully called. The fight lasted one hour and twenty-nine minutes. When Spring was declared the winner, Cribb seized his young victor in an embrace and carried him triumphantly around the ring, to enthusiastic cheers from the crowd.

* * * * * * * *

The verdict after the fight was that 'Spring turned out much better man than he was previously rated, though it was still urged that he was not a hard hitter. He used his left hand well and displayed cool-ness and command of temper.' Worryingly, after a fight he had totally dominated, Spring ended up with his face badly cut and some damage to his eyes. Painter had no complaints except for commenting on the excruciating pain he felt in his shoulder after his fall. One bad loser among the gentry, an 'influential amateur', unjustly accused Painter of taking a dive. Painter insisted he had been fairly beaten and that it was Spring's superior reach and strength that had made him impossible to best. Sadly, the brave and scrupulously honest Painter had to endure a few lordly insults for the rest of his career.

11

Spring Loses the Return

Painter's backers were so keen for their champion to make good his defeat that they placed a deposit for the return fight within a week of the match. On 14 April this was increased to £40 to cover a rematch on 7 August 1818, for a stake of 100 guineas. Mindful of Painter's accident in the first fight his side stipulated that there should be only eight stakes around the ring, two per side. Cribb dutifully signed Spring up for the return. This time the venue was Russia Farm, five miles from Kingston-upon-Thames.

Taking on Painter again was the sort of mistake even the best of managers makes. Spring was described as 'unfit and out of form'. Cribb, who had been in Painter's corner when he was destroyed by the brilliant Lifeguardsman Shaw on Hounslow Heath in 1815, obviously assumed even an unfit Spring could give the veteran another pasting, ignoring the fact that three of the four fighters who had beaten Painter got their comeuppance in return battles.

The fighters limbered up before a good crowd. Painter again had Harmer and Belcher in his corner, while Spring was looked after by Cribb and another new man, Clark. Both fighters started cautiously, warily circling, hands cocked. Spring was caught dreaming when Painter feinted and, as Spring made the necessary defensive ploy, planted a massive dig on Spring's eye 'which not only produced the claret copiously, but floored him like a shot'. The punters who had gambled on first blood and first knockdown whooped with joy as the favourite lay sprawled and bleeding on the turf. It was one of the hardest single punches Spring would take in his entire career.

The betting boys ran around like dervishes, clutching handfuls of blunt. Spring's chances of survival were reduced to even, as Painter received new backing at the bookies. Thanks to Cribb's calm corner work, the comatose Tom just about made it to scratch for the second round. Half asleep and with blood running down his face, Spring appeared as helpless as a day-old chick as Painter went to work to finish him off. Although reeling and stumbling, Spring managed by ducking, diving and clinging to avoid the finisher. In fact, the round ended with both men down and Spring on top of his opponent. A few of Tom's supporters were sufficiently encouraged to yell 'Bravo, Spring!'

In the third round Spring showed signs of recovering and he swapped blows with Painter with both men touching the dirt. In the fourth, fifth and sixth rounds Spring grappled with Painter and flung him to the ground. The seventh and eighth were messy affairs with very little clean hitting. Both men looked tired and both hit the deck. In the ninth both furiously competed, swapping hard blows without flinching. Then Painter landed an almighty blow on Spring's ear: with blood pouring from him, Tom went down. He had difficulty making scratch but when he did he gamely pursued Painter, landing lefts and rights until he had him down. For the next three rounds, Spring soaked up punishment, and in the fourteenth managed to sweep Painter off his feet. The crowd loved it. Someone called out, 'Do that again Spring, and you'll win it.'

From then on it was downhill all the way with Painter driving the Fownhope man around the ring, giving him the hiding of his life. Spring was seeing his tormentor though a veil of blood and sweat, absorbing the shock of the blows on every part of his body. His courage was admirable. Cribb should have pulled the lad out. The agony went on to the thirty-first round when Painter discharged a right-hand that landed flush on Spring's jaw. The Herefordian collapsed and the gamblers shouted the odds against him not coming out for the next round. Proud man that he was, he assumed the perpendicular once more. The fight continued to the forty-second round when Spring's resistance was finally broken. Painter measured him once more and landed a crunching blow to his head. The fight beaten out of him, Spring collapsed for the final time. The beating lasted just over one hour and four minutes.

Like Painter in their first fight, Spring had never recovered from that first-chance punch and had failed to show his true colours in the rest of the match. Even though he garnered considerable praise for the grit and stamina with which he went down fighting, Spring's first defeat, amateur or professional, weighed heavily on his mind, and he would bear the physical scars for the rest of his life. He begged Painter for a rematch. The older man declined the offer and instead, having avenged an unlucky defeat, Painter retired from the ring to run a pub in Norwich.

He still had unfinished business to deal with, however. Haunted by the unfair and persistent accusations that he had thrown the first Spring fight, Painter set off for London to clear his name. He took with him a certificate from an eminent surgeon which proved that the injury he had received to his shoulder bone 'prevented him using his arm at the time specified'. Painter was cleared of any wrongdoing and his 'integrity declared to be without a stain'.

Later, a group of gentlemen in Norwich challenged Spring to a third and decisive contest at 100 guineas-a-side, paying him a further £50 if he agreed to fight in Norwich, and an extra £20 towards his expenses. The contract was signed in Cribb's pub, with £50 to be put down by each party within three weeks of the signing. 'Gentleman' John Jackson agreed to referee the bout but it fell through. Painter instead fought one last time against Tom Oliver, a fight promoted by Tom Belcher, who backed Oliver. Painter won, but it was a poor fight, with both men 'reluctant to engage'.

Painter, with his reputation restored and his winnings in his pocket, became one of Tom Spring's loyal friends and often worked the Fownhope man's corner. Spring kept sharp at several benefits at the Fives and the Tennis Courts, sparring fast, skill-packed rounds with another exciting young prospect, Peter Crawley Their mock battles showed off their grace, speed of hand and foot and deft avoidance of punches swiftly thrown, while their pure youthful athleticism made them a hit with the Fancy. Like Spring, Crawley was noted for 'civility, respectful demeanour, straightforwardness, and good temper'. Both would eventually become English Champions.

12

Carter Upended

Fully fit and eager to fight, Spring was drawing comparison with another dangerous man, Tom Oliver, who had been beaten by Jack Carter on 4 October 1816 at Gretna Green, with the Marquis of Queensberry and Captain Barclay as umpires. Over 30,000 saw the fight, leaving 'the streets and houses of Carlisle and its vicinity… totally drained of the male population – females only were left to conduct business'. Carter won in forty-six minutes, then, responding to indulgent smiles and nudges from the Fancy, immediately claimed the title of Champion of All England. No one took the claim seriously except Cribb, who was so angry at this cheapskate claiming his crown, he offered to fight him for it. The two men eventually boxed an exhibition instead and although Cribb was out of condition, and four stone overweight, he exposed the self-styled champion in a brief skirmish.

Spring's connections now turned their attentions to Carter, who made considerable play of his victory over Oliver, touring country fairs to display his 'art' and peddling the myth that Cribb had refused to fight him. The bumptious Carter was expected to be a stiff test for young Spring. Carter, 'an ignorant mountain of a man', had once fought in conditions so cold that his opponent Jack Power was literally frozen. No one knew, or cared, that the unfortunate Power was dying of hypothermia as he slithered around stumbling into blows, his frozen hands uselessly dangling by his sides. The poor man died soon afterwards.

Contracts were signed for Carter to defend his 'title' against Spring. The stakes were small, £50-a-side with an additional £50 donated by the Pugilistic Club. Carter was installed as favourite, with Spring at two to one against. The two men met on 4 May 1819 on Crawley Down in Sussex before a vast crowd which included the Austrian Archduke Maximilian and the French ambassador, who watched the fight from their gilded coaches. Spring had Cribb and Tom Shelton in his corner while Carter was seconded by a recent victim, Tom Oliver, and the Irishman Dan Donnelly. Spectators were packed 100ft deep around the ring and sat perched in nearby trees to catch a glimpse of the battle.

★ ★ ★ ★ ★ ★ ★ ★

Just after the prelim – a lightweight contest between the brilliant Jack Randall and the 'Master of the Rolls' Jack Martin – Spring and Carter took centre stage. No one gave Spring a chance. He was a kid swimming out of his depth. The odds against Spring winning were now three to one with few takers.

Carter, 'an unstable, self-conceited, and when excited, a bullying rough', was determined to humiliate Cribb's boy. He entered the ring grinning and gesturing, making it clear that he considered the fight won before it was begun. Carter had a trick he often played on the inexperienced and the unwary. Immediately after shaking hands, he threw a quick, sneaky left to his opponent's chin. Cribb had primed his man to watch out for this sucker punch. Tom kept his distance for the first few minutes, padding round Carter, getting his measure. In the tentative early stages, as the massed crowds watched expectantly, waiting for Carter to destroy the young contender, only two punches of any worth were thrown. Both were landed by Spring.

Carter closed on the Fownhope man, grabbing him by the neck. After a brief, eye-bulging tussle, with the crowd hissing and jeering, Spring was flung to the ground. As the two men came up for the second it was obvious Carter was going to use his superior weight and strength to wrestle at every opportunity, to mess Spring about and wear him down. Spring wisely kept his distance, jabbing from a long way off. When Carter grabbed him, Spring resisted with great determination and, to Cribb's delight, he wrestled Carter to the grass. Some of the neutrals in the crowd were getting behind the underdog and there were cries of 'Well done, Spring!'

Spring began the third round brightly, moving in and sweetly catching Carter, who tried to escape. Carter held on grimly to Spring and both men toppled to the ground. Carter suddenly seemed to have no appetite for the task in hand and those who had placed their money on the 'champion' to win handily were astounded by his lack of venom. Spring nailed him again in the fifth and watched as the big man slowly subsided. At times, it was noticed, Carter was a little too keen to visit the grass.

In the seventh it was all Spring, the youngster peppering the big Lancashire man. To the crowd's disgust, Carter turned his back on his opponent and flopped to the ground. Spring was so incensed he 'pointed at Carter with contempt'. The crowd loudly hissed Carter's cowardly and disgraceful behaviour. In the eighth Spring chased after Carter, bashing him out of the ring to the obvious delight of the crowd.

Carter remained determined to hug Spring to death, and rounds nine to fifteen were dominated by his feeble grappling with very few punches thrown. His tactics were wearing down the lighter Spring who 'went down weak' at the end of the fifteenth. Noticing Spring's discomfort Carter upped the ante and caught Spring with a few ponderous swings. The round ended with both men on the ground. The seventeenth was another good one for Carter, and he punched Spring cleanly before throwing him. After a lecture from Cribb, Spring came out for the next round determined to reassert his superiority. He ran after Carter and punished him. Carter tried a big left hook, his famed punch, but Spring blocked it expertly and countered with a stiff right to the button. Carter fell like a dynamited statue. For the next four rounds it was all Spring, darting into the big man and punishing him to head and belly. 'Well done, Spring,' the crowd cheered.

By the twenty-first Spring was ten to eight to win. Despairing of getting past the youngster's jab, Carter resorted to dubious tactics. Suddenly it seemed, an observer remarked, 'as if Spring were fighting a bear rather than a man'. Like a great bull festooned with banderillero's darts, Carter lowered his head and charged into Spring's midriff. It was a crude act of desperation that was received with great disapproval from Cribb. Carter, who was bewildered, bamboozled and outboxed, finally lost his temper, while the superbly fit Spring stuck to his boxing and clipped and cuffed Carter, 'opposing science to the old-fashioned heavy hitting'.

In the twenty-fifth, as Carter was pinned on the ropes and being lambasted by Spring, the older man called out in despair, 'What are you at?' In the next round Spring waded in, Carter grabbed him and the rope broke, decanting both men out of the ring. They resumed with Spring grimly firing short, sharp but hurtful blows. By the twenty-ninth Carter was bleeding heavily at the mouth. It was one-way traffic with Carter taking severe facial damage and his right eye closing through bruising. Spring was outclassing one of the best men in England. As he grappled with the Lancashire man, Carter cried, 'Let go!' Spring was giving him a taste of his own medicine and he didn't like it. In the thirty-sixth, after Spring had again battered Carter out of the ropes, one ringsider sneered, 'Where's the champion now?' He had entered the ring in such a pompous manner; now it was humble pie time.

By the fortieth round, with the fight seemingly on an inevitable course, there was a shock. Carter flung a hopeful swing. Spring, perhaps a little too certain of his mastery, lost concentration and hit the deck with an awful thud. There was pandemonium as Cribb and Shelton dragged their stricken fighter to his corner. Quick to switch sides, the gambling fraternity were now taking bets on Carter to win. Cribb yelled and smacked and doused Spring until he was able to totter to scratch. Luckily Carter was in no shape to do anything but breathe heavily and scowl. Spring recovered and came right back in the next round, falling on top of Carter, an old trick, and knocking both wind and stuffing out of the big northerner.

Carter was holding now and pawing like a tired old bear trying to extract honey from a hole in a tree. Spring, too, was weak, his legs buckling every time Carter leant on him. Both men visited the ground at frequent intervals. Still, Spring landed several good shots which further rearranged Carter's visage. In the fiftieth Spring, whose recuperative powers were amazing, somehow found the energy to chase Carter across the ring and batter him through the ropes. To everyone's amazement Carter climbed back to his feet 'with the utmost sangfroid'.

In the fifty-fourth Spring put together a spectacular array of punches and very nearly wrapped things up. He caught Carter with a blow to the head, the best punch of the fight, and the 'champion' hit the deck like a row of tenements. 'Thunders of applause' greeted the event and 'a guinea to a penny' was offered on Carter surviving the round. Carter's corner got to work and just about succeeded in sending their man stumbling into the ring. Spring coolly measured him before sending him crashing again with another beautiful blow. The gamblers, in a froth of excitement, were offering ten to one on Spring. But the ferociously game Carter came back from the dead and landed two great lefts which shook the Hereford man. Spring survived but he was almost out on his feet. Frantically urged forward by Cribb and Shelton, Spring regained his senses and the initiative and Carter once more collapsed in a flabby, disoriented heap. The crowd went wild. 'Go it, Spring!' they yelled, grinning and clapping like seals at feeding time. 'You have not a minute to lose,' one gentleman said to young Tom. 'Give such a champion a finisher.'

Round fifty-seven loomed. Carter was again floored. In the next, Spring was 'punishing him on the ribs until he went down'. In the fifty-ninth, Carter was 'down like a log' and the round finished with an incredible volley of applause from the crowd. Carter was not yet done for and he connected with a couple of worryingly good punches in the next round, but by now all the support was behind the young man from the Marches. By the sixty-second Spring had beaten the resistance out of Carter, who could barely lift his arms. The Lancashire man was up and down like a yoyo, measuring his length in three successive rounds. Anxious to get the thing over and done with, Spring once more stalked the slow-witted hulk in front of him. The bemused Carter took a bad fall with the full weight of Spring on top of him. The big man lay like a corpse on the ground and, in spite of strenuous efforts to revive him, he was unable to be brought to scratch. Spring was declared the winner after one hour and fifty-five minutes. The post-fight verdict was that Spring's

> ... consummate tactics, defensively and offensively elicited general applause. Although never rash, he never shrunk from his work, and this triumphant defeat of the braggadocio north countryman placed him on a pinnacle of fame. If only Spring had been a punishing hitter he must have won in half the time.

In spite of the carping about Spring's lack of a 'finisher', beating the experienced, self-styled champion Carter was quite an achievement.

Unfortunately the legitimacy of Spring's well-deserved victory was questioned by a group of disgruntled Carter fans who, despite not even being present at the fight, sent a letter to *Bell's Weekly Despatch* in which they accused Carter of taking a dive.

★ ★ ★ ★ ★ ★ ★ ★

On 20 April 1819 Spring boxed an exhibition with Dan Donnelly at the opening of the Minor Theatre in Catherine Street. Both men 'were received with great applause'. Donnelly, who was in training for a fight with Oliver, boxed intelligently, used the ring nimbly and blocked several of Spring's best attacks, to great applause from the crowd.

One of Donnelly's gentlemen backers challenged Spring for £100-a-side, but the same gentleman similarly waved his cheque book at Shelton, Painter, Cooper, Richmond, Neat and Gregson. There was money to be made out of the erratic Donnelly, but the Irishman could not see the point in running, sparring and sweating just to get punched in the gob. He would much rather be chasing girls and downing whiskey – and who can blame him?

> *"Carlisle, May* 12, 1819.
>
> " SIR,—
> " You will oblige the Cumberland fancy by giving insertion to the following paragraph in your next paper.
> " Your obedient servant,
> " H. P.
>
> "The gentlemen of the Cumberland fancy have held a meeting after reading an account of the battle between Spring and Carter contained in your paper, and from other sources of information, and were unanimously of opinion that Carter made a cross of the battle. They have, therefore, come to the resolution of withdrawing all support from him in future: they will not back him, even if he were matched to fight an orange boy. All bets upon the battle have been declared void in the North."
>
> This nonsense elicited the following reply :—
>
> " SIR,—
> " In reply to a letter, signed H. P., from the Cumberland fancy, which appeared in your journal of May 16, I shall briefly observe that the gentlemen who acted as umpires at the battle between Carter and Spring are well known as men of honour and integrity, and had they detected anything like a cross, would have immediately made such a circumstance public. The battle money was paid without hesitation. The noble lord who backed Carter also discharged his bets upon demand ; and no refusal has been made in the sporting world to pay, that has come within the writer's knowledge.
> " Respecting the fight, sir, it was most certainly a bad one—a pully-hauly encounter ; in fact, it was nearly the same as the battle between Carter and Oliver, at Carlisle, but with this difference—the left hand of Carter was foiled, and Spring also proved the stronger man at the ropes. The Lancashire hero having thus lost the two only points for which he was distinguished, led to his defeat. Spring behaved like a man, and did not appear to have any hugging pretensions about him, had he not been dragged to the ropes. Carter was beaten against his will.
> " In giving insertion to the above letter, to prevent any improper allusions going abroad, you will much oblige
> "AN OLD SPORTSMAN.
> " *Tattersall's, Hyde Park Corner, May* 28, 1819."

Letter and reply.

The big-hitting Donnelly outlasted Oliver at Crawley Down in July 1819 but the proposed bout against Spring never got beyond the speculation stage. This may have been linked to the venereal disease which was said to have been the cause of Donnelly's out-of-sorts display in the latter stages of the Oliver fight. Rather than wait in London, the Irish warrior returned to Dublin to spar with 'Gypsy' George Cooper and Bob Gregson at the famous Donnybrook Fair.

13

Sparring in the West Country

Spring, meanwhile, set off on a more prosaic sparring tour through the provinces in the summer of 1819, accompanied by the ever-present Tom Cribb in his role as trainer and ersatz father figure. Cribb, still fêted for his demolition of Molyneaux, 'received in all places the ovation of a conqueror'. After years of irritating vacillation, the old coalheaver had decided finally to relinquish his title and was sizing up the opposition with the intention of matching Spring with a suitable contender for the championship. One man worthy of consideration was 'the renowned and accomplished Bill Neat, a foeman worthy of his knuckles'. Neat was a beautifully muscled, hard-punching young man with great strength.

Cribb, assisted by John Gully, had trained Neat in the early days. Indeed, Neat may at one point have been Cribb's first choice to succeed him as champion, before the two men fell out. Cribb, with Belcher, seconded Neat in his fight with Tom Oliver on 10 July 1818. Neat duly won that fight but was later described as 'little more than a novice who might be improved under the tuition of skilful and accomplished boxers'. There was no denying that Neat's right hand was the most powerful weapon in boxing. In the Oliver fight he was outclassed, panting for air and clearly in trouble, when he blindly swung and flattened Oliver. Still, with his intimate knowledge of Neat, and of the Bristol butcher's sole dependence on that big right hand, Cribb was quietly confident Spring had the skill and the nous to dismantle Neat if the match could be made.

Bill Neat.

Spring versus Neat was first mooted in the Greyhound Inn, in Broadmead, Bristol, during Spring's peripatetic summer tour. Over a drink or two, Cribb and Neat's handlers agreed a match at a 100 guineas-a-side, with 50 guineas to be put down as a deposit. Ten guineas of this were paid on the night with the remainder promised before the fight, which was due to take place on 6 October, halfway between London and Bristol. It was an attractive match, with the Bristolian's 'steam engine power' making him favourite among the Bristol cognoscenti, while Spring's track record secured the fancy of the London crowd. The neutral supporter simply licked his lips in anticipation.

* * * * * * * *

Cribb and Spring continued their sparring tour in good heart. The match they both wanted had been made: Spring would soon be champion. The boxers took in every market town fair in the West Country en route. These rural extravaganzas were wildly colourful, with quacks, strolling ratcatchers, itinerant magicians, hedge preachers, ballad mongers, firearms and perfume salesmen, common pedlars, hawkers and 'providers of small goods'. They attracted 'sharpers', pickpockets, chancers of every type, bright-eyed gypsies, 'curiosities' and 'freaks of nature'.

Respectable citizens naturally feared these outrageously uninhibited jollies might lead to 'the debauchery of Servants Apprentices'. One critic described fairs as 'the prolific seed plots and occasions of the most hideous forms of moral and social evil – drunkenness – whoredom – robbery – idleness and neglect of work,' where folk 'cast off all appearances of decency to plunge into every excess of riot, without shame or restraint.' To the roving pugilist and his team of trainers and sparring partners, on the other hand, fairs provided an opportunity to earn a few pounds during the lean summer months. There were plenty of cider-filled toughs looking to impress their friends by matching their limited skills and scattered wits against the professionals, who entertained the crowds by toying with such men before laying them out as painlessly as possible.

Spring's sessions with Cribb attracted huge crowds, making enough cash to afford a good dinner and a bed at the end of the day. Travelling from town to town packing in the crowds was an easy life. By the time Spring reached Hereford to visit relations and friends, he had money in his pocket and was as fit as a flea.

★ ★ ★ ★ ★ ★ ★ ★

Spring returned to London unaware that the Neat fight had been cancelled in his absence, and trained hard for the most important fight in his career. On the morning of the contest he and his entourage headed for Newbury, the agreed venue, but there was no sign of Neat or his backers. With the normally placid Spring in tow Cribb headed grimly for Bristol to seek an explanation and at the very least to collect Neat's £50 forfeit. Even on this score they were to be frustrated and instead of receiving the £50 due to him through the prior agreement and the sporting rules, Cribb had to settle for £25, with an extra £5 allowed for his expenses. Bitterly disappointed, Spring complained that the people who made the match at Bristol 'had not behaved handsomely' to him.

Neat's reason for skipping out on the eagerly anticipated fight was sketched out in a letter sent to Tom Belcher at the Castle Tavern:

> Bristol, 19 September 1819.
>
> Dear Sir,
>
> I am sorry to inform you that Neat, in taking of his exercise, fell down and broke his right arm: three surgeons were necessary to set it, and their expressed opinion is that twelve months must elapse before he will be well.
>
> From yours, &c.
>
> R. Watson

When word got out that Neat had in fact broken the arm while running down a steep hill known as King's Weston for a bet, Cribb was incandescent, claiming Spring was severely out of pocket due to Neat's irresponsible behaviour. And to chuck sand in the Herefordian's eyes, Neat's backers were trying hard to match the big novice against Thomas Hickman for Cribb's title.

14

Spring Ill and Contemplating Retirement

In October 1819, after an attempt to match Spring against Tom Shelton fell through, a match was proposed with the great Tom Oliver, whose backers asked for a match at £100-a-side. Cribb immediately agreed. Oliver put down a pathetic £5 as forfeit. The following night at Randall's pub they backed out and Cribb was handed the fiver. Spring's trainer then heard that Ned Painter's backers wanted a third and decisive battle with Spring. The challenge was accepted and Painter's initial stake matched. When that too fell through Painter was deemed at fault and forfeited his stake money. With no definite offers lined up, a dispirited Spring gave up on training and started to put on weight.

The Herefordian's route to the title was further thwarted when he was struck down by some mysterious virus and sent to bed. Cribb concentrated on running his new pub, the Union Arms, in Panton Street, Mayfair, serving those of the Fancy who still ventured there. A few drunken loudmouths, foolish enough to insult the great man, found themselves on their ears in the street: John Hauptmann, a German dwarf, complained that Cribb had hit him and took the ex-fighter to court. When the case was heard the 'beak' came to the conclusion that the miniature German had been asking for it. Meantime, Tom Oliver's backers had the nerve to put down a mere five sovereigns for their man to box Spring. The fight never took place and they again forfeited. Spring seriously contemplated retirement.

The amiable Herefordian's tribulations continued into December 1819 when he got out of bed and visited the Castle Tavern to enjoy a quiet drink with the sporting set. 'Over the gaily circling glass, in conse-quence of some trifling dispute over who was the best man', the ailing and unfit Spring was challenged to a fight by a bar-room philosopher and occasional boxer, the massive 'Uncle' Ben Burn, whose nephew Jem Burn, the 'Young Skiver', was a good fighter. The transplanted northerner was landlord of the Rising Sun in Air Street. Without consulting his manager Spring accepted the challenge. His reputa-tion had been impugned and he could do with the money – Burn 'fancying himself as good as any of them' was happy to agree a stake of £20-a-side. It was agreed that the two would meet the next day at one o'clock and a venue was hastily arranged. It being close to the eleventh hour they chose Wimbledon Common and shook on it. Although it was customary because of the interference of magistrates to stage fights well outside London, there were exceptions. Fights had been held in Hyde Park, Wormwood Scrubs, Kennington Common, Islington, Blackheath and Old Oak Common, near Ealing.

Wimbledon Common, a wild and secluded area of 1,100 acres, was inhabited almost exclusively by gypsies. Although seventeen fights were staged on the common between 1788 and 1823, it was better known as the scene of various duels, one involving Lord Cardigan – he of the infamous Charge of the Light Brigade – who wounded a Captain Tuckett in September 1840. In an earlier spat, Frederick, son of George III, the 'Grand Old Duke of York' of nursery rhyme fame, shot it out with the Duke of Richmond on 26 May 1789.

While the sickly Spring persuaded Phil Eales, a useful fighter and a man he met in the pub, to second him, Burn had the star team of Bill Richmond and Jack Scroggins in his corner. Yet such was Spring's reputation he was five to one to win. The two men stripped in the freezing cold and stepped into a ring supplied by the Pugilistic Club. A tiny crowd of less than 250 people turned up. The contest was described as a 'burlesque', with the pale-faced Spring understandably cautious. He picked his punches carefully, 'hit heavily, but seldom, and never gave away a chance.' The huge sixteen-stone Burn threw plenty of punches and grappled with his more illustrious opponent. He even managed with a wild swing to find Spring's weak eye, the one that was almost destroyed against Painter. This was the spur Spring needed and, knowing he could last a long fight, he pasted the big Durham man with lefts and rights, 'hitting Burn when and where he pleased for eighteen minutes'. Burn took some heavy blows and by the eleventh was 'compelled by weakness to give in'. Spring, gasping for breath and out of condition had yet again demonstrated the superiority of his method. It was a gritty display of guts and determination against a fully fit monster of a man. But the effort took its toll on Spring. After the fight he was so seriously ill Cribb ordered him to return to his bed where he remained for some time.

15

Cribb and Burn
Seek Revenge

When Neat came up to London to spar at his second Harmer's benefit Cribb was waiting. The old champion was still furious at the way he and Spring had been messed around. Cribb made a point of sitting ringside to watch Neat sparring. To say he was unimpressed by his former pupil's form is an understatement.

When Cribb tactlessly voiced his opinions in public, Neat responded in a letter that was sent to most London newspapers:

TO MR. T. CRIBB

I observed in a report of the sparring match for the benefit of Harry Harmer, that you, being flushed by the juice of the grape, took an opportunity of paying me a compliment, which I did not expect you had liberality enough to do; namely, that 'Neat was the best of the bad ones,' and that 'you would fight him for from £500 to £1000.' In answer to which, I inform you that I will fight you as soon as you like (the sooner the better) for from a glass of gin to £200.

All Saint's Lane, Bristol, 14 August 1820

WILLIAM NEAT

While on the road to recovery, Spring was invited to work Shelton's corner in his battle with Tom Oliver at Sawbridgeworth, Hertfordshire, on Thursday 13 January 1820. Spring was assisted by Ned Turner while Jack Randall and Tom Callas served in Oliver's corner. Shelton had a bandage tied around his right wrist, which he had severely cut eight months previously when a glass rummer (a drinking cup) shattered in his hands.

The two old bruisers swapped swings until the one-armed Shelton could take no more. As he sat on Turner's knee feeling quite dejected, Callas rushed over and asked him if he wanted to give up. Spring took great exception to this impertinence and a row was narrowly avoided. Oliver won in the thirty-ninth, 'to the surprise and expense of the knowing ones.' After the fight Shelton said he was sorry he couldn't have done better. A medical examination later revealed that, as well as his damaged wrist, the veteran had two broken ribs. Shelton fancied another shot at Oliver but it fell through because Oliver preferred a match with Spring, convinced that Spring was nothing but 'a sparring hitter'. Oliver was certain that Spring's so-called 'fine fighting' would not inconvenience him and he could hardly wait to get the Herefordian into the ring.

In the meantime, Ben Burn, upset at his defeat by a man who, according to some of the connoisseurs of the old ding-dong school, 'couldn't hit a dent in a pound of butter', persuaded his kinsman Bob Burn to challenge Spring for £100-a-side. Cribb put the offer to Tom's backers, who quickly put their money down. The venue was to be Epsom Downs on Friday 8 February 1820, but as the day approached, Cribb, worried about Spring's slow recovery, advised them to withdraw from the arrangement. They did, forfeiting the £100.

As was the practice of the time, the last man to know of the postponement was Bob Burn, who turned up ready to do battle. The ring was erected, spectators began to assemble, Burn threw his hat up and loudly declared he was ready to fight Spring, but the Fownhope man was at that moment sitting up in bed giving a soft-boiled egg a thrashing. As fight time approached, Bill Richmond asked if 'any gentleman present appeared on the part of Spring' but no answer came.

Bill Abbott, a journeyman boxer who beat Dolly Smith, Tom Oliver and Phil Sampson, was there as a spectator. He offered to fight but only for money. A whip-round was made which yielded £12. Burn declined, but a strapping yokel, whose only previous experience of milling was in drunken brawls, stepped forward. Abbott was seconded by Lifeguardsman Shaw and Hopping Ned, while the yokel had the considerable assistance of Bill Richmond aided by Clark. The fight began with Abbott 'putting a hit on the countryman that floored him like a shot'. On being picked up by Richmond the yokel dreamily asked three questions: 'Who done that?', 'What's that for?' and 'Where am I?' The broadly grinning Richmond replied, 'Why, you are in the Court of Chancery; and let me say, you are not the first man that has been bothered by its practice.'

★ ★ ★ ★ ★ ★ ★ ★

As if to fill the gap left by Spring's convalescence, Tom Cribb at forty years of age was sufficiently goaded by Carter to get back into his breeches, even if it meant he had to let the waist out a foot first! Carter had offended Cribb – barging into a private meeting, insulting those present and ultimately throwing a glass of wine, part of which landed on the former coalheaver – but besides, both men could use the money. The 'fight' was held in a crowded room in a pub in Oxenden Street on 1 February 1820. The two men had no sooner come up to scratch then the fight was over, with Carter lying in a heap on the mat. The old maestro just walked though Carter's feeble defence and destroyed him, handing out a severe thrashing in the space of one minute and leaving Carter begging 'that Cribb might be taken away from him, or he should be killed'. As *Bell's Life* reported, 'it was insolence punished'.

Bob Burn's backers again offered Cribb £100 for their man to be given a crack at Spring. Cribb knew Bob was a good fighter, he had seen him spar at the Fives Court and was impressed. Satisfied that Spring had almost fully recovered, Cribb accepted. The fight took place on Epsom Downs on a stormy Tuesday, 16 May 1820.

Burn was in good form after an energetic match with a man called Larkin which lasted twenty-one bruising rounds. The Corinthians, impressed by Burn's style and aware of Spring's well-publicised ill-health, for the most part decided to hedge their bets and put their money on Burn to win. He appeared confidently at the ringside with his seconds, Larkin, the man he had recently thrashed, and Jack 'The Nonpareil' Randall, a sterling little two-handed fighter 'who doubled up an opponent as easily as though he were picking up a flower, or pinching a girl's cheek.'

The string of vehicles that wound its way down the lanes to Epsom Downs that morning rivalled any Derby day. The ring was built with a hill on the northern side which allowed hundreds of keen spectators an unimpeded view of the arena. Burns tossed his 'castor' into the ring, and walked up and down waiting for Spring to appear. Randall tied his fighter's green colours to the stakes, where, eventually, Spring's blue handkerchief joined them. Spring was slow to come to the ring and many punters thought he had backed out because he was unwell. Others betted on him either being unable to punch with any power or even failing to finish the fight, but late money still made Spring the slight favourite, in spite of his problems.

Cribb and Shelton, who had fought and beaten Burn, were in Spring's corner. When Burn stripped his body looked in fine trim. He had lost some weight since he fought Shelton and had obviously taken his training seriously. Spring, on the other hand, looked in less than prime condition. Before the fight, the referee, 'an honourable baronet', lectured both corners on the need for sportsmanship. Jackson also demanded a clean fight without interruption from either corner.: 'Upon the men setting-to the seconds were to retire to the corners of the ring, and if any of them spoke to the combatants, that moment the watch would be thrown down' and the fight stopped.

Spring began slowly, waiting to catch Burn with a counter. The confident Burn tried a few hits but Spring back-pedalled, catching Burn with a 'facer'. Burn replied with a couple of blows. The two men clinched and suddenly Burn was on all fours on the floor. Spring had caught him with a venomous short right. The crowd roared, 'Burn can't win it.' Immediately the odds shortened. Burn decided to trade in the second and was decked again for his trouble, Spring catching him with a brisk combination. 'The big one can't fight,' the crowd jeered. Spring was now at two to one. In the third it became obvious that Burn, though superbly built and trained to the minute, couldn't fight. He did, though, manage to nick Spring over the left eye.

Realising the man was a bum, Spring tore into Burn in the third and battered him around the ring. Although Burn was staggering, flapping and utterly defenceless, Spring did not have the armoury to knock him cold. In the fourth Burn was leaking claret after Spring caught him with some punishing blows. The round ended with him again ignominiously sniffing Epsom grass. Although not fully fit, Spring was walking away with the fight.

By the fifth, though, it was crisis time for Spring. He was weakening visibly and being caught. One stinging punch from Burn grazed powerfully across Spring's scalp, removing a thatch of Spring's hair and leaving a bleeding and intensely painful bald patch. Spring overcame the setback by closing on the lumbering Burn and knocking him down.

Up to and including the seventh, Burn was on the floor in every round, sometimes dragging Spring down with him. But the eighth was a dangerous round for Spring. The two men grappled on the ropes with neither man able to gain the ascendancy. Spring was trapped, and his attempts to escape were sapping his strength. The crowd roared for him to go down and take a rest, but the stubborn Herefordian fought his way out of his predicament only to fall heavily on his head as he threw a punch.

By the ninth Spring looked tired and distressed, dropping his hands in exhaustion, but before Burn could capitalise he was again being pummelled by the fantastically game Spring. As he fell, Burn in his confusion, grabbed Spring by the nose. The fans screamed their disapproval. Burn hitting the dirt once again made them happier. In the tenth both men threw good punches, but it was Burn who was showing most signs of punishment with one eyed closed and his face bruised and cut. In the next round Spring went down from exhaustion, much to the concern of his backers and cornermen, but in the subsequent three rounds he caught Burn more or less at will and by the fifteenth, 'Burn's body and head were quite at his service'. Burn fell heavily and he turned to his corner to tell them he'd had enough – Spring was too strong for him.

Burn's corner told him to get back in there and fight. The big man tried but in doing so fell and twisted his leg so badly it was thought he had broken it. Even so, he was made to return to scratch once again, breathing heavily and looking pathetic. Spring went through the motions until the fight was stopped in the eighteenth. In characteristic fashion, the Herefordian had his opponent defenceless on the ropes in the closing moments but yet again raised his arms and walked away when he realised the battle was won.

For all his ill-health, and obvious weariness, Spring walked out of the ring virtually unmarked. The verdict was that Burn was 'a good trier and nothing else', who lost his confidence when Spring made him look foolish from the outset. The big man had gallons of pluck and his fair share of strength but no scientific method to his boxing. Once more, Tom Spring had shown the superiority of technique over brawn.

16

Spring Tames the Bull

Spring's next fight was a brief encounter with the boozy and belligerent Joshua Hudson, the self-styled 'John Bull' fighter, a man who had absolutely no time for 'fancy Dans' like Tom Spring. Hudson's Cockney ebullience and penchant for practical jokes did not endear him to the serious, clean-living Spring and there was a testiness whenever the two met.

The 'Bulldog Fighter' had a loyal friend in Pierce Egan, who enjoyed the Londoner's heartiness and often visited the boxer's Half Moon Tap. Indeed, he used the inn as the location for some of his famous Tom and Jerry escapades. Hudson, who didn't care for training, often fought well over weight and if his initial windmilling onslaughts failed to make an impact he usually ended up enmeshed in the ropes or on his back.

Spring and Hudson bickered while both were at the Cooper versus Shelton fight at Moulsey Hurst on Tuesday 27 June 1820. Spring, who had lost money on Shelton, refused to allow Hudson into the bedroom where the battered Shelton was recovering. Their arguing was overhead by Corinthians sitting ringside, one of whom mischievously offered Hudson £5 if he would fight one round with Spring. Always on the lookout for a good dust-up as well as a gambling opportunity, several gentlemen whipped out their wallets and between them they put down £20 for a proper fight between the two. Spring, who may have thought it time to teach Hudson a lesson, accepted. Besides, the £20 would be some recompense for his recent losses.

* * * * * * * *

Joshua Hudson.

The fight was wedged in as the fourth fight on a large bill, with Spring starting as the favourite to outbox the roly-poly Londoner. Hudson, wisecracking and full of confidence, had his brother Dave and Tom Owen in his corner. The fight commenced with Hudson, as usual, rumbling forward flinging punches from floor to ceiling. Spring swayed, parried and defended as best he could but the early advantage was clearly with Hudson. Egan reported from the ringside: 'Five or six rounds were sharply contested in which Joshua drew the cork of his antagonist.' However, as soon as the Cockney ex-butcher ran out of steam, Spring began to punish him severely. Hudson, bemused and bleeding, collapsed from a combination of exhaustion and the accumulative effect of Spring's accurately delivered blows. Conceding defeat, he left the ring and pocketed his £5 blood money. Spring, pleased to have chastised the aggressive Hudson, happily trousered his winnings. After the fight the battered Bulldog said words to the effect that Spring couldn't punch his way out of a paper bag. The truth was rather that the gifted Spring had sufficient skill to beat the likes of Hudson every day of the week and twice on Sundays.

* * * * * * * *

It was a difficult time for boxing. Most of the big names were either retired, dead or in the workhouse. Bare-knuckle fighting had become a dull and corrupt business. As a spectacle it no longer attracted wealthy, high-born backers. The days of Cribb, Gully and Jem Belcher were in the past. Gentleman Jackson, who had done more than anyone to keep boxing going, was disillusioned. Immortals like Mendoza sullied their reputations by making ill-advised returns to the ring. At fifty-seven years of age the little Jew took on another half-centenarian, Tom Owen. The fight was a disgrace, two wrinkled old men huffing and puffing, their toothless gobs flapping open with fatigue after a few minutes. The Pugilistic Club damned a sordid exhibition which resulted in the once-great dancing master Mendoza winding up bleeding and humiliated, his reputation in tatters. The ever-decent Jackson's whip-round among the old lags present fetched £20, which Jackson stuffed in Mendoza's pocket before the battered old milling genius was carted away. The Pugilistic Club, too, was in trouble, with its annual dinner in 1820 an embarrassing disaster. Only seven guests turned up. Where were the talented young great fighters who would stride forward, strip, flex their gleaming muscles, vault over the ropes like mythical gods and rescue boxing with skill and charisma?

The centres of excellence were no longer turning out men with a tangible hunger and determination to fight for a living. Those who were coming forward were feeble and inadequate men. Bristol, once the home of great men like Cribb, Gully, Jem Belcher and 'The Game

Chicken' Pearce, now offered 'Cabbage' Strong who, after his encounter with Jack 'Master of the Rolls' Martin in April 1820, was called 'the worst pugilist from the renowned Bristol nursery'. Everyone seemed fed up with boxing. Farmers, without whose cooperation many a great fight might not have been held, closed their gates to the rag-tailed mob who did nothing but rip out hedges, steal hens and trample crops. Fight fans were more disorderly than ever. A contemporary report vividly records the riot that ensued at a Josh Hudson fight:

> The immense multitudes closed in upon the inner ring in one mass, aided by plunderers of the most daring description, with whom some of the fighting men a desparate affray occurred, which ended in many broken heads. Such disorder was never before seen at a fight, and it is hoped never will again, or measures must be taken of a different kind.

What bare-knuckle boxing needed to halt the decline was a real champion, a sportsman who would set an example to others by his exemplary behaviour. There was only one contender for the post: Tom Spring.

★ ★ ★ ★ ★ ★ ★ ★

Cribb and Spring attended the Tom Oliver versus Ned Painter rematch on 17 July 1820 in North Walsham, Norfolk on a spying mission. Both got work as seconds to pay their expenses. Cribb, aided by Tom Belcher, worked Oliver's corner, while Spring, who had forged a friendship with Painter, was the senior man in Ned's corner, assisted by Paul. It was a hugely popular match. Colourful crowds wound like a giant crocodile over the hills and down the valleys to invade Norwich and, according to some reports, over 1,200 vehicles passed over the Cottishall Bridge into the city. The Fancy turned up in such huge and famished numbers that 'the place was literally drained of every article it possessed in the eating line in the course of an hour or two; and as to Hollands, Rum, Brandy, and Wine, the rapid demand for all these renovators of the constitution beggared all description.'

Also at the battle were the backers of Tom 'The Gasman' Hickman, an undisciplined slugger who was being slyly lined up for a match with Neat for a 'title' fight. Hickman wanted Spring first. Cribb agreed but only £5 was paid down by Hickman's side. This was always a bad sign and the Gasman's backers duly reneged on the deal after securing a fight with Neat.

Oliver showed up, 'dressed in white trowsers, a black waistcoat and a green greatcoat', but there was no sign of Painter. Cribb was getting agitated. Eventually Painter turned up, out of breath and without his coat. Then followed a dispute about the gate money, with Jackson ruling that it should be divided equally. Cribb took a friendly one-guinea bet with Spring that the fight would be off. The boxers settled their differences and entered the ring. Spring won the toss against Cribb for the shade. It was a cracking fight with both men in receipt of heavy punishment, the claret flowing plentifully, and both regularly taking a closer look at the texture of the grass.

The opposing corners worked efficiently, with neither Cribb nor his pupil mentioned in despatches. Spring had the last laugh though when the big-hitting Painter nailed Oliver in the twelfth, rendering him incapable of continuing. Poor Oliver was so shattered by Painter's final blow that he scrambled to his feet after an interval of dozing and, walking shakily up to his opponent, said, 'I am ready to fight.' 'No,' said Painter, 'I have won the battle.' At which point Oliver turned in aston-ishment to Cribb and said, 'Why have you not picked me up sooner?' Cribb replied with a smile, 'Because I couldn't wake you, Tom.'

At a dinner after the fight Painter announced his retirement from the ring to run The Lobster in his adopted town, Norwich. The same year Spring decided to follow his mentor Cribb into pub manage-ment. In assuming control of the Catherine Wheel, in Little St James's Street, Spring was joining no fewer than twenty-five other pugilists in the pub business. The venture lasted a year.

17

Spring Tackles Oliver

Fighting, not ale pouring, was Tom's profession and he was pleased to hear from Cribb that Tom Oliver's backers, 'anxious to keep the game alive,' were prepared to offer a match. Over a 'jolly' dinner at the Castle Tavern, 'the game Oliver was pitched upon to try to check the upward career of Spring. The stake of 200 sovereigns was good.'

The date selected for the fight was 20 February 1821. It was to be the first mainline promotion of the year and backers hoped it would mean a return to the huge gates of yesteryear. They needn't have worried. Spring's reputation had grown and the fight proved an enormous attraction. The only trouble, as far as the poor pedestrians were concerned, was that the venue was moved all over the place before a final site was agreed upon. Cribb initially agreed to fight at Salt Hill, Slough. However, while the spectators were mustering, the local magistrate sent for Oliver, who had arrived early, and extracted from him a promise that he wouldn't fight there.

On hearing the news, carts, coaches and pedestrians set off for the Magpie on Hounslow Heath. *Pugilistica* reported:

> The cavalcade proceeded down a lane at Arlington Corner, where the ring was formed in a meadow, and tired horses and rickety vehicles were put up by the hundreds: but here they were again stopped by Magisterial authority, and the ring was next formed at Newman's Field, Hayes, Middlesex.

Tom Oliver.

The string of carriages wound down the road for miles – the horsemen galloping and leaping over the hedges, the pedestrians all on a trot, and the anxiety displayed on every countenance to arrive on time. The surprise occasioned in the villages through which this motley group passed was immense. Children ran out of doors at the farm houses shouting, the 'Johnny Raws' were staring, the country girls grinning, the old folks wondering what was the matter, and asking if the French were coming, the swells laughing, and bowing to the females, and all the Fancy, from the pink on his 'bit of blood', down to the toddler, full of life and spirits, formed a most interesting picture.

★ ★ ★ ★ ★ ★ ★ ★

Oliver's management were convinced their man was one of the best 'in-hitters' in the game and they doubted Spring could stand up to their man's crippling body shots. Spring's strength lay in his ability to avoid punches and score with sharply delivered counters, and he had the will to endure pain and keep going when arms, legs and head ached. If only he could lose that niceness and just wade in and finish off weakened prey. As he had beaten most of the likely contenders the smart money was on Spring to win. Some dismissed the fight and the claims of either fighter, one critic describing them as being 'as inferior to their predecessors as a would-be tragedian would be to a Kean'.

Under Cribb's wise tutelage Spring was in prime condition, but Cribb knew Oliver would fight till he dropped. Born in 1789, Oliver was a thick-eared old warrior, with a mug like a map of the United Kingdom. He was still a formidable foe with his slashing, eye-cutting punches and he had the heart of a lion. His aggressive style meant that over his long career he took fearful punishment to land his own blows, even when fighting moderate opposition like George Cooper. He showed enormous courage when he clawed himself back from the verge of defeat to beat Painter in their first fight, after shipping so much punishment he could hardly see. In his losing fight with Carter he was carried from the ring 'in a state of stupor, and completely deprived of sight'.

Oliver also lost to Dan Donnelly when the Irishman's handlers had managed to get their man to the ringside sober and in some sort of shape. Although Oliver fought with his usual leonine courage, with over £100,000 wagered on the result, the Irish cleaned up. Oliver did have some success in his next fight, beating another veteran, Tom Shelton, on 13 January 1820 at Sawbridgeworth in Hertfordshire.

****

There were a few noblemen among the crowd, mainly older gentlemen who followed the honest trier Oliver as Cheltenham coves would a trusty old steeplechaser. Oliver had Owen and Richmond in his corner, while Spring was in the capable hands of Cribb and Painter. Oliver was sporting his trademark striped stockings. When Spring asked after Oliver's health he replied with a smile, 'Pretty bobbish'. The joshing ceased when they two men toed the line. Both looked in fine fettle. The first round was quiet with plenty of cagey circling. After a light exchange of punches, they grappled and both went down. 'Oliver must win it,' one old gentlemen croaked. In the second, Spring settled into his smooth boxing and caught Oliver with a stiff punch that knocked the older man down. Spring's followers shouted, 'That's the way to win it.'

Boxing superbly in the next round, Spring hit Oliver at will, cutting his lip and knocking him down again. For the next few rounds Spring piled up the points, tenderising Oliver's face. In the sixth, Spring dazzled Oliver with a variety of punches, including two great body shots. By the seventh Oliver was blowing and missing. Spring threw him heavily, knocking the wind out of him. As Oliver lay seemingly concussed, Owen ran to him calling out 'Hallow, Tom! What is the matter – are you going to sleep?' Oliver was indeed comatose but Spring allowed him to recover. Oliver grabbed and hugged for all he was worth and Spring 'showed great forbearance, and allowed him much latitude'. By the tenth the fight should have been stopped. After taking a savage cut to the eye, Oliver fell the floor, doused in his own blood.

Worse was to come. In the fourteenth Spring grabbed Oliver in a headlock and rained such a combination of blows upon his face that it became one distorted mess of blood and bruising. Poor, outclassed Oliver fell to the floor, utterly poleaxed. Both fell in the next, with Spring's full weight on top of the battered veteran. When Oliver hit the floor, the thud was sickening. When time was called he seemed unconscious and the fight over. But after being allowed a long half-minute to recover, Oliver came up to scratch looking like a man who had been run over by a brewery wagon. He stared into space then put his mitts up. 'He's a brave creature,' one old friend said. 'He's an extraordinary man,' another pensioner agreed. Oliver had to take great punishment in the next three rounds. Spring was just too good for him and chased his foe around the ring, beating him to the punch and switching from head to body, before felling the big man with ease. The next rounds were like a training session. Spring had improved so much as a fighter. Was there anyone in the country who could live with his speed and brilliant technique?

In the eighteenth Spring caught Oliver with a punch as he was dropping to the floor. A few in the crowd thought it was a foul blow. Spring allowed Oliver to recover before savagely walloping home some superb body blows. Spring had obviously worked on this part of his game with Cribb, the most savage of belly punchers.

By the nineteenth, Clark, a friend of Oliver, thought he would stop the slaughter by throwing his hat into the ring. It was kicked out and the fight continued after Owen dragged Oliver to his corner where Richmond tried to retrieve the situation. The front seats began to empty as several of Oliver's fans left the scene of their old hero's painful humiliation. In the twentieth Oliver decided to make a last stand and he blazed away with all he had but it was laughably inadequate. Spring brushed him aside and continued to inflict pain and cut him up. In the next round, thinking Oliver had quit, Spring went to put on his coat against the chill February winds when, to his surprise, Oliver trundled up to him for more punishment. Spring calmly let fly with several punches and Oliver, not for the first time, noisily measured his length on the ground.

Surely this must be the end! But no. The crowd were angrily encroaching and in a madhouse of chaos and confusion the two men endeavoured to fight on. Oliver was beaten to a standstill but he pigheadedly refused to give in. Even his backers, men not normally concerned with humanity, cried out to have the one-sided fight stopped. 'Hold enough,' they yelled. 'Take him away.' But with Richmond in his corner Oliver knew he would have to die and be dissected before the towel fluttered. By the end Oliver's supporters could do little but pity their man's stubborn courage. Batttered from one side of the ring to the other, the old campaigner refused to yield.

He was led up to scratch one more, 'reeling like a drunkard who had swallowed two quarts of Deady's primrose', and was again battered onto the ropes. As he lay there, a helpless target, someone in the crowd cut the ropes and let him down gently. Oliver sat bemused and disoriented on his second's knee, unable to come out for the twenty-sixth. It was over at last in fifty-five minutes. Those who had despised Spring for being a powderpuff puncher and not gung-ho enough for their taste only had to look at Oliver's face to be answered.

****

The post-fight verdict was that Spring 'had won the battle three times before it was over'. A combination of speed of hand and thought, quick reflexes, long reach and fancy footwork thoroughly confused Oliver, who was systematically dismembered. Spring's stock rose after this fight. The great Pierce Egan, while feeling sorry for Oliver, was mightily impressed by Spring who 'by his superior mode of fighting on that day, raised himself considerably in the estimation of the Fancy in general; it must be a good man indeed to beat him; in fact, the ring was much surprised that Oliver could do nothing with him.' 'It's no use arguing,' Oliver said afterwards, 'Spring is too clever, too strong for any of us.'

A correct Statement of the BATTLE

BETWEEN

Spring & Oliver

For One Hundred Guineas aside, at Newmann's Meadows, Hayes, Middlesex, on Tuesday, February 20, 1821.

Yesterday was the beginning of Gymnastic Sports, and at day-break in the morning the western road was all bustle with the usual equipages, from the lordly barouche to the sweep and costermongers' *sets out* intermixed with the *Bermonsey dennets* and *sedate rattlers*, and all seemed upon an e-quality. The *raincrites* as game as the *Norwich bull,* started after their Monday night's diversions, and no adequate idea can be conveyed of the confused scene when the Fanciers approached the ring. When a great event is on the eve of being decided, much interest is excited; and, from the diversity of opinion respecting this battle, on which the best judges were at variance, a corresponding interest prevailed.

Of the biography of these heroes of the day's play, it will be sufficient to be brief. They are first-raters of the present day, but as inferior to their predecessors *used up* as a would be tragedian to a Kean of the present day. Both men beat Painter in their first battles, and both were vanquished by him in their second battles. Carter beat Oliver easily at Carlisle, and Spring beat Carter with the same ease at Crawley. Of their fighting, Spring has length and strength of his adversary, and he beat Carter as the latter did Oliver, by hugging him, and half hanging him at the ropes of the ring. But Oliver is the best in-hitter, and fancied himself superior, Spring being a light hitter of his weight.—The groupes of horse and foot which had assembled at Slough, Salt-hill, &c. on Monday, were disappointed in *taking* ground, as the *Beaks* sent for Oliver, and without offering to molest his person, took his word that he would not fight there.—The Magpies, on Hounslow Heath, was the next rendezvous, and from thence the cavalcade proceeded down a lane at Arlington Corner, where the ring was formed in a meadow, and tired horses and ricketty vehicles were put up by hundreds; but here they were again stopped by Magisterial authority, and the next ring was formed at Hayes; but two thirds of the pedestrians, and half the horses were beat.—Seconds—Crib and Painter for Spring, and Tom Owen and Richmond for Oliver.—Guineas to Pounds on Oliver.

Spring versus Oliver.

While Oliver bore all the signs of a severe beating, Spring, on the contrary, had not the slightest mark on his face. Egan, who had seen more fights than anyone and who knew the form book backwards, compared Spring with Jem Belcher, Cribb and Gully, putting the Herefordian in the same bracket as the greatest bare-knuckle fighters of all time. After the fight Cribb considered Spring his rightful heir as Champion of All England. He was not the only one who did. Among the crowd who watched Spring box that day was an Eton schoolboy who without his master's knowledge had hopped over the wall to see the fight. His name? William Gladstone.

On the Friday after the fight Spring, in a spirit of gentlemanly solicitude, called on Oliver, who sportingly whispered through battered lips that he 'had entertained an opinion, before the fight, he was the strongest man' but Spring 'was too long for him'. According to Oliver, Spring 'had a head for fighting, and a man only wins by chance if he hasn't a head.'

* * * * * * * *

On being informed that Neat intended to fight Hickman for the championship title, Cribb was furious. Tom Spring, he said, was his worthy successor. At which point the venerable old champion once again declared his retirement, naming Spring Champion of England. So Spring had a nominal hold on the title but even he would admit his hold was tenuous. In order to decide the matter in a more unambiguous fashion, Spring challenged Neat, offering the Bristolian the not inconsiderable sum of £500 to decide once and for all who was the real Champion of England. Neat's backers were studiously disinterested. Spring was an awkward customer; he was fast and he could box. He might make Neat look ordinary.

While Spring was now poison when it came to finding fights, he was much in demand as a second. He worked for anyone who asked him, including the vicious Phil Sampson, 'the Brummagem Youth' who had been matched against Spring's nemesis, Josh Hudson. Sampson was a vain and bad-tempered individual who spat venom at friend and foe alike, but he was very popular with the upper crust, who admired 'the bounceable young fellow'. With Hudson in the other corner it promised to be an epic battle all over again. The two men had fought before, Hudson winning a thrilling fight during which he accidentally landed the point of his knee on the fallen Sampson's 'private parts'. Although the incident brought tears to the Brummie's eyes he accepted Hudson's apology.

Spring was assisted by Randall, with the ever-present Oliver acting on behalf of his friend Hudson. The fight took place on Saturday 3 March 1821 on Banstead Downs, Surrey. Enjoying a mutual respect after their recent battle, Spring and Oliver exchanged smiles as they went up to tie their fighter's colours on the ringposts.

Hudson was built like a beer barrel but he could fight. It was another terrific contest with both men scoring knockdowns and drawing claret by the magnum. Hudson, showing great guts and determination, overcome a mauling in the eighteenth when Sampson hit him with everything but the ringposts. The 'Bulldog Fighter' took it all and came back to batter Sampson to the deck. Sampson struggled to his feet and attacked once more. It was hectic stuff and the crowd enjoyed it hugely. Round twenty-eight proved to be the last as both fighters, red with blood and dizzy with weakness, toed the line like a couple of drunks on Brighton pier. Although Hudson had taken massive head shots throughout the fight, the blows only made him madder and more determined to win.

It was this indomitable grit that finally wore down the game Sampson. In what proved to be the final round Hudson came to scratch with his lower lip hanging like a piece of pork liver. His eyes were all but closed and he swayed like a sapling in a hurricane. Sampson was in even worse condition and toppled over before Hudson could even try to raise a tired fist. It had been the sort of fight that renders the second's job obsolete, and all Spring and Oliver had to do was provide the knee and the bottle between rounds and watch the two men attempting homicide. Hudson did extraordinarily well to beat the highly-touted Sampson but the result was a tribute to Spring, who had made Hudson look mediocre when they fought.

In a public advertisement of 25 March 1821, Spring challenged all comers to try to take his 'title'. The ad ran for months but there were no takers. It seemed no one regarded Tom Spring as the champion except his 'old Dad'. Meanwhile Spring had plenty of offers from pub philosophers whose heads were spinning and blood was boiling. Spring was done with that sort of stuff. He was no longer interested in fighting some cowardly hungover drunk for a tenner at the crack of dawn. Cribb fielded each belligerent request with diplomacy. The connections of Sutton, a famous black prizefighter, also wanted Spring. The offer was tempting but just as the day approached the arrangement was cancelled.

18

Spring Marries

The year 1821 was a big one for Spring, and not just in boxing. His next engagement was 'one of a more tender kind, a match made for better or for worse'. Unfortunately, there is little of consequence written about Spring's bride and what is recorded is not complimentary. Downes Miles wrote, 'We wish that our personal reminiscences did not unpleasantly remind us that, as regards the lady she was all "worse", and never showed signs of "better".' What we do know is that a certain Elizabeth Griffiths from the city of Hereford had agreed to marry the finest young heavyweight in the kingdom. Packing his presents and laughingly accepting the ribald jibes and congratulatory back-slapping of his pugilistic peers, Spring caught the coach back to Hereford. Tom was quietly elevating himself socially. His bride was the daughter of William Griffiths, a schoolmaster at the City Member's School in Commercial Road, 'the next house to Mr Simister's rope-walk'.

The ceremony took place on 26 June in St Peter's church, a modest red sandstone edifice built on ancient foundations and equipped with a chancel dating from the twelfth century and featuring a solid copper key measuring 31in long as a weather vane. Among the plate was a capacious silver-plated flagon rumoured to be the largest in the county and capable of holding enough cider to render most of the congregation legless. The Reverend John Duncumb, Rector of Abbey Dore, a man of considerable local acclaim, was brought in especially to conduct the service, a rare honour for the former Tom Winter from Fownhope whose father was incarcerated in a debtor's prison.

Left: St Peter's church exterior.

Below: The marriage certificate.

Duncumb was born in Sussex in 1765 – where his father held a living in the gift of a man whose early interest in Tom helped the youngster launch his career: the Duke of Norfolk – and went on to compile an unfinished but valuable *County History of Herefordshire.*

After the ceremony and the inevitable altar kiss, the tall Spring and his diminutive wife stood outside St Peter's on that sunny day in the shadow of the Booth Hall, a venerable pub Spring would one day return to manage. The *Hereford Journal* briefly recorded the match, sniffily referring to the finest heavyweight in England as a man 'known in gymnastic circles'.

The confetti was still in the Hereford gutters when the newly-weds packed their bags and set off for London with the bunting hanging from their carriage and the cheers of friends and relatives ringing in their ears. Tom kept in touch with boxing by acting as second, assisted by Hickman, for the sulphuric Phil Sampson when the Birmingham button-maker fought Charley 'Gybletts' Grantham for £50-a-side at Moulsey Hurst on Tuesday 17 July 1821. Sampson boasted that the match would be his inside twenty minutes, but Gybletts put on a bravura show to clip the youth's wings in one hour and twenty minutes. As all the 'flash' money was on Sampson, heavy losses were mulled over in the riverside inns that night.

19

Spring at the Coronation

Later that year the unthinkable happened, when Tom Spring, the unpolished rustic from Fownhope, Herefordshire, was invited to join a team of the top eighteen fighters in the country to act as ushers at George IV's Coronation on 24 July. The fighters were selected by 'Gentleman' John Jackson. Aided by Watson, 'a distinguished amateur', and with a little encouragement from Cribb, Jackson selected men he could trust.

The Prince of Wales's interest in bare-knuckle fighting was originally fostered by his appearance ringside as a gay young blade with a penchant for boozing and gambling. He became a regular, attending a number of fights including the bloodfest between Richard Humphries and the 'Bath Butcher' at Newmarket in 1786. Jackson had first met the Prince in 1788 when boxing at Smitham Bottom near Croydon. The nineteen-year-old fighter was slipped a banknote by the Prince after a particularly skilful demolition of his opponent. He went on to defeat the Prince's favourite, Daniel Mendoza, for the title on 15 April 1795.

* * * * * * * *

Now a sad and portly fifty-seven-year-old and in such poor health that many wondered if he would live to be King, George was determined to have the finest fighters in the land at his Coronation, not merely as spruced-up, oversized pages but as bodyguards. The celebration was going to be the most kitsch, the most elaborate, the most fantastic public event ever seen. No expense would be spared. There were many terribly poor and disenfranchised citizens out there who might just find the whole tacky exhibition a little provocative.

Cartoon of the Coronation.

Months were spent in preparation. Tiers of seats were erected in Westminster Hall, with a raised floor, a dais with boxes at the sides for the royal family, and the inevitable triumphal arch. The King's path was strewn with herbs selected by His Majesty's herb lady, Miss Fellowes, aided by her six maids in ivory gauze dresses and Medici ruffs. It was a scene straight out of *Blackadder*. Benjamin Haydon was so bowled over by the herb-scented virgins that he tossed off a dreamy ditty: 'The grace of their action, their slow movement, their white dresses, were indescribably touching'. There was 'blue and gold brocade for the altar, a specially woven blue and gold Wilton carpet on the altar steps and the sacrarium floor' and 'crimson velvet and sarsenet for the royal box'. Twenty-eight tailors, six gold-lace-makers, several specialists in robe-making, two sword cutlers and two goldsmiths were recruited. Endeavouring to encourage a spectacular love-in with his wary subjects, the Prince spent £25,000 of public money on his own gaily embroidered costume – not including the cost of sending someone to Paris to examine the quality of the French Emperor's robes so that the Prince of Wales's would be altogether more beautiful, and with a longer train! The resultant costume was so weighed down with gorgeous threads and jewellery that the new King almost passed out. The crown that sat on top of his false curls contained 12,314 jewels and cost the equivalent of £5 million in today's money.

It was going to be the coronation to top all coronations – especially that of Napoleon in 1804. Yet in spite of the mounting expense, perhaps because of it, response from those invited was muted. 'Application for Seats to see the Procession,' an official reported, was 'owing to the apprehension of tumult very slack.' In the event, many of the boxes and galleries that had been so painstakingly erected were left vacant, and there was a suspicion that the crowd were paid to cheer – although there was nothing new in that on royal occasions!

It was hardly surprising, therefore, that the King might need a little insurance in the shape of eighteen of the top pugilists in the land to keep the rabble's filthy fingers off the childish monarch's fat neck. The King, who for breakfast consumed, 'two pigeons, three beefsteaks, three parts of a bottle of Moselle, a glass of Champagne, two of Port and one of brandy', was so vilified by the press that he paid George Cruikshank £100 not to lampoon him. Cruikshank took the bribe but continued with his insulting drawings.

What a sight it must have been for Tom Spring, the poor young man from Herefordshire. One minute he was plucking pheasants at the back of a butcher's shop and punching a sandbag at the rear of a dusty little cottage in Fownhope, the next standing scrubbed, shaved, ramrod-straight and dressed up like a doll right beside the new King in an overdecorated Westminster Hall. The old bruisers must have felt ridiculous, dressed in their adorable scarlet coats trimmed with gold lace, with blue sashes and white silk stockings. The *Annual Register* of 1821 described them as 'Splendid, and in some instances grotesque'.

The heavyweights waited, nervous and impassive, sweat beading on their foreheads for it was a bright sunny day, their big-knuckled hands clasped in front of them. Spring, tall and erect, his handsome countryman's face only marred by that Painter scar, stood side by side with the man who made him, his mentor, the great Tom Cribb, both of them guarding the entrance to Westminster Hall.

'The manly appearance of the "big ones",' Egan wrote, 'attracted the notice of most of the great folks who were present at the august ceremony.' The old pugs stood shoulder to shoulder, their battered faces serene. These enormously tough and heavily-muscled working men, in their ludicrous page boy suits, stood like a pride of old lions, ready to spring into violent action should anything befall their King. Along the line from Spring waited some of the most famous bare-knuckle fighters England ever produced: Tom Belcher, Tom Oliver, the fiercely-English-and-damn-proud-of-it Josh Hudson, Jack Carter (who resisted the temptation to show off his twin talents, clog dancing and standing on his head while tossing off bumpers of ale), the stylish black fighter Bill Richmond, Ben Burns, Harry Harmer, Harry Lee, Tom Owen, Harry Holt, Peter Crawley, Dick Curtis, Ben Medley, Purcell, Phil Sampson and wily Bill Eales. But no 'Sir' Dan Donnelly, allegedly knighted by his friend, the Prince.

The real reason the biggest, roughest and best boxers in the country were recruited to guard the new King's every gold-slippered step quickly became apparent. Queen Caroline, on receiving news of the Coronation, hastily prepared to return to London to spoil the Prince's party. When the *Observer* reporter Vincent Dowling, 'The Oracle of the Ring' (who later edited and published the seminal *Fistiana*), got wind of the Queen's intentions, he rushed to France to document her progress. In order to beat the opposition to the sensational story, the intrepid Dowling made a storm-tossed nocturnal Channel crossing to arrive in London triumphant with the news.

Full of Germanic high temper, the irate Caroline turned up at the Abbey demanding admission. On hearing the commotion, the flat-nosed, thick-eared pugilists rushed to the door en masse. Cobbett wrote: 'When she got to the door, and made an attempt to enter, she was actually thrust back by the hands of a common prize-fighter.' The Queen, whom Lord Hood thought 'looked like a blowsy landlady', was booed by some sections of the crowd and cheered by others. Nowithstanding her rank, the pugilists were ready, with sinews taut as banjo strings to repel the fragrant invader and her supporters.

After the ceremony, Jack Carter and Phil Sampson – who were 'reared in the hard schools of canal navvying and a Birmingham button factory respectively' and could hardly keep their thumbs out of the soup – and the comfortably upholstered Tom Cribb and Josh Hudson, both bursting out of their flash tunics, helped staff serve a sumptuous lunch. The menu, which cost over £25,000, was a gastronomic nightmare of soups, fish, roast joints of venison, beef, mutton and veal, vegetables with 'appropriate gravies', cold ham, pastries, seafood, and 3,271 jellies, sluiced down with 9,840 bottles of wine and punch. After lunch the King's champion rode in to formally challenge the King's authority by a cod throwing-down of his gauntlet three times. It wasn't taken up, but as the shy young man selected for the role galloped into the hall to the sound of trumpets, 'the horse defecated dramatically'.

When the official aspect was over and the King taken away, it was a signal for the hungry hordes in the galleries to descend like uncaged rodents onto the half-eaten feast and grab anything they could lay their hands on. Pies, cakes and wine were spilled and trodden into the priceless blue-and-gold carpet as the noisy and undisciplined crowd crammed their faces with food and their pockets with golden cutlery and the finest cut glasses. The scene encapsulated the vulgar King's image and the standards he had himself set. But it was a memorable day for Tom Spring – one he would never forget. Who cared if a few killjoys saw his involvement as a result of a bloated and cowardly King's need for the protection of a bunch of heavies in ornate garb? In turbulent times the main consideration was that the King, sedated on the grand occasion with laudanum and alcohol, shouldn't suffer the same fate as Perceval, the Prime Minister who in 1812 was murdered in the lobby of the House.

The fighters were allowed to tuck into what was left of the food and were required to return next day to keep public order. Lord Lennox was delighted at the dignified behaviour of the boxers. 'Nothing,' he said, 'could exceed the good humour and forbearance that characterised their proceedings.' Each man was delivered a personal letter of thanks from Lord Gwydyr, the Lord Great Chamberlain, and the King donated a gold medal which was later raffled and won by Tom Belcher, who wore it with pride until his death.

20

Back to Boxing

Spring's more normal routine of battles and betting was rejoined when he was invited to second, with Hickman, a boxer called Lenney against the most brilliant lightweight of the time, Dick Curtis, the 'Pet of the Fancy'. The location was Moulsey Hurst and the date, 24 October 1821. Curtis was the most glamorous fighter around, who dressed in a 'white upper-benjamin with a brilliant canary yellow fogle around his throat, and a white beaver of the most fashionable mould'. Spring admired the engaging 'Pet' and he learned a lot from him, including how to improve his wardrobe. The swashbuckling little boxer strolled to the ring arm in arm with Tom Belcher, then President of the Daffy Club. But the betting boys at ringside were taking money on Lenney to cause an upset.

As Spring tied Lenney's colours to the ringpost Belcher cracked, 'I'll bet you a trifle that I take them down'. His ebullience seemed justified as Curtis began the fight like a cobra striking, flooring Lenney in the first round. The fight continued in the same vein, the lithe and speedy Curtis throwing fast clusters and sliding away from the counters.

In the fifth round he dropped Lenney with a corker of a right-hander which caused another great lightweight, Jack Randall, who was sitting ringside, to exclaim, 'What a beautiful fighter!' It was a perfect exhibition of ringcraft, with the game Lenney so totally outclassed the fight should have been stopped in the ninth. It dragged on for another twenty painfully one-sided rounds with Lenney absorbing punishment from the Pet's flashing fists. When the battle was over,

Curtis's hands were swollen from the beating he had given the luckless Lenney. It was generally held that no one could hold a candle to the glamorous lightweight, but in the end he fell victim to his own invincibility. The Pet ran out of opponents, and lost his fine record by being forced to concede weight to another fighter, also seconded by Tom Spring.

* * * * * * * *

Towards the end of the year Spring took another pub, the Weymouth Arms Tavern, in Weymouth Street, Portman Square. After the palpitating excitement of fighting, the acclaim, the travelling in style, the cosy inns, the adoring fans, and a wad of cash in his breeches pocket, it must have seemed tame. Elizabeth was hardly the beaming and buxom barmaid required to entice new customers off the street and into a tiny, dim little inn in a London backwater.

However, the two of them worked hard preparing for their opening dinner on 6 December 1821. Jackson presided and 'the swells numerously mustered.' It was an important occasion for Spring. Jackson was such a revered personality that his presence at Spring's humble inn sent the appropriate message to those with money and influence. 140 guests sat down 'to a prime dinner, served up, in excellent style, by Spring in person. The evening was dedicated to harmony and good fellowship.'

Christmas approached with the promise of an increase in trade but with no sign of a title fight. That honour had gone to Hickman, 'the ferocious, determined, neck-or-nothing man' who was matched with Neat for the title on Tuesday 11 December on a freezing Hungerford Downs. The 'Gasman' was an absolute phenomenon. He had beaten the accomplished Peter Crawley and thrashed the scientific George Cooper twice in a total of thirty-one minutes. Spring was naturally disappointed to miss an opportunity but at least he could earn a little money as one of Hickman's seconds and be able to observe Neat at first hand, in case their match came off.

One week later Sampson fought again. It looked like easy money against Bill Abbott, who, it was rumoured, 'had trained under the auspices of Mr Lushington' – in other words, he was on the beer. Abbott's appearance, though, suggested quite the opposite. He seemed fit and confident, and he had Spring in his corner assisted by the Herefordian's old friend, Shelton. Sampson also had a brace of good men on his side, Jack Randall and Tom 'Paddington' Jones. The Birmingham Youth was favourite at seven to four.

As Abbott stepped up to scratch he looked the image of 'Tom Cribb in his early fighting days' while 'Sampson asserted he was never so well in his life before'. It had the makings of a good fight. In the event, though, it was the same old Sampson. If he didn't nail his man in one of his wild rushes, he tended to walk into lamp-posts. He huffed and he swung and he charged head down, he was knocked over and he got up and did it all over again. In the fourth he fell and got Abbott's knee in his guts, at which point 'in the ecstasy of the moment, the cabbage-plant heroes offered five to one that "the Birmingham ware" must soon be disposed of'. In the seventh, 'a distinguished sporting man from Newmarket offered a guinea to a bottle of beer' that Abbott must win, 'but no taker appeared'. Sampson looked very second-hand by the forty-third, when the fight was stopped in Abbott's favour.

21

Spring, the Gasman and the Fight of the Century

When Spring again agreed to second the Gasman in his 'title' fight against Neat, he wasn't to know the blood-spattered contest would go down in history. Spring was just pleased to be there to take a good look at Neat. The match caught the public imagination. The handsome and charismatic Gasman was popular among the blades, who turned up in colourful droves to cheer him on. Wheeled vehicles of every shape and size galloped to see him display his boxing prowess. Faces gaunt, fierce, hirsute, pampered, polished or pimpled, snored, grinned or stared out of every speedily passing window. Egan wrote:

> The delicate fair ones were seen peeping from behind their window-curtains. The fight was a good turn for the road; the lively groups all in motion. Tradesmen were leaving their counters to have a york at their doors; country girls were grinning, the joskins staring; the old folks hobbling out astonished; the propriety people stealing a look; with all their notions of respectability and decorum. The fun met with on the road going to a mill was a prime treat, and more good characters were to be witnessed than at a masquerade. Carts, hay-wains and drays of all sorts lumbered noisily over the cobbles while lightweight coaches hauled by thoroughbreds tore along at great speed, their spinning wheels flinging dust into the eyes of the tattered children who with smudged faces laughed and smacked their hands with glee at the unique parade unwinding before them.

Coaches and four, sometimes six, were driven flat out by egocentric men who, according to George Borrow in *The Romany Rye*, 'considered themselves mighty fine gentry, nay, the most important personages of the realm, entertaining a high opinion of themselves.' Cocky, boastful Hickman, against the hulking 'Bristol Butcher' with an explosive right fist, predictably drew a massive crowd, and farmers were hiring out their haywains to the toffs at £25 a wagon.

The fighters and their seconds arrived early. Helping Spring to keep order in the incandescent Gasman's corner was his friend Tom Shelton. Spring would have disagreed with Borrow's description of his fellow fighter as 'grim savage Shelton, a civil word for nobody, a hard blow for anybody'. The two had a cordial relationship and worked many a corner in quiet harmony.

In spite of their weight differential – Hickman was conceding two stone – on paper the Gasman and the Butcher seemed evenly matched. Neither was obsessed with the finer points of boxing and both were powerful hitters. Neat was the better bred of the two with a 'school education that was superior to that bestowed on the generality of those who turn to the ring'. He also had excellent men looking after him in Tom Belcher and Harry Harmer. With all to play for, the Fancy took their seats. William Hazlitt, the great essayist, who was once asked to step outside by Jack Randall when the brilliant lightweight 'was more full of blue ruin than of good manners', took his place ringside and opened his notebook.

On his way to the fight Hazlitt had shared a coach and 'exchanged civilities' with a shifty gambler and fixer who handled Hickman's affairs for a while. The man was John Thurtell, about to become nationally infamous as a brutal murderer. With two others, Thurtell robbed and killed a fellow gambler named Weare. The crime and the resultant trial made sensational news with 'penny-a-line' merchants making fortunes printing off and selling sheets full of real and imagined facts about the case. William Thackeray wrote that as far as murderers went, 'John Thurtell was the flower of the flock'. As a member of the Fancy he was an expert on 'fighting dogs and men, bears and badgers.'

Thurtell told Hazlitt how a fighter should train. 'Exercise and abstinence,' he said, 'abstinence and exercise. A yolk of an egg with a spoonful of rum in it first thing in the morning, then a walk of six miles till breakfast with a plentiful supply of tea, toast and beefsteaks.

Then another six or seven miles till dinner-time, and another supply of solid beef or mutton with a pint of porter, and perhaps, at the utmost, a couple of glasses of sherry.' Thurtell, son of a respectable Norwich Alderman, had been introduced to boxing by Ned 'Flatnose' Painter, Tom Spring's friend and only conqueror, who ran the Anchor Pub in Norwich. Another connection.

Hickman was favourite. On 12 June 1821 he had demolished Oliver in twelve minutes, while it took Neat an hour-and-a-half. When they'd sparred at the Fives Court to raise interest in the fight, Hickman impudently walked up to the Bristol butcher and, measuring him from head to foot with a contemptuous gaze, sneered, 'What are you, Bill Neat? I'll knock more blood out of that great carcase of thine, this day fortnight, than you ever knocked out of a bullock.' Hazlitt thought Hickman's actions were those of a frightened man and he unfavourably compared the Gasman with 'civil, silent men' like Cribb, Jem Belcher and Hen Pearce.

The Gasman talked a good fight but it didn't sway John Gully, a shrewd judge who had sparred with Neat at Jackson's gym. He was so impressed by his fellow Bristolian he betted heavily on Neat to beat Hickman. 'If a fine, young, strong, fourteen-stone man,' Gully reasoned as he nursed a pint of ale in the Three Tuns at Newbury, 'could not defeat a twelve-stone boxer, then there was no calculation on prize-milling at all.' Egan agreed. Mr Gully, he said, was a 'cool, sensible man, not a slave to passion in these matters'.

Hickman, exuding confidence, swaggered to the ring wearing a white top hat and sucking an orange. Puffing out his chest he raised his right fist and said, 'This is the gravedigger.' He then shook hands with Neat and asked, 'How are you?' Neat's reply is not recorded but it was probably in Anglo-Saxon! As Spring stood smiling at his man's antics Hickman continued to posture shamelessly, treating his doleful, bandy-legged opponent with utter contempt.

The Gasman had borrowed every penny he could lay his hands on, including £200 from his wife, who came from quite a well-off family, to bet on himself, even though he was giving away weight and inches to 'the great, clumsy, long-armed Neat'. In total, £150,000 was laid on the fight – an enormous sum.

Hickman, who was built like a miniature Roman god, won the toss, allowing Neat the watery winter sun full in his eyes, then sprang savagely at his opponent. He landed 'five blows in as many seconds, three first and then following Neat as he staggered back, two more right and left.' the Bristolian collapsed under the sudden pressure. 'Neat,' Hazlitt said, 'seemed like a lifeless lump of flesh and bone, round which the Gasman's blows played with the rapidity of electricity or lighting.'

Happy with his handiwork, Hickman sat on his second's knee and winked at the crowd as he mentally prepared for an early visit to the hot tub. Remarkably Neat recovered from the sustained barrage, lifted his two great fists, gritted his teeth and, ignoring the 'lump as big as a hen's egg' on the side of his head, stood like a mute monolith in front of his tiny, fiery opponent.

The Gasman rattled across the ring and again belaboured the static Neat with punches from every angle. He was determined to destroy Neat. He had placed a large bet on winning the fight within sixteen minutes, a feat he had accomplished on five similar occasions. Everything was going swimmingly. The Gasman was unmarked and full of pep. Spring and Shelton were counting their bonuses. Fired by a fierce desire to get the job over and done with and retire a wealthy man, Hickman swung mightily at the huge target in front of him, Neat, with the baleful eyes of a murderer, sidestepped and crunched the incoming Hickman with a right hand that ripped his face open and felled him. 'How do you like it?' one excited London dandy asked another. 'That blow has just cost me, I am afraid, 100 sovereigns,' his friend archly replied.

John Gully looked down at the fallen Hickman and said, 'That blow has won the fight.' Spring and Shelton worked frantically to get their man up to scratch, dosing him with brandy and, no doubt advising caution, at least until his head was completely cleared, steering the Gasman back to the furnace. Hickman 'grinned a horrible, ghastly smile' – there was to be no respite. Suicidally he tore into Neat to land his famed 'whisker blow' but Neat now had the measure of him and felled him again with lefts and rights. 'There was little cautious sparring,' Hazlitt observed, 'no half hits – no tapping and trifling, they were almost all knockdown blows... It was one of the most brutal fights ever seen.'

At the end of the fifth, Belcher, Neat's second, felt relaxed enough to shout into the Bristolian's ear, 'That's the way, it's all your own. You'll win it my boy: only a little one now and then for the Castle.'

Spring and Shelton knew theirs was a lost cause. Hickman was not up to the job. But the Gas still raced in, even though he was choking on his own blood. Neat measured him coolly once more and floored him with an enormous punch to the abdomen.

In the seventh, Hickman did not rush in. He simply had not got the energy. Instead he stood quietly, covered in bleeding contusions and breathing heavily as if gathering his wits and his strength. 'Be ready my boy, he's coming,' Belcher said. Shelton and Spring were concerned at Belcher's constant interference on Neat's behalf, and at last Shelton complained to Gentleman John Jackson who sat close to the ring.

Tom 'The Gasman' Hickman.

In the eighth Hickman, laughing like a lunatic, charged across the ring once more only to be impaled by a massive right fist. Hazlitt watched awestruck as 'Neat made a tremendous lunge at him and hit him full in the face'. Pierce avowed it was 'one of the most tremendous right-hand blows ever witnessed. The eyes were filled with blood, the nose streamed with blood, the mouth gaped blood.' *Pugilistica* said Hickman 'went down like a log and when he rose he clawed at his eyes and howled, "Where's Neat? I can't see him. I am blind."' The man deemed one of the most exciting and dangerous knockout specialists in the kingdom, who had shattered good fighters, was staggering around like the victim of a bomb blast.

'It was doubtful,' Hazlitt wrote, whether Hickman 'would fall backwards or forwards.' In the end, he seemed to hang suspended for silent seconds before falling back, his hands in the air and his face a lifeless, senseless mask. As the Gasman lay prone, the only movement in the ring was the blood spouting from his broken visage. Spring rushed to his stricken charge screaming 'Gas! Gas! Gas!' But Hickman was totally unconscious, a deadweight as Shelton and Spring dragged him back to his corner. At last the Dudley man opened one manic eye. He was facing death.

Remarkably Hickman survived. In the next round Neat seemed content to play with his battered foe, allowing him to retrieve his senses. Hickman repaid the Bristolian man by connecting with a wild punch that sent Neat down. Downes Miles commented: 'An experienced boxer of the London ring would have taken advantage of this circumstance, and not have given the chance away. It was a tragic fight, one-sided but due to Hickman's insane bravery, fascinating.' Hazlitt watching open-mouthed, observed: 'To see two men smashed to the ground, smeared with gore, stunned, senseless, the breath beaten out of their bodies; and then, before you recover from the shock, to see them rise up with new strength and courage, stand steady to inflict or receive mortal offence, and rush upon each other like two clouds over the Caspian... this is the high and heroic state of man who doesn't feel pain.'

By the beginning of the eleventh round Hickman was in a dreadful state. It wasn't improved by Neat nailing him with another sleep-inducing right. Hickman fought on for another seven painful rounds with no hope of winning, but eager to strike the one blow that would save him from the poorhouse. Knowing he had him licked, Neat plodded forward, his big fists hiding a square jaw. It was an embarrassingly easy victory. Another man with a big punch had been exposed. The London fraternity were cleaned out and returned to the Smoke with 'pockets to let'. But there was no complaint. Hickman had fought his heart out and gone down fighting.

The result of the fight was carried to London by carrier pigeon, the birds arriving at 3.30 in the afternoon. Neat, the much-ridiculed, big-hitting novice had earned his place in the sun, in literature and in history. Bristol was as raucous as if there had been a declaration of war. The streets were dark with men wanting to read the account of the fight in the *Bristol Gazette*. The boys selling the paper had placards by them which read:

<blockquote>
Bristol Illuminated,
London in darkness,
The Gas extinguished by a 'Neat hand'.
</blockquote>

A modern fight fan might wonder why Spring or Shelton didn't pull Hickman out of the fight. Shelton was a friend of the Gas. Surely he wouldn't want to see him take such punishment? The answer is that it was against the rules. If the cornermen had shown compassion, the opposing ruffians in the crowd would have joined forces and rioted. There was masses of money riding on the result. Later the rules were amended, forbidding outclassed fighters from being dragged and bullied to the scratch.

After the fight Hickman, who had previously so antagonised both the Fancy and the wealthy backers with his foolish and insulting behaviour, drew massive sympathy from the crowd. He had lost every last penny of his own and his wife's money. Lavishly, he was praised for his pluck. Jackson, who had refused an offer to referee the fight, went to the Gasman's side and whispered, 'I am collecting a purse for you Tom.' Mr Elliot, at the time Hickman's backer but later to swing to – and disappoint – Spring, lost a huge sum on the outcome. Neat went up to his defeated prey and shook his hand then, turning to the cheering, stamping crowd, picked out a familiar face and snarled, 'You always said I couldn't fight – what do you think now?' 'Not much.', Spring might have been thinking as he relished the prospect of relieving Neat of his cardboard crown.

Hazlitt asked Cribb, who was at ringside, what he made of the fight. 'Pretty well,' Cribb dolefully replied. He still harboured a grudge against Neat for stealing his title. Now, having seen Neat, he knew his 'boy' had the skill and the brain to combat the butcher's brawn.

After the fight a commemorative medal was struck bearing the legend 'The good old English Custom of Deciding a Quarrel'. Hazlitt wrote the most famous boxing report of all time, 'The Fight', published a year later in the *New Monthly Magazine*. It became a literary classic. Hickman's blood-letting was not in vain; he was immortalised. What fight fan would not thrill to that opening: 'Reader, have you ever seen a fight? If not you have a pleasure to come...'

****

A year later Hickman, fully restored to health and having just taken over a pub, was racing home with his backer Tom Rowe from watching Tom Shelton beat Josh Hudson on Harpenden Common. As it careered across Finchley Common, their frantically driven gig collided with a loaded farm wagon. Both men were decanted under the wheels and killed. *The Annals of the Sporting and Fancy Gazette* said 'there never was seen a worse driver than Tom Hickman who was spoilt by gentlemen who lavished praise on him and gambled huge amounts on his fights.'

Hickman, only twenty-seven years old, was popular among fighters, who were massively represented at his graveside. Everyone was there except Tom Spring, with no reason given. Cribb was listed as one of the pallbearers but 'cried off in consequence of a restive horse, on the preceding evening, near Stockwell, having thrown him off and fallen upon him.' In reality, Hickman was an unpleasant man, who in his truncated, violent life had bludgeoned defenceless old Joe Norton to death after some trivial argument, regularly beat up his wife and once broke the back of Cy Davis's dog in a fit of temper.

The presiding vicar said of Hickman: 'The unfortunate man had not time for repentance, but was killed like a moth, trod upon like a grasshopper, run over like a dog.' The celebrated fighter was buried eighteen feet underground to prevent body snatchers from digging up his beautifully proportioned corpse.

The fight fraternity rallied around Hickman's widow and her two young children. Jackson arranged a benefit at the Fives Court on

5 February 1823 at which 'all the first-rate pugilists will produce a grand display of the Art of Self Defence'. Most of the top names contributed, including Cribb and Tom Spring, whose sparring with Bill Eales garnered considerable praise and helped raise £133 13s 6d for the cause.

22

Cribb Abdicates At Last

Neat, basking in the glow of his success over Hickman, hoped he would now be taken seriously as a fighter. He was sick of being 'chaffed as a nobody'. Now he could name his price as he toured fairs and clubs giving exhibitions. But he was definitely in no hurry to defend against Spring, who was still supping at the servant's table as far as fighting went.

Cribb tried to arranged a bout for Spring against a little-known fighter named William West. They were set to box on 12 March 1822 but nothing came of it. On 18 March, Spring was recruited by his old pal Eales to second his protégé Dick Acton, who was down to fight Kendrick, a black pugilist, at Moulsey Hurst. Randall and Hudson handled Kendrick's corner. Acton was the outsider but won the match in thirty-two rounds, rattled off at cracking pace inside thirty-five minutes.

Spring must have missed the atmosphere of the big promotions: the tension and excitement, the badinage, the satisfaction of winning and the company of the men who idolised him. Behind the bar at the Weymouth Arms he was just another pint-puller, a nearly man with a veneer of sporting excellence that barely separated him from the bores and the shiftless drunks who frequented his pub. He was neither a dashing Dick Curtis, a hail-fellow-well-met Josh Hudson, a smooth and respected 'Gentleman' John Jackson, or a big-hitting Neat. He was a good boxer, he was fair and sporting, but was he exciting? No. The gentry never took to him like they did to Sampson and Hickman.

Tom's misery was compounded when his father Joseph, an inspiring first teacher, if a poor role model, died on 29 May and was buried beside Fownhope church.

While Spring regularly attended fights either as a second, a whipper-out or a mere spectator, his own career had ground to a halt. He again contemplated retirement. Cribb knew his 'boy' had the skill and experience to take Neat's crown, and was determined he should have it, but Spring didn't want the fight. He got used to eating well and drinking more than an athlete should.

On 18 May 1822 Cribb persuaded Spring to accompany him to the Fives Club, where the old champion intended to formally announce his belated and long-awaited abdication. The club was packed to the skylights with the Fancy and the swells. Backers were there with new money and old. Square-shouldered pugs were crammed together. A few prematurely emancipated women provided a touch of elegance. In their lofty 'suite' gentlemen took snuff while snootily observing the goings-on below. 'Never in the history of British boxing,' it was reported, 'did a more distinguished crowd gather' than that which joined to pay their respects to the great old champion. Portly and happy in drink, Cribb was in rare form, singing and chanting with the best of them. He climbed the stage to tumultuous applause and so many feet stamped on the bare boards that dust rose in the club's dim, fight-hallowed air.

Staggering a little, and ostentatiously wearing his old threadbare lion-skin championship belt, Cribb theatrically slapped down a bag of guineas and bellowed, 'Not while I have a drop of blood in my veins will I let my title go without a fight.' The Fancy roared, 'Bravo Tom, bravo.' Cribb dabbed at his maudlin eyes with his kerchief and called for his 'boy' to step forward. To loud cheers Spring picked his way through the throng, bowed to the crowd and announced, 'My lords and gentlemen; my Old Dad, as I'm proud to call him, has retired from the prize-ring altogether, and as I have stood next to him for some time past, I mean to stand in his place till I am beaten out of it.' The crowd whistled and hooted, while the gentlemen in their private eerie nodded sagely.

★ ★ ★ ★ ★ ★ ★ ★

" *Castle Tavern, Holborn, Wednesday, March* 12, 1823.

" William Neat agrees to fight Thomas Spring for £200 a-side, in a twenty-four feet ring, half-minute time. To be a fair stand-up fight; to take place on Tuesday, the 20th day of May. The money to be placed in the hands of Mr. Jackson. The place and distance from London to be left entirely to Mr. Jackson. An umpire to be chosen by each party, and a referee to be named on the ground. £50 a-side is now deposited in the hands of Mr. Jackson. £50 a-side more to be deposited on Monday, the 31st of March, at Mr. Belcher's, Castle Tavern; and the remainder of the stakes of £100 a-side to be completed on Monday, the 5th of May, also at Mr. Belcher's. The above stakes to be put down between the hours of eight and eleven o'clock on each evening. The above deposit, or deposits, to be forfeited, in case of either party not appearing on the specified evenings to make the money good."

Contract for Spring *v.* Neat.

On Monday 12 June 1822 Spring, assisted by Bill Eales, was at Moulsey seconding Dick Acton against the talented but unreliable Jem Ward. The latter won handily in six blistering rounds, leaving the shoemaker unconscious in the ring for three minutes before he could be moved. On the same day, after the sport was concluded, it seemed the match everyone wanted to see was finally made. Spring would at last box Neat for the title.

Interested parties were invited to a 'sporting dinner' at the Castle Tavern on 12 November to discuss the matter. This only made a confused situation even more tangled. Neither Spring nor his backer, Mr Elliot, put in an appearance. Belcher put down £200, of which £150 had to be forfeited to Neat because Elliot was deemed to have broken the contract. At another dinner, this time at the Old Tun on 16 November, Spring apologised for the mix-up. He said he was told by Elliot that the latter 'would make it all right' and that he 'was now ready to make a new match for £200-a-side'.

At yet another dinner, this time at Harry Holt's Golden Cross in Long Acre on 22 November, the chairman urged both parties to tie up the much-anticipated fight, but Elliot again did not appear. Moreover, Belcher said that since the first talks had been held Neat had taken to the bottle and he (Belcher) could not guarantee his condition. 'Neat was acting like a bird out of a cage,' Belcher said, with the 'gaily circling glass continually up to his mouth.' His man would need training, not to say sobering up. Neat had left for Bristol and Belcher 'had no doubt from his gay disposition, he was playing the same sort of game there.' Belcher promised to write to him there immediately and endeavour to make the fight. Spring said since the fight had failed to materialise he too had missed training and was in the same condition as Neat.

He added that his backer, Mr Elliot, had deserted him, leaving him severely out of pocket. He expressed his keenness to fight Neat, after which he intended to 'quit the prize-ring forever, to attend to his family and business'. There were loud cheers, and shouts of of 'Well said', 'Manly', and so on. Spring said he was prepared to give Neat time to get in condition.

At a well-attended meeting at the Fives Court on Thursday 28 November 1822, Spring was booked to spar with an old opponent, Jack Carter. In an impassioned plea from the ring, Spring again challenged Neat for £200-a-side and said he was prepared to put the stake money down there and then. He claimed impatiently that too much time had already been wasted, and again declared his intention to retire from the sport after this one all-important fight. The match must be made 'now or never'. Cries of 'Very fair!' came from every corner of the Fives Court. 'Well spoken, Cribb's boy,' a well-dressed gentleman said as he pushed forward and placed a hand on Spring's arm. It was Lawrence Sant, Corinthian, sportsman and Wandsworth brewer. Anxious to discuss Spring's prospects Sant got into an earnest huddle with Cribb. Without knowing Elliot's position, a deal was done. Spring and Carter then put on a good exhibition.

Sant contacted Tom Belcher, matchmaker, second and landlord of the famous sporting watering hole The Castle Tavern, to inform him that he was prepared to put up £300 for Spring to fight Neat for the championship. Neat, who won £1,000 beating the Gas, was in no hurry to risk his 'title' against such a smart fighter as Tom Spring, but the public wanted the fight. The news that Spring and Cribb were waiting to hear came at last: Neat was ready to defend his crown.

> *" Red Lion, Hampton, June 12, 1822.*
>
> " Mr. Elliott, on the part of Thomas Spring, and Thomas Belcher, on the part of William Neat, have deposited £50 a-side, to make a match on the following terms:—W. Neat agrees to fight T. Spring on Tuesday, the 26th of November next, for a stake of £600 (£300 a-side), in a twenty-four feet ring, half-minute time. The place to be named by Mr. Jackson. within forty miles of London, on the Bristol road, and the umpires to be chosen on the ground. The second deposit, upon the above conditions, £100 a-side, to be made at T. Spring's. Weymouth Arms, Weymouth Street, on the 12th of July, between the hours of four and eight o'clock. The deposit to be forfeited by the defaulter. The remainder of the stakes to be made good at T. Belcher's, the Castle Tavern, Holborn, on the 12th of November. Mr. W. S. has received, and is answerable for, the deposit of £100."

Second contract.

Sant, Cribb and Spring descended on Bristol to try to get Neat signed up. They met at Sam Porch's tavern near the Bristol Guildhall where backers were found to cover Sant's stake. A date for the fight was agreed, both fighters signed a contract but – due, it was intriguingly said, to some difficulty between Spring's 'betting agents' – the fight was called off. Neat's side demanded a £150 forfeit. Sant paid and the fight was on again, this time with the solid figure of Jackson holding the stake. Jackson also agreed to oversee the preparation of the ring and organise some way of controlling the more rumbustious fight fans. Jackson's method was to treat the hooligans to a good whipping. It was, Jackson said, 'the only thing they understood'. The new contract was signed over another good dinner at the Castle Tavern on 12 March 1823.

The following week, on 19 March 1823, Spring was at Moulsey Hurst seconding the Brummagem Youth in his return fight with Bill Hall. Spring was assisted by Jem Ward. In the other corner stood chubby Josh Hudson with 'a friend from Birmingham'.

After snorting and pawing the ground, Hall streaked out of his corner. Sampson sidestepped like a cartoon matador and clipped Hall on the nob as he trundled past, felling the Brummie on the spot. Upon resumption Hall went berserk, chasing after Sampson and pelting him with everything he had. Sampson took it all, then absolutely and totally nailed Hall between the orbs with a Sunday punch that sent him to the floor with a thud. He lay there motionless, without as much as a preliminary twitch. The crowd was stunned at the ferocity of it. Hall looked dead.

It was with some relief that the habitués of the Castle Tavern greeted Hall at eight o'clock that very night. Hall said he was 'out' for twenty-five minutes and was bled twice. He showed no ill-effects except for the incisions the surgeon made to tap his claret.

23

Spring Arrested and the Title Fight Threatened

The crucial match between Spring and Neat was to be contested near Andover. After his hammering of the Gasman, Neat was considered the most terrifying boxer around, the Sonny Liston of his era. It was an enormously attractive match. The betting men were convinced that Spring would not be able to regain his former speed nor have the resilience to stand up to Neat's hitting. The Fownhope man would be simply brushed aside by the Bristol butcher's raw power.

Forswearing all alcoholic potions and reckless snacking, Spring monastically prepared for the battle of his life. While Neat had recent experience in the bloody theatre of real fighting, Spring had not engaged in a proper fight since he had beaten Oliver in February 1821, twenty-seven months previously. He went into training in Brighton with Tom Shelton, who had just signed up for a fight with Hudson. The two men pounded the commons and the lanes and punched holes in punchbags and each other in preparation for this career-defining skirmish. Spring sparred with the youthful enthusiasm of those gilded days in the barn behind the cottage in Fownhope. He sharpened both wits and mordant skills, and worked on speed and stamina. Neat was no less eager. The fight was a gravy train for all concerned and Spring, nearing the end of his career, could certainly do with the money.

* * * * * * * *

Then came a serious setback. While taking a break from training in Brighton for the Neat fight, Spring was recruited with Tom Shelton to act as 'whippers-out' at a modest fight on Brighton Downs between Daniel Watts and James Smith. They patrolled around the ring with bull whips, assisting a mounted supervisor in crowd control duties. Spring also had a watch in his hand during the fight which indicated he was doubling as time-keeper. In Watts's corner stood a couple of unknowns, Hazeldean as bottle-holder and Sherwood as second. When Smith died from his injuries after the fight, Spring and Shelton, along with the other two men, were arrested and charged with 'complicity' in Smith's death.

Spring lied under oath, saying he was nowhere near Brighton at the time and Shelton said the fight was made days earlier and neither he nor Spring knew anything of it until they arrived in Brighton. Their testimonies were rejected and Sir David Scott, the local magistrate, ordered the men to be detained in a pub until the evidence was considered. A stream of flat-nosed visitors made the boxers' stay in custody not an unhappy one. Eventually Spring's backer Mr Sant intervened and explained to the magistrate Spring's position *vis à vis* the upcoming title fight. On offering to pay a £100 surety against the unlikely event that Spring might get into further trouble, both he and Shelton were released. Spring was criticised for being 'imprudent for a man in training' but the title fight was saved. Spring immediately put £100 on himself to win.

* * * * * * * *

Neat had his training quarters above The Angel in Marlborough where he was visited by the famous Quaker philanthropist Elizabeth Fry. Leaving her two daughters below, she ascended the stairs to confront the surprised Neat and Tom Belcher, who was supervising his training. 'I understand, friend Neat,' Mrs Fry said, walking up to the muscular half-naked Bristolian, 'thou art about fighting a prize battle. Dost thou not know it is very sinful? Be advised, friend, and give it up.' Neat was tongue-tied but managed to blurt out that if the fight were cancelled he 'would be a heavy loser'. 'If it be the lucre of gain, friend Neat,' Mrs Fry smiled, 'I will recompense thee.' With that she rooted in her handbag, but before she could pull out a wad of notes Belcher intervened and showed her to the door. When the newspapers got hold of the story they went to town, with all the licence and imagination that only they could muster. Neat remembered Mrs Fry's visit and years later he ruefully remarked, 'I'd rather have faced Tom Spring for two hours than Mrs Fry for twice the money'.

* * * * * * * *

When the chosen battleground was revealed – 'a field about one mile short of Andover, opposite the Princess Charlotte pub' – the combined magistrates of Berkshire, Wiltshire, and Somerset moved in, clutching writs banning the event. Desperate to know the new location, Corinthians besieged Jackson's home at Pimlico on the eve of the fight, clamouring after information. Hinkley Down in Hampshire was finally chosen.

The layout of the land was perfect. Much like at Epsom, a hill at the back of the field created a natural amphitheatre, ensuring that the crowd got a good view. Spring walked out from Andover with Mr Sant to inspect the venue. 'It was so beautiful a spot,' Spring said afterwards, 'no man could grumble to be well licked on it.'

The Bristol man had Belcher as second and Harry Harmer as bottle-holder. Spring, meanwhile, was served by Cribb and a Mr Hancock, but specifically requested that Ned Painter should also be in his corner. Painter immediately left his pub in Norwich and headed for Hinkley Down.

Upward of 30,000 spectators began to assemble from dawn. One report put the attendance at 40,000. Spectators came from all parts of the country and some took the boat over from Ireland to see if Neat could destroy Spring the way he had dismantled Hickman. The large number of tall, craggy men with rearranged features showed how many pugilists had made the trip. This was a fighter's fight. The ringside bookies thrived on the numbers and the atmosphere, filling their satchels with heavy bets on both fighters.

The role of ringmaster fell again to Gentleman John Jackson, who performed his duties with aplomb. 'I have refused to be referee,' he told the massed crowd, 'that I may walk about and attend to the ring.' He then reasoned with the gentry and those closest to the action to move back and give the men room to fight. 'Only the umpires and the referee,' he said 'can be stationed close to the ropes.' The nobles respectfully shuffled back a few inches.

At one o'clock Neat arrived arm in arm with his backer, Mr Harrison. Belcher, followed by Harmer, threw Neat's hat into the roped square amidst thunders of applause. About ten minutes later Spring appeared, accompanied by Mr Sant and Ned Painter. Cribb was already there waiting for them. Spring very coolly walked up to the ropes, and dropped his hat inside. Then Neat's orange-yellow colours were tied to the stakes by Belcher and the speckled blue, for Spring, placed over them by Cribb. The two fighters stripped and faced each other across the turfed ring. Neat was massively structured, his muscles binding him like steel hawsers. Spring was trim and alert, in the best condition of his life. Downes Miles concluded that 'Two finer young men could not have been opposed to each other, or a more equal match made.'

Spring shook hands with Neat and said, 'I hope you are well.' 'I am very well, thank you. I hope you are,' Neat cordially replied. The parties shook hands. At that moment there was universal silence: 'Neither from the blue billies for Spring, nor the yellow canaries for Neat, was heard the slightest sound – all was awful suspense and expectation for the opening of the pleadings.'

In the immediate run-up to the match, Spring had gone from outsider to favourite. Downes Miles described Spring's aspect before the fight as 'fine as a star, strong as an ox, light and active as a deer, and confident as a lion.' There was little doubt that Cribb's methods, learned from Captain Barclay, had been most successful.

From the first round it was obvious that Cribb had carefully worked out a 'rope-a-dope' routine, much like Ali did against big-hitting George Foreman. Spring, like Ali, had been out of the ring for a considerable time. Inactivity makes the legs go. So at every opportunity, instead of relying on his sure-footedness and vastly superior boxing, Spring moved inside the arc of Neat's ponderous swings and held on grimly. In the first round both men took stock and the first eleven minutes saw little but tentative sparring until Neat threw a blow to Spring's jaw, which Spring parried. The Bristol man made the amateurish mistake of holding his right hand cocked ready to throw it, and the cagey Spring easily blocked, turning his head to slip the blows or diffusing their force on his arms.

Neat's only weapon nullified, Spring went on the offensive, catching the immobile butcher with stinging lefts and rights. Neat looked confused. One Cockney at ringside turned to a mate and said, 'What do you think of Spring's light hitting now then?'

Neat chased Spring into a corner and was about to lower the boom when Spring, with all the agility of his little friend Jack Randall, wriggled to safety. After a brief flurry of slaps and jabs Spring moved in and, with a deft throw, sent the embarrassed 'champion' sprawling on the grass. The crowd roared; Cribb smiled. Spring was no Hickman. He was going to set Neat as many conundrums as he could. The London Fancy were yelling, 'Spring forever. He can fight for a day and a night into the bargain. Seven to four on Herefordshire!' Even at this early stage of the fight, those with money on Neat were already concerned. Spring – the 'lady's-maid fighter', the 'light tapper', the 'china-man' – was connecting with solid blows in defiance of the hammer-fisted Bristolian.

In the second round Spring stuck to his boxing, unbalancing Neat with swift jabs to the face and hooks to the belly. Neat marched purposefully onward, swinging punches, determined to disturb Spring's equanimity. As he came within range, Spring caught him with a viperish shot on the left eye. Blood spurted. In his excitement Spring yelled, 'First blood, Neat!' This seemed to confuse the Bristol man. He was hurt but managed to stay on his feet. After another barrage of swift, accurate punching, Neat capsized, going down with all limbs flailing.

As he sat on Painter's knee, Spring joked, 'It is as right as the day. I would not take £100 to £1, and stand it – he can't hit me in a week.' Neat's corner was anxious, amazed at the ease with which Spring was handling their hero. Neat's yellow-rosetted supporters, who had bet masses on the right result, were muttering and grumbling.

In the third round, it was obvious that Neat needed to uncork a big right hand, both to encourage his fans and to unsettle Spring, who had relaxed into an ominous routine of steady, thoughtful boxing. Spring held his guard high at all times, ready to counter, as advised by Cribb. When Spring threw a punch and Neat parried, the bemused Bristolian smiled appreciatively at the applause he received. 'Well stopped,' Spring said condescendingly. Neat finally landed a big right-hander which bent Spring's ribs and caused him to grimace and drop his hands for an instant, but the Bristol man was too slow to follow up and missed a great opportunity. There was another brief moment of danger for

Spring when in leaning back to avoid a determined Neat onslaught, he was trapped on the ropes. 'Now's the time,' Tom Belcher shouted, 'get at him.' But instead of wading in with all guns blazing, Neat surprisingly took a step backward. Spring instantly seized the initiative and tore into the 'champion'. After a set-to he threw him, both men falling but crucially with Spring uppermost.

What had become of Neat's bone-crunching punches? Why was he playing into Spring's hands by slavishly following the script Spring had worked out with Cribb?

In the fourth there was still no encouragement for those who had staked their shilling on a Bristol victory. Neat began to look a beaten man. His punches, wrongly delivered, were way off the mark and his defence was non-existent. He was completely bemused. Instead of using his unrivalled power to overwhelm his nimbler opponent, Neat struggled to get past Spring's watertight guard. Spring was now sufficiently confident to forget his defence and just walk up to Neat, who lay on the ropes, lay hands on him and throw him. As Neat hit the ground with a tremendous thump Spring dived on top of him, pounding the breath out of the listless Bristolian and triggering 'shouting like thunder from 30,000 persons'.

Neat plodded to his corner with his right arm dangling uselessly. While sitting on Harmer's knee he grimaced and explained to Belcher he had broken his arm in the fall. The unsympathetic Belcher pushed his boxer back into the fray.

Coming up to scratch for the fifth Neat was obviously struggling, while Spring seemed as fresh as if he had just strolled into the ring. Satisfied he had softened up his prey, Spring

> ... put in a belly-go-faster – Neat staggered – Spring followed up with a second, which took Neat off balance. As he was going down, Spring caught him at the back of the neck with a blow that sent him topsy-turvy. In falling Neat's right arm was under him. Time was called – Neat was manifestly disabled.

What was supposed to be a murderously bloody war was petering out into one-way traffic with Neat clattering to the boards every time Spring got near him. The disappointed crowd yelled abuse at Neat who was stumbling around. The umpires called on Belcher and warned him 'it was stand up fight and Neat must take care of what he was about'. Jackson, sitting ringside, on the fighter's side as always, told them that Neat had gone down as the result of a punch. One punter in the crowd, a man named Martin, bellowed '£1,000 to £100 on Spring!' At the end of a one-sided round Belcher came to the ringside and whispered to Jackson that Neat's arm was broken. 'I perceive it,' Jackson said, 'but I shall not notice it to the other side.'

In the sixth, Neat, holding his injured arm awkwardly, tried his best with his left but Spring clobbered him to the deck. In spite of the fact that he was still fresh and winning easily against a disabled man, Spring remained cautious. He had seen first-hand what Neat did to Hickman and he was taking no chances. As if to prove him right, Neat roused himself and in a sustained attack landed a heavy blow to Spring's side, which the poker-faced Tom took without flinching. Boxing cleverly, Spring dominated the remainder of the round, nullifying Neat's feeble attempts to extricate himself from the web Spring had woven round him. 'We can fight for a week in that manner,' Belcher sneered as Spring made no effort to press home his advantage. 'Yes,' Painter said, 'but we have got the general.' The jibe inspired Spring to open up and he peppered Neat and noisily dropped him to his knees. The crowd, who knew they had lost their money, now had no time for their fallen hero. The Canaries were not singing any more as they gloomily witnessed the gradual humiliation of their erstwhile favourite.

In the eighth, after receiving more punishment and going down again, Neat got up wearily, walked up to the surprised Spring and shook his hand in surrender. He confirmed his arm was broken and he could fight no more. The crowd, used to seeing beaten men grittily sliding about in their own blood, felt cheated and they heartily jeered Neat. What was he about, this paper tiger? What a conman. He was a certain to win. He was a proud man; he had the punch. So what went wrong? There were dark suggestions that the fight was fixed. Rumour had it that masses of money was placed at the last minute on Spring, even that some gamblers got their bets on after the fight was officially over. The matter was settled when two surgeons came forward and examined Neat's arm. They confirmed that a small bone was broken.

* * * * * * * *

A FULL AND AUTHENTIC ACCOUNT OF THE FIGHT BETWEEN

SPRING AND NEATE,

On Tuesday, May 20, 1823, near Andover, in the county of Hants, for the Championship of England, and 400 Sovereigns.

This high Court, of which the jurisdiction is confined exclusively to England, was held on the 20th of May, according to the ancient usage of chivalry, in the open air, near Andover, in the county of Hants, in a circular space, 24 feet in diameter, which for the convenience of judges, the counsel, and the parties, had been previously enclosed with ropes. The site chosen for this Wager of Battle—by which was to be decided the title of *Thomas Spring*, to the office of Champion of England, claimed by *William Neate*, was a field on the left hand side the road, about one mile short of the Town of Andover, in the county of Hants aforesaid, and opposite to a certain Inn of Public House, commonly called or known by the name of the Princess Charlotte. About ten minutes before the honr of one the respective parties to the suit entered the lists—in this court usually termed ring. In support of the damandant, *Neate*, appeared as senior Counsel, or in the language of this Court second, Sergeant Thomas Belcher, a practitioner of unquestioned skill, and great exprience—Mr. Harry Harmer assisting him as junior counsel, or bottle holder—an office peculiar to this Court, but indispensable from its forms and practice. For the respondent Spring, appeared that sturdy and invincible practitioner, Sergeant Thomas Cribb, who never yet lost a name in the Court of honor, The bottle and the lemon were held by his junior Counsel, Mr. Hancock. The judges having announced the opening of the Court, order was with some difficulty otained—a circumstance which will not excite surpise, when it is known that more than 40,000 spectators are computed to have been present at this awful trial for the Championship of England. In the multitude which inclosed the ring, we noticed the most able practitioners in this Court from almost every county in England ; and not a few who had crossed the sea, which divide Britain from the sister Island for the express purpose of witnessing a trial, on the issue of ,which was dependent, not only the honour of the parties to the suit, but the heavy lots of *Blunt* posted by their backers. At length the parties peeled, a term familiar in this Court, signifying the doffi g the upper garments, a ceremony always practised in this Court both by the parties and their Counsel, who by immemorial usage, invariably plead in buff. The ring being divided into two equal parts by a line or scratch in the centre, the parties to the suit shook hands, and the respective Counsel retiring to some short distance the opening of the trial was announced. At this moment there was universal silence, neither from the blue billies, for Spring, nor the yellow canaries, for Neate, was heard the slightest sound—all was awtul suspense and expectation for the opening for the pleadings.

1. Nearly eleven minutes were exhausted in scientific preliminary sparring—when Neate let fly a blow intended for the jowl, but which was parried—alias stopped, by his antagonist, who returned, though not effectively. A rally followed, which, terminating in a close, Spring threw his man—9 to 1 on Spring.

2. Cautious sparring—no effective hitting—but beautiful science on both sides. Neat's tactics were evidently intended to rouse the temper of Spring, but or this point he was immoveable. At length Neat received on the left eye, but kept on its feet. At the end of the rally he was again thrown. And it began to be *suspected by the Canaries*, that there was a bit of a *mistake*.

3. Sparring, with extreme caution on the part of Spring, whose right arm never moved from a position in which he could strike, without preparing for the motion—counter-hits were exchanged, and Spring in stepping back got upon the ropes, when Neat, instead of following up the advantage, retreated. Spring instantly followed him up, and after a rally, had the best of the throw, From the first round there had been very few takers of odds, and here, the *yellows* seemed greatly lowered ir spirits.

4. Neat tried to ruffle Spring's temper, but in vain. Spring still kept his right arm ready for instant action, and at length throwing in a tremendous blow in the *Neck-hole*. Neat went off his legs clean under the ropes. Any odds on Spring—and some of the *yellows* went off in despair.

5, 6, 7. The quantity of *business* not considerable, except in one instance, when Neat put in a very heavy blow on Spring's left side, but Spring invariably had the best of the throw.

8. On coming to the *scratch*, Neat was evidently distressed, while Spring appeared without a scratch—fresh as when he began—and as cautious as if he had all his work to do. Sparring and counter-hits, of little consequence. Spring at last put in a *belly-go-fister*—Neat staggered—Spring followed up with a second, which took him off his balance, and as he was going down, Spring caught him at the back of the neck with a blow that sent him *toward .... .* alling, Neat's n ht

arm was under him. Time was called—and Neat came to the scratch with his right arm manifestly disabled. He held out his hand—which Spring shook, and the Judges immediately pronounced a verdict for the Champion of England.

Two surgeons came forward and examined the arm, the small bone of which was broken. Neat was conveyed in a chaise to the bush, at Andover, and put to bed.

Thus is settled, for the present, the CHAMPIONSHIP of ENGLAND, to which Spring has fairly established his title, until some competitor for pugilistic fame can show a better.

The result of the battle was anticipated after the first round—and, from the fourth, was not doubted even by the *Yellow Canaries*, as tho friends of Neat were termed, from wearing his colour. That of Spring and his friends was blue.

It is generally acknowledged that Neat never had a chance of winning ; his dependance was on the possibility of ruffling Spring's temper, in which, however, he completely failed. The steadyness of Spring never for a moment forsook him, and a more beautiful display of pugilistic science has been rarely seen. It had been said, that the blows of Spring would not tell. "He can't make a dent in a pound of butter," was no uncommon expression of opinion before the "Trial "—a trifling mistake which we apprehend the extraordinary force and velocity with which his right *hammer* was thrown, will have completely corrected.

By an unfortunate coincidence, the Eton *Montem* took place yesterday—and the usual conveyances being previously engaged for that occasion—very few of the assembled multitude had the fortune to find their way to Town till this afternoon. Only a few knowing ones, " up to snuff," aware of the difficulty, had made his necessary provision for reaching town last night.

The fight lasted 33 minutes.

Betting before the battle, was *guineas* to *pounds* for choice.

Spring and Neat.

The truth was that Spring had been yet again underestimated. One hit was all Neat needed 'to spoil the science of Spring'. But he had neither the wit nor the skill to land it. Like Foreman, Neat was out-generalled. The experts summed up the debacle: 'Neat had an opponent of superior talent to himself pitted against him. To give punishment, and to avoid being hit, is deemed the triumph of the art of boxing.' At ringside one John Gully, who had previously backed Neat to beat Hickman, craftily switched his allegiance to Spring and won £100.

It had been a woefully disappointing fight. Neat, rated by some to be the best fighter in England, had miserably failed to live up to expectations. One point made concerned Neat's apparently facile demolition of Hickman: it might have looked easy for Neat but the Bristol man had in fact shipped tremendous punishment before he managed to extinguish the Gas. Jackson, as usual, passed around the hat among the disgruntled Bristolians and handed Neat £47 19s. The fallen battler was carried to the Bush at Andover, and put to bed. Spring called to see him later in the afternoon, after he had had his broken arm set. Neat greeted the new champion saying, 'I am not beaten. I lost the battle by the accident.' Spring knew better but said nothing as he pressed a tenner into Neat's hand and departed for London.

The new champion, sporting a black eye and with his right arm in a sling, waited until the carriage cleared the confines of Andover before shyly tying Neat's canary yellow fogle around his throat. As his carriage passed though towns and villages crowds waved and cheered. Later, Neat, encouraged by the mischievous Belcher, demanded an inquiry into the result. But there was truly no great mystery to be unveiled. One spectator who witnessed the fight said, 'If Neat had possessed four arms instead of two, he never could have conquered Spring.' Another wrote:

> It is generally acknowledged that Neat never had a chance of winning; his dependence was on the possibility of ruffling Spring's temper, in which, however, he completely failed. The steadiness of Spring never for a moment forsook him, and a more beautiful display of pugilistic science has been rarely seen.

As far as Neat was concerned, he was a beaten man before the fall. Most of the Fancy agreed on that point.

Spring's triumph was loudly acclaimed in London. Every pub owned or managed by a pugilist was packed, Egan reported that 'Belcher's house, the Castle Tavern, was like a fair; Randall's was crowded to suffocation; Holt's hadn't room for a pin; Harmer's was overflowing, Shelton's was like a mob; Eales' was overstocked; and Tom Cribb's was crammed with visitors.' Several songs honouring the new Champion were hastily penned.

Neat, it seemed, had every butcher in the West Country gathered noisily around the ring to support him. *Blackwood's Magazine* printed a poem mildly mocking the Bristol meat men and their broken hero. It included the lines:

> In the shambles of Bristol, among Butcherly people
> There was blackness of sorrow...
> Cleaver, and bloody axe, steel, hand-saw, chopping-block, hatchet,
> Lay in grim repose...

His wounds healed, Neat returned to his butcher's shop in Bristol to see lads selling these disparaging sheets in the streets.

On 22 May 1823 Spring was guest of honour at Tom Shelton's benefit, having also agreed to spar a few rounds with his old friend and trusted cornerman. The champion's appearance meant the house was full. Unfortunately, due to his damaged hand, Spring could not box. Even so, after a few energetic bouts, the champion was 'loudly called for' to say a few appropriate words. Spring climbed into the ring, his arm still in a sling. 'Gentlemen,' he said, 'I return you my sincerest thanks for the honour you have done me today, and I hope my future will equally merit your kind attention. I promised a set-to with Shelton; but having met with an accident, I trust you will excuse me; at all other times, you will find me willing and ready to obey your commands.' This signalled loud cheering.

Spring was thanked by Shelton and also by Belcher, who said Neat would be attending his benefit on Tuesday 27 May 'in order to convince the amateurs that his arm was broken in the fight with Spring'. Gentleman John Jackson then entered the ring and presented the new champion with £200: 'his reward for victory'. With regard to the controversy surrounding Neat's insipid capitulation, Jackson confirmed that he, 'in the company of two eminent surgeons', had seen Neat and that there was absolutely no doubt that the Bristolian had broken a bone in his arm.

SPRING & NEATE,

MAY 20, 1823.

TUNE, (*Jack's return'd from Sea.*)

The Bristol men thought right
To back a man call'd Neate;
But Winter, (who could fight)
Determin'd his defeat;
Defeat he did right true!
For Winter prov'd a Spring!
Who made Neate close out,
Before he left the ring.
Fol lol the ri tol le &c.

Neate said he'd conquer Spring,
But Spring to prove his strength;
Turn'd Neate round like a sling,
Then laid him on his length;
Now this was round the first,
And then t'was eas'n to four!
Neat round Neate's face was burst,
And two to one the rotr.
Fal &c.

In second round I mean,
When Spring did queer Neate's nob,
He fibb'd him neat and clean,
(T'was nearly up by Bob.)
Neate still stood up for more,
But he had such a milling
That ere the fun was o'er,
T'was a guinea to a shilling.
Fal &c.

It was on the twentieth day of May last,
Such a Battle was fought that never yet past,
'Twas for the great Championship they did contend,
To decide the dispute and put that to an end.

CHORUS.

Spring for ever, ever, and ever,
The Champion of England huzza and huzza.

Tho' Neate did so boast that his strength it was
great,
But after three rounds he saw his defeat;
Spring several times knocked him down, each made
the ground ring,
And the shouting was loud in favour of Spring.

This great battle did rage fourteen minutes or more,
Spring with his fine science then made him give o'er
The bats then in the air were merrily tost,
Some hundreds of thousands were then won and lost

Now Bristol is beat it is in a bad plight;
All the *Elms* they could muster was brought to the
fight,
And immediately they began for to bet,
But now they complain they have pockets to let.

There is the dandy from Holborn, that made this
great fight.
He assured his friends that all would be right,
But instead of being right, it has proved to be wrong,
Now the dandy from London will quickly be gone.

The dandy's word is nothing, he contriv'd for to
fling
Ten pounds of Neate's forfeit that is due unto Spring,
The whole of the money he promised for to pay,
But now he has refused what will the world say.

Spring's the *Champion of England !* who can it
deny ?
No one dare oppose him the world he'll defy,
He fought like a lion the battle did win,
He is the Champion of England, that glorious Spring

MR. NEATE came from Bristol, elated with pride,
And, boasting his science, our towns-men defied,
Who knew very well what he came there about,
And that was his Business to knock him about.

CHORUS.

Heart of oak in our man,
Who always was ready,
Undaunted and steady,
To fight and to conquer again and again.

They had a set-to Mr. Neate work'd away,
His friends thought for certain he would win the day;
Spring laugh'd at their folly in raising a shout,
Its being determined to knock him about.

Mr. Neate was extinguishing—the booster was beat,
And the pride of his spirit was drawn out so neat,
This vanquishing hero went back to his place,
His friends followed after in wretched disgrace.

Two songs.

SHEEP'S HEAD,

On the Loss of the Fight;

Being a curious and diverting DIALOGUE which took place on
Wednesday morning last, between himself

And a Bullock's Cheek,

Concerning the Fight between Spring and Neat.

Walking through Bull Paunch Lane on Wednesday morning last, I
perceived much consternation prevail throughout the neighbourhood;
every thing was still for some time; but at length the following plain-
tive strains struck my ear, which seemed to emanate from a solitary
Sheep's Head that hung on a crook, and appeared to be addressed to
a humble *Cheek* that was placed on a shelf below

Head.—Oh, dear! dear! here's a pretty mess of a job; patience
bless us, what will become of us all ! Nothing going forward now ;
here I hang quite neglected, and almost alone ; bad market to day,
and worse expected to-morrow.

Cheek.—Sure enough here I lie, not so much as looked at; but I
suppose we are doomed to remain here as a kind of stock on hand, for
I neither hear the surly moan of the sturdy bull, the lowing of cows,
on whom twenty summers have shone, the blair of a calf, doomed for
slaughter ere a Sunday had dawn'd on it, the grunt of a hog "from
shipwrecked saved," or the bleat of the old tup, whose progeny covers
the fertile hills and vallies of Somersetshire. Oh, dear ! what a death-
like stillness reigns around. Whence the cause of all this ? Is it on
account of the blight this SPRING ? Things are not NEAT-ly done
now-a-days.

Head.—SPRING ! SPRING ! There is something ominous in that
word : it strikes dizziness into my very brain. The victory he has so
NEAT-ly obtained over him who has hitherto been conqueror over
every competitor, has driven those who has hitherto dealt out death,
with an unsparing hand to almost every living creature but man, to
bring death home to themselves, either by pistol, knife, or halter !!

Cheek.—But something has been said about the Float, where many
of our fellows have gone before us, after having graced the market a
fortnight : and mayhap some of our masters are gone there seeking them
again once more to grace their vacant crooks.

Head.—I beg you'd put aside all joking ; I cannot relish it at all ;
it is far beyond a joke to lose every thing but one's life. And you know
dear Cheek that we ought to pity those who never pitied us.

Cheek.—Well, well, I allow it, it is not a subject for joking ; but I
allow it is a very bad job ; but we should make the best even of that.

Head.—So we should ; and I hope from this time it may be a lesson
to those who have sported with what it would have been advisable to
have gone to a better market with. *Andover* market won't do ; no, no,
for it is not only *Hand-over*, but I am sorry to add, that it is *Done-over*
and *All-over.*—Farewell ; should I hear any thing further I will com-
municate it to thee.

Printed by H. Shephard, Bristol.—I printed by T. B. Watkins, Hereford.

'Sheep's head'.

Spring at twenty-seven
years old.

As champion Spring was not too proud to second 'Slashing Gypsy'
Cooper in his fight with Bishop 'Smuggler' Sharpe on Tuesday 17 June
1823 at the Old Maypole, in Epping Forest. Although the nobles hated
cantering 'over the stones' to witness battles in Essex or North Kent,
they were prepared to make an exception to see the exciting Cooper,
who had beaten several good men. Bill Richmond helped Spring
minister to the Gypsy while the rugged pairing of Josh Hudson and
Phil Sampson did likewise for Sharpe.

The battle was bloodless until the fourteenth, when Cooper gave
Sharpe a severe cross-buttock which left him embarrassed at Hudson's
feet. 'It's no good,' Hudson laughed, 'I have seconded Bishop seven
times, and none of the coves could ever make a mark upon him.' By the
twenty-sixth, both boxers seemed to have caught a dose of Hudson's
verbals as they cussed, cuffed and grunted as pleasantly as if they were
in a snug somewhere.

In the forty-fourth Jack Martin leaned into the ring and fluttered £50 in Cooper's face, saying the dough was his if he could only win. But by the fifty-third the 'Slashing Gypsy' could slash no more. 'Use your right hand and you must win it,' Spring hissed in Cooper's ear. 'I can't,' Cooper hissed back. 'I have hurt my shoulder.' With that, he collapsed after an enthusiastic assault by the Smuggler, who was getting bolder by the minute. The fight, which had promised much but delivered little, was stopped in the fifty-sixth after a discussion between Cooper and Spring. An examination confirmed that Cooper's collarbone was broken.

24

Spring Returns to Hereford as Champion

Spring, having at last achieved his life's ambition, returned triumphant to his native Herefordshire to look up old friends. He was also to receive a solid silver trophy to commemorate his great achievement. The money to buy the cup and have it suitably inscribed was raised by William Pateshall, surgeon at the Hereford lunatic asylum. Pateshall canvassed the many city pubs, who contributed enthusiastically. Cash was raised by the Fancy Tavern, the Black Swan, the King's Head, the Half Moon, the Coach and Horses, the Sun Tavern, and the Nag's Head. The trophy, which featured a cock, 'a symbol of courage', was made by Grayhurst Harvey and Co. of the Strand, London, at a cost of £56 10s.

The trophy would feature an engraving of a boxer copied from 'a good figure of Spring' sent to the engravers by Pierce Egan, who acted as project consultant. 'The subject we put upon it is indifferent to us, providing there are not more figures than the drawing we send,' Grayhurst Harvey wrote to Mr Pateshall. The price included 'inside gilding', two elegantly chased handles, a fluted pedestal, 'apples and ornaments, and a Cider Butt, resting upon a stand as a handle for the cover'. The 'two game-cocks at the close of a battle, one standing over the other' were a reminder of Spring's interest in cock-fighting. The finished trophy weighed between sixty-five and seventy ounces and was large enough to hold 'a gallon of the nectar divine'.

The inscription read:

Springs subscription.

	£ s d
Fancy Tavern — — — — — — —	8 .. 14 .. 0
Black Swan - - - - -	5 .. 0 .. 0
Kings Head - - . .	4 .. 5 .. 0
Nags Head -	1 .. 17 .. 6
Half Moon — ~ . . .	~ 3 .. 0
Coach & Horses . - - .	.. 5 .. 0
San Tavern - — - . .	~ 2 .. 6
Hotel - -	2 .. 10 .. 0
J. B. Watkins . - . .	21 .. 2 .. 0
Billiard room - _ - .	1 .. 2 .. 6
	45 .. 1 .. 6
Mr. Watkins bill - -	1 .. 14 .. 4
	46 .. 7 .. 2
Robert Lane by J. Cooke - - - —	1 .. 5 .. 0
	£ 44 .. 12 .. 2

List of subscribing pubs.

1823
TO THOMAS WINTER
Of Fownhope, in the county of Hereford.
This cup was presented
By his Countrymen of this Land of Cider
In token of their Esteem for the Manliness and Science
Which, in many severe Contests in the Pugilistic Ring
Under the name of
SPRING
Raised him to the proud Distinction of
THE CHAMPION OF ENGLAND

Spring was presented with the trophy at a rousing dinner in
Hereford with friends and family. Emotional speeches were made
and cider despatched by the barrel. Spring's visit was fleeting though

London 25th August 1823

Sir,

We duly received your favor, & have been considering, & consulting with Mr Pierce Egan respecting the alterations you propose for the Cup, he has furnished us with a good figure of Spring which accords with your ideas in regard to the manner of standing, the head & arm we are afraid cannot be moulded in any form to look well as handles, and we would recommend you giving up that idea, & allowing us to form one with Trophies as ornaments, and a Cider Butt resting upon a Stand as a handle for lower, this Mr Pierce Egan says is the best thing that can be put, and it is our decided opinion it will look very well, the expence of gilding inside will be from £4:10 to £5.—

We think we can complete it in the course of two Months, waiting your reply we are Sir, Your most ob't Serv'ts

Grayhurst & Harvey & Co—

Letter from engravers mentioning Pierce Egan.

and, weighted down with silver, he quickly returned to London to resume his career. It was his turn to be a hot property and offers poured in for sparring exhibitions. After his skilful defusion of the explosive Neat the purse required to tempt Cribb to consider a title defence had been ratcheted considerably upwards. Having got Spring back to fighting trim after his long lay-off, his backers were understandably keen to cash in. Having vanquished all the serious English contenders, Cribb began looking overseas for a challenger who would draw the crowds and whom backers would consider good enough to test the finest boxer in England.

The most likely candidate was the Irish Champion Jack Langan, who had been observed on a sparring tour of the north of England. When he passed the Manchester theatre, Langan saw a billboard advertising a sparring exhibition between Tom Cribb and Tom Spring, 'Champion of England', and announcing that Spring was prepared to accept challenges from any pugilist in the world. Without hesitation, Langan challenged Spring for £100-a-side. It was refused but Cribb later negotiated a larger sum. The Irishman was aggressive, which would suit Spring's style. A former merchant seaman and mercenary soldier, Langan was intelligent, charming and handsome. What is more, he was a foreigner. From his fights with Molyneaux, Cribb knew a touch of xenophobia did no harm when it came to selling tickets.

A preliminary meeting was held in London on Thursday 23 October 1823 at the Castle Tavern. Agreement was quickly reached and Belcher, acting for Langan, put down a deposit of £50 of the £300-a-side stake. A confident Spring immediately helped himself to odds of £100 to £80 that he would win the fight. The backers of both fighters dined together at the Castle on 1 December to thrash out the details. Neither boxer was present. Cribb was due to put down a further £150 but was £50 short. Belcher argued that Cribb must put down the whole of the required figure under the terms of the contact. Cribb, who was not wealthy, idly boasted that 'if the other party wished it, he would make the £300-a-side good immediately, or would increase the match between Langan and Spring up to 1,000 guineas.' The chairman helped Cribb out of his embarrassment by agreeing that both parties should pay £100 of the amount stipulated by the contract.

In the meantime Spring accepted an invitation to second Jem Ward, assisted by Abe Belasco, for his fight with Josh Hudson on 22 November on Moulsey Hurst. Jack Randall and Peter Crawley acted for Hudson. When he saw Hudson stripped, one Corinthian commented, 'He is in no condition at all.' Ward, in contrast was in such fine form that 'a sculptor might have long looked for such a model of a pugilist'. Both men went into the fight with verve, landing blows ferociously and giving a fine demonstration of boxing science and grit in the process.

By the tenth, Hudson's face was a jelly, prompting the former apprentice butcher Spring to smile and say, 'I should like to have a calf's head as fat as that.' Crawley retorted angrily, telling Spring to speak softly in case Hudson overheard if he didn't want to see

John (Jack) Langan, the
Irish challenger.

his own face still more cruelly treated. Showing enormous courage, Hudson overcame the far more talented Ward in the fifteenth. When Spring brought the tottering Ward to the centre of the ring the crowd bellowed, 'Take him away. Don't hit him Josh.' Instead Hudson put out a hand and gently pushed Ward over. Although it was agreed that both men put up a good fight, Ward was criticised for not being more aggressive when he clearly had the science to beat Hudson. It was the twenty-seven-year-old Hudson's sixteenth victory.

* * * * * * * *

On 1 January 1824, Spring's connections met with Langan's for dinner at Cribb's. At the head of the table was Cribb's silver cup, which Spring won along with the title. Next to it stood the massive solid silver trophy Spring had brought back from Herefordshire. Over a hearty dinner, sluiced down with fine wines, several of the influential backers and 'amateurs' of the boxing world discussed the coming match with gusto. Since neither protagonist put in an appearance, Spring was represented by Cribb and Langan by Belcher. 'At the call of time' both parties lit their cigars, topped up their brandies and haggled over the next instalment of the purse. Both stumped up the full amount.

It was to be 'a fair stand up fight – half-a-minute time to be allowed between each and every round'. When the Irish contingent present attempted to raise the temperature by insisting their man would 'lift the laurels from the shoulders of Spring', the English champion's backers laughed and immediately offered two to one on Spring to win. Josh Hudson bullishly boasted he would give £2 to fight Langan for £200-a-side, and he would take £10 to fight Spring for his title and £200. His extravagant gestures were met with indulgent applause from the jovial crowd.

The fight would be staged halfway between London and Manchester, and arrangements were posted at Cribb's inn. Spring was a two-to-one favourite and brisk business was done at the bookies, with one punter laying £300 to £100 on the Englishman to win. Knowing too little of the Irishman's ability, many kept their blunt securely in their pockets.

The *Hereford Journal* reported: 'The fight has excited as strong a feeling in the country, as the anticipation of an expected battle during the war.'

25

Worcester Prepares for the Fight

The first choice of venue for the showdown was Birmingham Heath. When that fell through, the promoters tried Whittingham Heath near Lichfield. There were problems there too, so Warwick Racecourse was suggested. The businessmen of the town were very keen but as they could raise only a derisory £40 towards promotional costs the 'Commissary refused to accede to the shabby proposition'. A better offer was hastily made but by then, much to the chagrin of the tardy Warwickshire businessmen, the fight had been switched to the Pitchcroft at Worcester with the full blessing of the magistrates.

The cathedral city was an ideal location. It was not far from Birmingham and just over 100 miles from London, It had good roads, a navigable river, the Severn, and was on one of the oldest drover's routes. For a population of 26,000 there were over 100 pubs. John Wesley described it as 'one of the liveliest places in England'. The fact that the champion hailed from nearby Herefordshire would draw large numbers of his supporters who had never seen him fight.

The Pitchcroft had altered little since the day in 1558 when, according to records, 4½ acres of meadow were sold to the corporation by one Thomas Wylde. It remains a valuable amenity. These days, rather than playing host to bear and bull baiting, cock fighting and duelling, it's a little tamer, with toddlers toddling, boys kicking ball, young cricketers hitting sixes and horses leaping fences.

* * * * * * * *

In the run-up to the match, preparations were made on a Herculean scale. On Monday and Tuesday, vehicles of all sorts rolled into town. Rooms were swept, beds prepared and meat and drink delivered by the cartload. Innkeepers were smiling and chambermaids were saucy.

> An armchair and bolster were worth a half-guinea, and many had to lie with their feet to the fire. Up to eleven on Wednesday morning there were constant arrivals, a throng of persons both Corinthian and plebs, on horseback on foot, and in carriages of every description.

The jaded condition of the horses, and the fagged appearance of their drivers and riders, bespoke the lengthy journey many had made: not a few of the poor horses were beaten to a standstill, and very many of them to an absolute death.

The public houses were overflowing with famished guests, the stableyards with hungry steeds. Such was the consumption of provender that in very many instances, both master and servant were doomed to go hungry. 'The adventures at the inns,' it was said, 'would furnish twenty farces.'

From dawn on that cold January morning the city was wide awake and alive with anticipation. Armies of Langan fans oozed out of shebeen and shed, doss-house and lean-to, their feet caked with the glutinous mud and horse dung that covered lane and road to a depth of six inches. Yelling in the dark they headed down to the Severn-side for the fight. Many of the poorest had slept all night in ditches, kept alive by singing, enthusiastic chatter, cheap booze and smoking their clay pipes. As they shuffled and jogged to the Pitchcroft, the ring was already assembled and a goodly crowd milled around looking for somewhere to park themselves and gnaw their loaves of bread.

In the centre of the town crowds waited patiently in the freezing cold for Tom Spring to appear. Clumps of Irishmen, hands in pockets, kicked stones as they waited for Langan. Their breath coming in puffs, bare-headed and bare-handed men, women and children lined the roads, keeping their eyes on every entrance. At last, just before noon, a great shout went up as Spring's carriage approached the town, the pale winter sun losing itself in the black of the coach and four horses and glinting on the scarlet red of the postillions. 'A cacophony of rattles, bells and hunting horns' echoed off the town's narrow stone walls and time-warped houses. Spring smiled and waved like a prince to his adoring subjects. He was a celebrity, a sporting hero, one of the most famous men in England. He had risen in the classical style from nothing to be mentioned in the same breath as royalty and the great poets and explorers of the time.

Langan, who had also conquered poverty, was a worthy opponent. Langan, a redoubtable warrior, had once, although stabbed several times and bleeding profusely, beaten off a mob of Portuguese muggers who had jumped him while he was on shore leave in Lisbon. It was said of him that 'a gamer man and a fairer fighter never contended for a stake'.

Mounted toffs, their horses plumed and groomed, endeavoured to barge their way through thick mud, sullen pedestrians and pools of brackish water to get to their advantageous seats. Rickety scaffolding had been hastily erected before the gaze of the magistrates who turned a blind eye to the illegal bout, partly because a large number of influential aristocrats were expected to be present. As the crowd swelled, the promoters ordered two more wings to be tacked onto the main stand. The poor paid up to ten shillings for tickets and gambled their children's suppers on the result. Boat owners moored their craft on either side of the grandstand close to the river bank.

It paid off, as enough agile young ruffians risked their lives scrambling to the top of the rigging, where they dangled like monkeys bawling and catcalling to the upturned faces below. Latecomers snaffled up the last few tickets for precarious perches two stories high, which were already moving in the cold morning breeze and which by fight time were leaning crazily. Thousands who tore their clothes and endured cuts and abrasions scaling walls and straddling fences were rewarded with a free view of this once-in-a-lifetime battle.

The twenty-four-foot ring was two feet from the ground, covered with turves and sprinkled with sawdust with eight iron-capped stakes each marked with the letters 'P.C.' The freshly hewn wooden stakes were driven into the earth and a leather bag holding money gambled on the outcome dangled from one of the posts. The stake money itself was held by a gentleman. The loser would get nothing except a thrashing and a whip-round.

Pierce Egan.

The surrounding area, a flood plain, was churned into an oozy mess by all the activity of the crowd of thousands. While the area closest to the action was protected from the mud by the wagons providing safe accommodation for nobles and their friends, away from the ring nowhere was free of water. Several lads who tried to leap the ditches on their way to the stands ended up sprawled headlong in the mire, an object of entertainment for the local country lasses. London swells, suffering the after-effects of the port they had so copiously quaffed the night before, 'were to be seen sitting down in the mud more coolly than if loafing on a sofa.'

By ten o'clock, over three-and-a-half hours before the fight was due to commence, every ticket was sold. Stragglers who had travelled vast distances pleaded for spares. Taunted by the huge crowd they tried in vain to access the muddy field. At ringside the finest sporting journalists and artists of the day congregated. Estimates of the attendance reached over 50,000. According to Egan. they included:

> the proprietors of splendid parks and demesnes, inmates from proud and lofty mansions, groups from the most respectable dwellings; thousands from the peaceful cot; and myriads from no houses at all – in a word it was a conglomeration of the Fancy. Peers, MPs, yokels of every cast, Cockneys, and sheenies who cast away their salaries without a sigh to witness the grand mill.

All over England navigators had lain down their spades, itinerant farm labourers skipped work and tinkers put away their pots and pans to make their way to Worcester. Dodgy coves, drawn for miles, assembled to relieve gullible gents or swooning ladies of their gold fobs and diamond rings. Pimps, footpads and pickpockets worked the throng like bees buzzing through a pollen-rich flowerbed. Bawds brazenly offered their tired wares, shamelessly flashing their muddy, knickerless thighs. Cardsharps with hands and brains as keen as cut-throat razors milked the poor of their last coins, quacks sold exotic cure-alls in thick brown bottles, and religious zealots with eyes like threepenny bits sold newly-minted gospels.

Pierce Egan sat, as always, a stovepipe hat on his head, pad on his lap, pencil at the ready. In bumpy coaches or at ringside in the rain, knee-deep in mud in some desolate field, he composed his pithy, witty and wise columns for the *Weekly Despatch* and the *New Times*, as well as freelancing articles to regional papers. Egan shared a loved of bare-knuckle fighting with the Cruikshank brothers, George and Robert. Indeed, George, who was also ringside, being 'not averse from using his fists in an up-and-down tussle' and having a penchant for 'gig-driving, badger-baiting, rat-matching, dog-and-duck hunting', was looked upon 'as a kind of Tom Spring'.

26

The Bloody Battle

Around the ringside hung the pall of cigar smoke as the nobles lit up. Smoking was gradually replacing snuff but there was enough of that too, and a fair number of concealed bottles and flagons containing all manner of alcoholic concoctions to protect the frozen spectators from a premature death. The bluntless far away from the ring amused themselves by yelling abuse, pouring cider on the heads of those below, and relieving themselves from their dangerous perches.

At ten minutes to one a great cheer went up on all sides of the ground at the appearance of Ned Painter. Smartly attired in a flannel jacket, Painter had silk fogles in Spring's colours tied around each knee, which confirmed his position as a second to the champion.

Five minutes later there was a huge shout as a swathe appeared in the crowd to allow Spring's entourage up to the ringside. The smart carriage belonged to Captain Barret, one of Spring's backers. Out of it piled a crumpled knot of sporting characters, including the great past champion Tom Cribb, who had built Spring's career with paternalism, skill and sagacity. Now more solidly proportioned than ever, the eternally popular Cribb was greeted by a tremendous roar.

Spring, who had finished his preparation on Captain Barrett's country estate, arrived looking suitably smart in 'a blue dress coat over which he wore a brown upper tog, with brown kersey-mere small clothes and jockey boots'. Saluting all corners of the arena, Spring threw his hat into the ring. Another roar rent the chill air and scattered the gulls perching on the ships' sails.

Spring shed his clothing in his carriage and walked to the ring with Viscount Deerhurst who would act as timekeeper. The champion was protected against a chill wind by a coat thrown over his shoulders. Around his waist he wore a scarf bearing his adopted colours – white bird's eye dots against a navy blue background. He also wore an unusual belt. When asked to comment on the fight, Spring calmly expressed complete confidence, and when he produced his pocket watch to check the time, an incredulous witness said, 'there was not the slightest tremor or shake of the hand.'

There was no sign of Langan. Sir Henry Goodrich, Langan's umpire, viewed the Irishman's empty corner with disgust. Colonel Berkeley, who was to referee the contest, stepped into the ring and asked, 'Where is Langan?' The crowd grumbled. Many had been up all night and their patience was not limitless. 'Why don't you go it, Spring?' yelled a cider-filled yokel. 'I can't fight without him,' Tom replied. 'Note that down, Mr Reporter', grunted Lord Molynoux sarcastically from the ringside. Egan licked his pencil and scribbled furiously.

Then, at the stroke of one o'clock, the warm-tempered Josh Hudson arrived, accompanied by Tom Reynolds, Langan's erudite friend and facilitator. When both men were seen to be wearing Langan's black fogles, a derisory outburst of fist-waving and yelling erupted from the Londoners, Spring fans to a man, while roars of approval went up from the Irishmen clinging to rickety stands and lofty rigging. Upon setting eyes on Spring's blue fogles, Hudson guffawed, 'I'll give a hundred to one we shall see those colours on their mugs before it is over.' Spring slid into the ring to a thunderous ovation.

Suddenly there was an enormous splintering of wood as the flimsy wing of one of the temporary stands slowly crashed to the ground, decanting 1,500 swearing and screaming spectators into a 'promiscuous heap' in the mud below. Fans rushed the ring to avoid being flattened and horses tethered close to the ringside reared in alarm. Wild eyed, some broke free, plunging and panicking as they dragged carriages and gigs across the Pitchcroft, their drivers powerless to stop them.

On witnessing the catastrophic scene, Spring blanched. For a few frightening moments, all was chaos. One doting aristocrat was 'frantic with agony, as he had the moment before placed his son on the scaffold as a place of safety'. But within a short space it became clear that, while several spectators were bruised or worse, most were limping safely away from the wreck of the stand, and no one was killed. 'Thank God,' Spring said, 'I would not have had it happen while I was fighting for a hundred thousand pounds.'

The area was cleared and the ring repaired, but there was still no sign of Langan. Spring was entitled to the whole stake if the Irishman failed to appear – and a few thousand spectators would have been seriously disgruntled. Eagerly the mob pressed forward, reducing the size of the ring to that of a hen coop; if the fight did take place, the boxers would have to fight nose to nose. But where on earth was Langan? Cribb was furious and roared, 'If you don't come Mr Paddy, from Cork, the stakes will be given up.' Suddenly there was a cry from somewhere in the crowd. 'Josh Hudson, Josh Hudson – Langan's here.' Hudson rushed into the crowd and, to wild bellowing from the fans, returned with the Irish champion. Instead of flinging his hat into the ring with a flourish as was the custom, Langan carefully leaned over the ropes to place it carefully and modestly in place. The combatants shook hands and Langan ducked into the confined ring, almost filled to bursting by Spring's incredible number of burly helpers. As well as his second and former opponent Ned Painter, Tom Oliver, Phil Sampson and Israel Belasco all clustered around the champion.

When the two men stood side by side it was clear this had the makings of a great fight. Spring, weighing 13st 4lb, was in fine condition, trained to the hilt and muscled like a thoroughbred. The champion calmly waited. On noticing Spring's odd-looking belt, Reynolds, Langan's second, objected, saying, 'If you persist in fighting in such a belt I shall put one on Langan.' Spring immediately took off the belt even though he always wore it in the ring. First blood to the Langan camp, and second too because when they tossed a coin for choice of sides, Langan won. As 'the sun was shining very brilliantly considering the time of year', it was a good toss to win.

As both men toed the line Henry Downes Miles noted 'The bust of Langan was much admired for its anatomical beauty', but his 'legs were thin; his knees very small, and his loins deficient as to strength. He did not exceed twelve stone four pounds and he was nearly two inches shorter than his opponent.'

Impatient to get going, Spring gestured for Langan to come on and fight. Langan simply smiled and cocked a thumb to his nose. In the Irishman's corner, Hudson yelled, 'Fight away, Jack, he can't hurt nobody.' He seemed vindicated when Spring made first contact with a powderpuff left that hardly impressed his opponent. After a further exchange, Hudson and Reynolds yelled 'First blood!' Spring disagreed but Hudson maintained that his lip was cut. In response, Spring feinted adroitly with his left and threw a right which landed flush on the Irishman's left cheek. Still Langan kept his guard up well, preventing Spring from capitalising until he finally landed with a powerful left that caused Langan's right eye to 'twinkle'.

After nine minutes of prying and teasing, the round ended. Shrewd gamblers had already seen enough to know it was going to be a long fight between two capable boxers. Langan was backing off, bobbing and weaving, and making the counter-punching Spring do the chasing. A few yelled odds of twenty pounds to five on Spring, but many more waited to see which way the wind would blow.

Spring came out for the second determined to bide his time and avoid Langan's less-than-deadly punching. He even began to drop his hands and flick out harmless jabs. This showboating gave Langan the incentive to attack. The Irishman 'tried a short, right-handed blow at Spring's breadbasket which fell short.' When the champion threw a decent punch in return, Langan proved adept at blocking.

As the two fighters circled each other, another temporary stand suddenly gave way, crashing to the ground beneath its weight of fight-frenzied humanity. Downes Miles wrote:

> The round was thrown into utter confusion...The shock paralysed the ring for a while. Both men drew back, and suspended the fight. The countenance of Spring, whose face was towards the accident, underwent that sort of sensation which did honour to his feelings and to his heart – he appeared sick with affliction at the circumstance. He put up his hands, indicating that his mind was perplexed whether he should quit the ring or proceed with the battle.

Again, no one was badly hurt and the battle went on. As the fight was restarted Spring seized the initiative and caught Langan with a heavy blow to the left eye. Langan went down, but dragged Spring with him as he fell.

The third round started with Spring again dropping his hands and inviting Langan to try his luck. Langan responded by flinging a couple of left-handers but Spring jumped back out of harm's way. Hudson, intently watching Spring's every move, yelled to Langan: 'Take care of your plum-pudding, boy, he's coming.' Spring responded with a terrific punch, but Langan traded blows and the Irishman's supporters erupted in applause. Spring quickly silenced them with a tremendous blow to Langan's nose, then a brief flurry of punches which put him on the floor.

At the commencement of the fourth, Langan tried a few speculative shots but the Hereford man slipped away from them with ease. Langan pursued the champion and trapped him on the ropes. After Spring was forced to block a powerhouse blow from the Irishman, both men went down with Langan on top.

In the fifth things got even more uncomfortable for Spring when Langan dashed from his corner and hit him with a combination of a punch and headbutt. Spring was bowled over and out of the ring when the ropes broke. The boxers were sent to their corners while repairs were effected. 'You had the great man down, at all events.' Hudson sneered. But it was Langan's 'left peeper' that was nearly closed as he came out for the sixth. Changing tack, the Irishman grabbed Spring. In the ensuing tussle the champion fell full on his head. It was proving to be a very uncomfortable afternoon for Spring.

In the next round Langan took a blow to the stomach. Spring was ahead on points, but only just, and Langan, 'with the fighting instinct of his race', came back into the fight in the eighth when 'he fought manfully and proved himself worthy of the Land of the praties'. He threw Spring and his greater determination won him the round. 'Bravo Langan,' came the cry, 'it's not so sure now that Spring will win.'

The Irish contingent waved their fogles and yelled with delight, imitating Langan's milling among themselves in the muck and the debris of the collapsed stand. After nearly half-an-hour of fighting, neither man had succeeded in subduing the other. It was an open fight, with the bulkier Spring making heavy weather of subduing the Irish light heavyweight. In a violent struggle on the ropes, with the smaller Langan showing bullish strength, both men went down. The displaced spectators now crowded around the ring, further limiting the space in which the antagonists attempted to fight. The whips were brought out and a few of the closest invaders soon wore painful red stripes on their faces but still the crowd pushed in, desperately seeking the best view of the action.

Spring *v.* Langan.

The eighth was lively, both men scoring until 'Langan finely stopped a right hand but received a left on the cannister – both down.' 'Go in to him,' Tom Reynolds exhorted, but Spring was ready for the collision and both men hit the grass again. Spring scrambled to his feet unmarked. In the ninth round, both men boxed elegantly, with Spring having some success before they grappled. Again the two men fell.

The tenth was Spring's finest round, when he outwitted and punished Langan. Boxing beautifully, he had the crowd shrieking as he battered Langan around the ring. Driving the Irishman into a corner, he feinted with the left and as 'Pat dropped his head to avoid the memorandum, Spring who had thrown out the bait for the purpose, caught him in the chin with the right hand in fine style. This was the worst round so far for the Irishman.'

The tenth round bored the freezing spectators as neither man seemed to want to take charge. Spring 'put in a slight nobber' and Langan a left-hand hit that 'touched the body of his opponent'. It was hardly blood-curdling stuff on a cold winter's day. There was no doubt that

Langan's style was giving the champion problems. The eleventh and twelfth were similar rounds, with nothing much happening and both men content to wrestle. Time and again they visited the turf, taking turns at being uppermost. In the thirteenth the wounded Langan, fighting like a deranged windmill, knocked Spring to the ground. In the next, Spring jumped on Langan as he fell and all but squeezed the breath out of him as he lay prostrate and pinned among the mucky boots of his fans.

As he sat on his second's knee, the loquacious Irishman chattered gaily away. Hudson, in surly fashion, told him to shut up and get on with it. The contender was still strong, while the champion seemed to be tiring. Langan came out smiling. 'You see, I am always ready,' he said. In the ensuing struggle Spring went down. It was remarkable how easily the smaller Irishman could throw the champion. In the fourteenth, Langan, 'as gay as a lark', and Hudson, his cornerman, bantered pleasantly. 'My boy, I can fight for a week,' Langan said. 'For a month,' Hudson replied, 'if you get no heavier blows than you had received already.'

As the rounds progressed Spring 'tapped his opponent's claret with a capital and powerful hit on his smelling bottle, and closed Langan's right eye as close as a prison door.' Fortunes swung from one to the other, with Spring's jabs skilfully pecking away at Langan's head until it 'displayed a most hideous appearance, blood issuing at every pore.' The odds on a Langan victory had now drifted out to 20-1 against, but Langan refused to capitulate even as Spring was pummelling him at will. In the sixteenth, after a fierce battery of punches landed on the Irishman's severely altered nose, Langan raised a hand to explore its new contours and laughed through the blood on his face.

Both men were cut up and showing signs of weariness. Spring went down again, this time clumsily tripping over Langan's feet. In spite of the brutal conditions both men refused to take advantage when the other was in trouble. In the seventeenth they rolled along the ropes trying to get the upper hand when Langan threw Spring powerfully to the ground. As they struggled on the wet turf Spring fans cried 'Langan is biting him!' A spectator countered, 'No such thing, he fought like a man all through.'

Round after round followed a similar pattern. Even the champion's fans, who understood his tactics and who had been vocally supporting him, began to tire of their man's apparent inability to lay the Irishman out. By the nineteenth there were cries of 'Go to work, Spring!' The champion waved a hand and said, ' All in good time.' Enjoying the moment, Langan shouted, 'I am ready for anything.' The light-hearted way the two men were treating the title fight was illustrated by an incident in the twenty-first round. After throwing Spring out of the ring Langan reached out a hand and, 'with much jocularity and good nature', hauled the champion to his feet. 'If I sent you down,' Langan said wittily, 'I have a right to pick you up.'

With the ring all but totally swept away by the encroaching crowd, the cramped, muddy and lawless conditions played into Langan's hands. Deprived of the space to slip punches, counter and fire back his elegant jabs and hooks, Spring was drawn into a crude wrestling match at which Langan was most effective – Spring went down more times than in any other fight. As the men tired, the fight went on, more falling and wrestling than boxing. After an exchange in the twentieth when Spring battered his opponent to his knees he walked over to Langan and 'good-naturedly patted him on the shoulder. He felt he had a brave man before him. Bravo Spring!' In the twenty-second Langan returned the compliment. He had Spring down and, instead of making the best of it, 'with the eccentricity of an Irishman' he raised him by the arm, to laughter from the crowd. After an exchange of falls Spring took charge in the twenty-seventh, battering Langan with his aching hands. Gritting his teeth he repeatedly floored his opponent but could not keep him there. By the end of the twenty-eighth, both had visited the ground almost every round. It was an unfortunate clash of styles. There was too much holding. But the more aggressive Langan was now ahead on points.

In the twenty-ninth Langan tossed Spring out of the ring. The crowd's allegiance shifted. 'Bravo, Langan!' they chorused. By the thirty-second Spring had stirred himself enough to hit Langan in the mouth with a couple of facers, but they seemed to have little effect on the brawling Dubliner. An old backer of Spring, sitting ringside cried out in exasperation, 'How bad Spring fights today.' Langan seemed to have energy to burn while Spring's weak hands were swelling. At the start of the thirty-fourth round Langan walked purposefully up to Spring who promptly decked him with a nobber.

Outside the ring was turmoil as fans of both men fought with sticks, fists and boots. The referee, Colonel Berkeley, strongly objected to the cramped space in which the two men had to fight. The battle was now reduced to little more than mauling as a large crowd was being pushed towards the ring by the unruly mob behind. 'Nothing less than a company of the Horse Guards,' an eye witness said, 'could have made out a ring, so closely jammed were the spectators.' Frustrated by the hampering conditions, Hudson turned on the spectators who had invaded the ring, snatching a whip from a bystander's hand and laying about him violently. He was assisted by Oliver, one of Spring's seconds. The berserk old fighters whipped and slashed until the mob backed off, not a few of them getting their faces sorely cut in the process. The ring cleared, Hudson again pleaded for fair play. 'Only give us a chance,' he said, 'and we can't lose it.'

As the fighters came up to scratch for the thirty-eighth round, Langan laughed, saying, 'You have done nothing yet.' 'All in good time,' replied Spring. 'I shall do it at last.' Langan grunted and landed two meaty blows on Spring's head. Both men fell and Cribb, unable to get out of the way, was flattened. The next few rounds were even worse, with few correctly delivered punches. Langan was so outreached he found it best to stick to his grappling. 'He is the best Irishman ever seen in the ring', one spectator said. 'He is the gamest man alive.' Another added, 'What a pity it his backers had no more judgement than to place him in opposition to Spring.' The champion won the round but was visibly weakening. The fighters closed and had a long try for the fall. Increasingly, the issue at stake was 'to see who was the best wrestler, Hereford or Donnybrook'. The ring was slippery, the fighting bloody and laboured. The bluntless pressed forward, their guttural tones mingling with gentlemanly expletives as the well-to-do, fearing for their lives, ordered their drivers and servants to lash out on all sides with their long whips.

The boxers heroically butted, slapped and gouged. Sweaty and growling, they went at it like pitbulls in a cage. The rounds grew shorter as both men went down from exhaustion. By the fifty-sixth round attempts to clear the ring had proved fruitless and a dense throng pressed the ropes on all sides. Spring tried to disentangle himself from the octopus tentacles of Langan and somehow found enough leverage to belt the stubborn Dubliner with two facers. The Irishman was slashed around both eyes. By the end of the fifty-eighth 'it was difficult for those persons who were placed only at a few yards distance from the ring to see the fight'. By the fifty-ninth Cribb had seen enough to know that his man was in danger of losing by accident as the crowd was so close. Urged on by his corner, Spring tried hard but Langan threw him like a rag doll.

His hands broken and bleeding, the Hereford man charged forward again in the sixtieth round, but in the narrow confines of the diminishing ring his greater height, weight and skill were nullified. The bookies were now offering odds on a Langan victory. The few who could see the fight were at last getting their money's worth, as both fighters scored. It was a grim war, a battle to the death. The sight of Langan's face smothered in blood from the attention of Spring's mangled hands was a bonus for the Londoners. Which would give in first, Spring's battered mitts or the Irishman's courage? The crowd edged closer, ignoring the constables' long poles and the whips of the old pugilists. Ensnared, both men fought valiantly in a space so confined they would have been more at ease in a sawpit. Cribb spread his large arms out to protect his man, but was so pressed upon by the crowd that in a violent rage he declared he would 'give a floorer to any person who stood in his way'. He made no distinction for the venerable men of the press: Vincent Dowling, Henry Downes Miles and the pugilistic Poet Laureate himself, Pierce Egan. The old champion was distinctly unimpressed. 'Here's a pretty go,' he sneered, 'a set of fellows with books and pencils in their hands pretending to be reporters. A parcel of imposters. I don't care! I'll hit anybody!'

The fight ground on, both men throwing punches so slowly it looked as if they were fighting in fast-drying cement. By hitting, holding and going down on one knee, Spring gained a few seconds respite, but neither man had the strength to knock the other cold. Langan had taken fierce punishment but if anything seemed the fitter of the two men. Gasping for breath, Spring closed on him, cuffing him and trying desperately to get leverage.

In the sixty-third he was beating the Irishman to the punch, looking as if he had gained a second wind. But in the very next round Langan drove Spring across the ring. 'Go to work, Erin-go-bragh,' Hudson yelled, 'Spring has no hits left in him. You must win it. Go in, Jack! You will soon spoil his fine science.' After a brutal struggle, Langan threw Spring and landed on him. Spring was pinned and the breath knocked out of him. Cribb dashed forward and dragged his stricken 'boy' back to the sanctity of his corner. He was weak and ashen-faced but Cribb got him to scratch on time.

A contemporary report of the fight.

Remarkably, Spring recovered sufficiently to batter Langan to the ground in the sixty-sixth. 'That's a settler', a ringsider said. ''Deed it's not,' replied a Paddy, 'Spring'll not settle his account this time.' 'Spring's tired of it,' Hudson roared, urging his man on. Covered in blood and snot, his frail hands broken, Spring responded to Hudson's insults by smiling and saying, 'Well done, Josh, chat away, I'll give you all you can do, except winning.' The Herefordshire man kept up the pressure in rounds sixty-seven, sixty-eight and sixty-nine. In round seventy he had the best of it but still Langan seemed to retain his will to fight. Determined to go out on his shield, he continued to flail, cursing his inability to nail Spring who, dredging energy from somewhere, administered 'heavy punishment with both hands'.

By now the ring was a seething mass of spectators, many of them armed and stirred up by the bloody spectacle they were witnessing. Spring was unable to move and the referee was powerless to act. 'I am so disgusted with the treatment I have experienced,' Colonel Berkeley said loftily, 'I will give up the watch. It is impossible to stand still a second without being assailed with a cut from a whip or a blow from a stick.' Despite the conditions, the two men fought on with 'nothing foul attempted by either man', though the ebullient Hudson objected when he felt Spring had too long an interval on Painter's knee. 'Do you call this fair play?' he roared. 'How many seconds is Spring to have?'

During the interval at the end of the seventy-second round Spring was left in no doubt by Cribb that he was not satisfied at the way the fight was going. The Hereford man left his corner fired up to finish the job. Langan, in contrast, emerged from his corner looking weak and bewildered. Spring, his loins girded, blasted Langan, who toppled but came up to scratch for the seventy-fourth round. 'Go and fight!' bellowed Cribb. Spring, now sensing victory, went for the Irishman, battering the challenger around the ring. Langan rested his bruised face and battered head on Hudson's like a tired baby before being propelled back into the fight. Spring attacked again and delivered a mighty blow to his opponent's head. Langan collapsed at the feet of the champion, his eye closed and his face smothered in blood. It was all Spring now, and the crowd pleaded with him to finish off the Irishman.

Langan insanely staggered out for the seventy-sixth like a drunk cadging a nightcap. He was almost asleep on his feet. Spring cut up the Dubliner with his broken hands. The fans roared approval, their voices thickened with ale. Delving into some primitive reserve, Langan showed 'he was not extinguished' and mauled and mullocked his way through the round. Both men were smeared with blood and mud, their bodies feverishly hot in spite of the cold wind blowing up from the river. Spring had never fought such a tigerish opponent and Cribb and Painter deserved great credit for keeping him in the fight. But the betting boys, traditionally good judges, now had Spring at twenty to one.

Langan went down slowly and quietly, like a suicide slipping into a cold canal. His seconds resisted calls to concede defeat, and Reynolds 'rushed to drag his man back to his corner only to have difficulty getting him off the ground'. As Langan sat half asleep on Hudson's knee, gentlemen sitting ringside pleaded for him to be pulled out of the fight. 'It is impossible,' they argued, 'he cannot meet Spring any more at the scratch.' They were right. When time was called, Langan was insensible to it, and though Hudson tried his best, shouting, slapping and cajoling the Irishman, it was to no avail. After thirty seconds had elapsed Langan opened his eyes only to be told the fight was over. He was outraged and said 'his seconds had no right to give in for him', adding that he 'could fight for another forty rounds'. 'Don't leave the ring, Spring,' rough Irish voices growled menacingly, as Cribb and Painter went over to Langan's corner to reason with his seconds. 'Don't let so good a man be killed,' said Painter. 'He does not know at the present moment what he is talking about.'

The Irish mob pressed forward demanding an official decision, and was granted it when Colonel Berkeley lifted his voice above the tumult. 'Langan did not come to fight when time was called,' he pronounced, 'therefore he has lost the battle according to the rules of Pugilism.' Langan screamed, 'I am not beaten – clear out the ring, I can fight for another four hours.' He was gently ordered to remain in his corner.

After seventy-seven rounds, Spring stood as the victor. He raised his bruised hands and the crowd cheered him wildly, tumbling down from the stands to mob their battered hero. He was still the Bare-knuckle Champion of All England. As carrier pigeons arrowed from ringside, carrying the result to London and Herefordshire, Spring stood quietly in the centre of the ring, his face nicked, his bleeding hands aching.

The ever-practical Jackson passed the hat around. There wasn't much in it, but it was topped up by Egan who managed to cajole £12 16s from the gentlemen sitting ringside. John Gully – a multimillionaire in today's currency – lobbed in a fiver. Spring, meanwhile, went to Langan's corner and shook his dazed victim's hand. Elated as he must have been, the champion conducted himself with the 'unassuming manner and gentlemanly conduct which has ever been a marked feature of his public career'. To his admirers, he was 'a perfect model

A battered Langan lies defeated.

of what an English boxer should be, and a more honourable man does not exist.' The defeated Langan crawled abjectly from the ring and, draped with fellow countrymen, he staggered through the mud, heading for town and a hot bath.

While Langan was being consoled by his friends, the champion was whisked away in his shining coach, glad to escape the mud-spattered crowd who pressed their dirty noses to his carriage. The driver whipped the horses to a gallop, and Cribb, Painter and Colonel Berkeley animatedly discussed the battle. The jaded Spring was ready for a leisurely soak in a sudsy tub to soothe his pain and mend his wounds. His hand, which he smashed early in the fight by hitting Langan's head and breaking the knuckles, was oozing blood through its swathe of bandages. As darkness fell on the freezing stonework of the old riverside taverns and warehouses near Pitchcroft, Spring slumped in his carriage, listening to the snorts of the galloping horses and heard the ring of their hooves on the road out of Worcester.

THE
GREAT FIGHT
BETWEEN
SPRING AND LANGAN.
BY W. MITFORD.

Tune—The Cuckoo's Nest.

Come all you milling coves, both of high and low degree,
Do'nt grumble at misfortunes, but listen unto me ;
It is of British courage I now intend to sing,
And the hero of my harmony's bold Winter Spring.

Now, the fame of this pugilist had reached the Irish shore,
When Langan prick'd his ears, and says he, I'll travel o'er,
I'll do my best to serve him out, and make old Ireland ring,
And I'll meet this English champion in Winter or Spring.

When he came up to London, he figur'd at the Fives,
He was quiz'd by the swells, as to bottom and to size :
When a match was soon agreed upon, that in a roped ring,
For two hundred gold Sovereigns he should fight Spring.

'Twas on a winter's morning to Worcester they drew,
They both look'd well, and shewing game, like Lions they set too,
When they got from semiquavers into semibraves to sing ;
And the battle terminated with it's Well done Spring.

Now Pat, though defeated, says he, my darling friends,
I'll meet the boy in summer, and I'll make you all amends,
Upon a stage, I'll him engage, not in a roped ring ;
And I'll turn the tune to Langan, boys, instead of Spring.

Oh, your bullying dear Pat, it shall never me confound,
I will meet you on those terms for five hundred pounds,
Within a hundred miles of town, your forces you may bring,
And so table down your blunt, I'm your man says Spring.

On the eight day of June, they to Chichester went down,
Attended by the Fancy both from country and town,
With looks as bold as Hercules they leapt into the ring,
This day must prove the best of us, says Langan to Spring.

For the first seven rounds, oh, they both made gallant play,
But Spring he stopt ; hit right and left, then quickly got away,
When he gave to him a facer, and floor'd him on the ring,
Which made the bets at two to one, with bravo Spring.

Now Langan strove to wrestle and to bring him to the ground,
And he fought, though piping weak, until the 77th round ;
When he coud'nt come up to the scratch, for time had taken wing,
And the laurel still adorns the brow of bold Tom Spring.

(Edgar, Printer.)

Song for Spring.

THE
Champions of England and Ireland,
SPRING AND LANGAN.
SHORTLY will be Published, by Subscription of
One Sovereign each, a highly-finished COLOURED EN-
GRAVING, 23 Inches by 13, REPRESENTING the
AMPHITHEATRE, containing upwards of 30,000 Persons,
in which, the above PUGILISTS CONTENDED; the GRAND
STAND forming the Centre. The Drawing (which has been
much admired for its Correct delineation), from Sketches taken
on the Spot, by JAMES CLEMENTS and JOHN PIT-
MAN, will remain on View, at Deighton's Library, 53, High-
street, Worcester, until Saturday next, the Thirty-first Instant.
Subscribers' Names received at the Library, and the Prints
will be Delivered in the Order of Subscription.
Worcester, January 26, 1824.

Advertisement in the *Hereford Journal*.

News of Spring's latest heroics reverberated around the country, as inky-fingered printers engaged barely literate hacks to scribble topical doggerel in a pugilistic vein. In pubs bursting with raucous celebrants, punters grabbed these still-wet sheets and sang discordantly, elbow to elbow, raising voices and beakers to their man, Tom Spring.

The sweatshops around Worcester and Staffordshire were work-ing overtime, churning out ugly figurines of both fighters joined at the waists in combat like Siamese twins, heavy useless jugs, crude plates and plaques, all with hastily drawn, laughingly unrepresenta-tive images of both fighters. These would be sold cheaply on street corners, at fights and fairs and in pubs where the Fancy congregated. A century-and-a-half later, fans would still be combing junk shops and flea markets in Cardiff and Birmingham for these crude sou-venirs. 'Collector's items', more carefully designed and wrought in the finest Worcester and Staffordshire china, were made in limited batches.

The *Hereford Journal* gave a 'vivid, round-by-round report 'which helped spread the news to the market towns and outlying village of Spring's native Herefordshire. On the Prospect, the highest point in Ross-on-Wye, fellows who had drunk more than was sensible stripped to the waist to re-enact the great fight. The pubs quickly emptied as men rushed to watch and goad the fighters. It ended tragically, when

'In jumping over a spiked gate to witness one of these fights a man named Chamberlain slipped, was caught by a spike, and killed.'

Meanwhile, in his prison cell in Hertford, John Thurtell, con artist, gambler and occasional fight promoter whose name would be commemorated by Hazlitt, Borrow, Lytton, Lamb, Scott, Carlyle and De Quincy, was preparing to die on the scaffold the following morning for his involvement in the sensational killing of card sharp and shyster William Weare. Thurtell broke off prayers to asked his gaoler, 'It is perhaps wrong in my situation, but I should like to read Pierce Egan's account of the great fight yesterday.'

The following morning, as Thurtell, wearing a spotted fogle – the necktie associated with Jem Belcher, the great Bristol fighter – took the slow, shackled amble to the gallows, many of his old friends were arriving in Hertford tired and mud-stained after a mad gallop from the fight to see him off. Egan, who had established a bond with Thurtell and scooped the rest of the press by gaining an exclusive interview with the condemned man, was already at the courthouse taking notes. In the Fancy's collective psyche, Spring's victory and Thurtell's death were entwined.

27

Honours and Controversies

Tom Spring's first official engagement after retaining his title was to visit Manchester, to be regaled by a group of businessmen and collect a fine trophy called the Manchester Cup after a hearty, backslapping dinner. Langan was in attendance and in a short speech challenged Spring to a return for £100-a-side. Spring said he would not fight for less than £500-a-side. The champion had had enough of blood-letting and was ready to pursue other interests. He returned to his adopted London, to be hailed once again by the cognoscenti, the literati and the nobility, but when he arrived there was a letter waiting for him from Tom Reynolds, Langan's second. It was the first of many claiming foul play. Langan, Cribb, Spring, Reynolds and Hudson all rushed to print with accusation and counter-accusation.

Before long, Langan too travelled to London to cash in on his new found fame. The Irishman's scrapping qualities, his sportsman-ship, humour and 'bottom' appealed to the aficionados. He walked into the Tennis Court at ten o'clock on 19 February, accompanied by Reynolds. Spring appeared half-an-hour later and the men who had so recently knocked each other into oblivion 'cordially shook hands'. After a spot of banter, Spring challenged the Irishman to affirm or deny the recently published accusations. Langan professed that the fight had been clean and that he harboured no grudge against the champion, but added, 'I was rubbed out of the last fight, my own confidence is not diminished. My friends will back me and here I challenge you to fight for 500 pounds a side on a similar stage to that which Cribb and Molyneaux fought on. I am ready to put money down to make the match.'

Spring declined. He would not box in a smaller ring. For the long-reaching scientist it had to be twenty-four feet or nothing. Langan spoke with passion about his fight with Spring and welcomed an early return, providing 'it was a more pleasant and agreeable mill than the last one'. The offer was repeatedly made to Spring but he steadfastly refused.

* * * * * * * *

Still the vitriolic letters flew in all directions. Most of Langan's were written by Reynolds and most of Spring's by Vincent Dowling. Regarding the scurrilous suggestion by Reynolds that Cribb had manhandled Langan, Spring's party wrote: 'We are requested by friends of Cribb to say that the statement in Reynolds' letter of Cribb having struck Langan is utterly untrue – Cribb being incapable of so unfair and unmanly an action.' As to the suggestion that Reynolds had the temerity to strike Cribb while defending Langan, the *Hereford Journal* said: 'If it be true we can only say he took advantage of his situation, as we are convinced he would not dare to do so anywhere else.'

Wounded by Langan's inexplicable assertion that Spring refused to fight on when he himself was prepared to do so, Spring published an aggrieved response in Pierce Egan's *Life in London*, in which he renounced his intention to retire. As a sensitive and proud man, Spring said he could not accept a jibe that questioned his courage. But the goading of the champion had finally achieved the effect Reynolds and Langan desired: Spring would defend his title one more time. The publicity and rancour generated in the inns and the fighting clubs, and in the columns of the magazines and newspapers, would ensure the return would be a financial bonanza. It would also mean the reluctant Spring could earn the sort of money that would enable him to retire permanently from the ring.

Langan accepted the champion's invitation to come to Cribb's to discuss a rematch. The room above the tiny pub was packed to capacity and many a would-be attender was denied entry. Both combatants bore scars from their championship battle. Langan had bruises on his face and healing wounds over both eyes. Spring's eye was blackened

"SIR,

"Your paper, and others of the public journals, have of late teemed with idle correspondence on the subject of my fight with Langan. Of Langan I have nothing to say, but that I consider him a brave fellow in the ring, and a good fellow out of it; but in order to put an end to all further chaffing, and to bring our matters to a clear understanding, I have only this to observe: Langan, at his own benefit, publicly stated that " he was ready to fight any man who called himself Champion of England, on a stage, for from £300 to £1,000." Now, I have been pronounced the character he describes, and I am ready to fight Langan, or any other man, for £500, in a roped ring on the turf, or for £1,000 in any way that himself or his friends may think proper—on an iron pavement if they choose. This is my final answer to all challenges; and I shall be at the Fives' Court to-morrow, at Turner's benefit, and come to the scratch if called.

"I am, sir, yours most respectfully,

"THOMAS W. SPRING.

"*February* 24, 1824."

Letter from Spring.

and he carried his right arm in a sling. Tom Belcher arrived with Langan, who looked dashing in a military cloak After the arrival of Jimmy Soares, president of the Daffy Club, the doors were locked 'to prevent an improper rush' and a guard was placed on the stairs to prevent any unwelcome intrusion. Langan took a glass of wine and drank to Spring's health. All present returned the compliment. Cribb, 'who was very lame', deserted his bar 'to hobble upstairs to meet Belcher to argufy the topic in a parliamentary style'. Belcher put a contract on the table which he said Langan was prepared to sign.

As the fighters haggled about what sort of stage to box on, Egan quoted Cribb, who famously said he would fight anywhere: 'upon a stage, the top of a house, in a ship, or in any place you think proper'. Spring, though, was reluctant to fight on the smaller, uncovered, boarded stage because it would suit Langan's grappling style. With his mobility and giant strides the Hereford man would prefer a larger ring covered in turves or matting. In the end, aware that it was definitely to be his last fight, the champion acquiesced. Now he was even more determined to win.

With the staging issue decided, Spring set himself to nitpicking every last full stop and comma in the contract. He questioned the size of the deposit, the date of the match, the day for paying the last instalment of the deposit and who should pay for the stage. He suggested Langan should pay the full amount as it was the Irishman who wanted it. Langan smiled and replied. 'See now Tom, say nothing about that, for if I win, and I think I will, I'll bear the whole expense of the stage myself. But that's neither here nor there. I hope the best man will win; and though we are going to fight, it's myself that would go a hundred miles to serve you, for I have no antipathy towards you whatever.' Reynolds wanted the contracts signed on St Patrick's Day at his benefit but Spring was obstinate, saying that he did not 'wish to lend himself to this additional attraction to the public'.

Langan laughed his way through the evening and would not hear a bad word spoken of Tom Spring. When the contracts were signed and Soares was appointed stakeholder, Langan and his entourage 'made their bows' and repaired to the Castle Tavern to 'finish the evening'. Spring met up with Langan again on 13 March at Jack Randall's pub where they paid £100 each towards the stake money. Langan in fact put up £200 out of his own pocket. Firm friends now, Langan hushed the Irish in the audience who began to abuse Spring when Langan attempted to drink the Herefordian's health. Langan said all he wanted was 'a comfortable and pleasant mill', and both men signed to fight on 8 June 1824.

Odds flew as the drink was downed and Langan and Spring exchanged friendly banter. A bond in blood had been forged between the two men that would last a lifetime. Spring offered the Irishman odds of £70 to £40 which Langan snapped up. Spring then offered £580 against £168 that he would win the battle. Langan helped himself to that too. The remainder of the evening 'was spent with the utmost good humour by all parties'.

* * * * * * * *

Meanwhile, a great fight fan died in far-off Greece. On the evening of 19 April 1824, after being caught in heavy rain in an open boat, the once hyperactive Lord Byron, a man whom his 'pastor and master' Jackson had warned against taking too much out of himself, succumbed to a virulent fever. His last words – tame for a man whose life was devoted to drink, fighting, love and debauchery – were: 'Now I shall go to sleep.' As the great poet lay like a pale, plucked and crippled little bird on a cold marble slab in swampy Missolonghi, Tom Spring, the young potboy he met in Cribb's pub and now Champion of All England, was contemplating his last fight. The morning after the great romantic poet died the Greek government ordered thirty-seven guns, one for each year of his age, to be fired from the batteries of Missolonghi at sunrise. All public offices were closed. Musical instruments were silenced, dances were cancelled and the taverns were closed.

In London the poet's friends made up for the Greeks' enforced solemnity. A benefit for Spring was held at the Fives Court on Tuesday 1 June. There was a massive turnout. Even the gallery was crammed, and its complement of swells, MPs and gentlemen, accustomed to being sequestered comfortably away from the press and the hoi polloi, were forced to squeeze together for a glimpse of the action. From a window Spring addressed the huge crowd milling in the narrow streets below. Anyone could take the floor to make a point, however fatuous. The round-bellied, rouge-cheeked Josh Hudson used the opportunity to challenge the champion once more, 'or anybody else', for a stake of 200 sovereigns. This provoked quite an uproar, mainly of laughter.

Slowly and deliberately Spring mounted the stage, to be greeted by a barrage of applause. He confirmed it had been his intention to retire after the first Langan fight but 'he was so taunted, vilified and abused' by the Irishman and his backers that he felt honour-bound to grant the return match, after which he was determined to quit the ring for good. Although, he added with a smile, while 'he did not wish to fight again, if anyone wanted to fight it must on his terms, 500 pounds a side, and he was prepared to put a 100 pounds down and the fight to take place within three months.' There was 'general and reiterated applause'.

Hudson then made a remark that first astounded, then drew prolonged booing and hissing from the knowledgeable audience. The championship, he said, had been given to Spring, while he had fought his way to fame, beginning at five pounds, then tens, then twenties, 'til he got to a hundred'. He did not, he said, understand about being backed for 500 pounds, but he could raise 200 pounds, 'not for Spring in particular', he insisted, but for 'any man in the world to try how they would like him.'

Spring ignored the boorish Cockney's insult and begged silence. 'I never wanted the title,' he said, 'and I wish to retire from fighting, if the people will let me.' The championship was merely nominal, and of no advantage to him, but 'having fairly obtained it', he was 'desirous of retaining it'. This remark drew 'universal cheers, and cries of Bravo! Bravo!'

"THE IRISH CHAMPION'S DECLARATION TO THE SPORTING WORLD.

" GENTLEMEN,

" Mr. Spring, in his letter, speaks of his wish to avoid 'chaffing, and bring matters to a right understanding' between him and me. To show you, therefore, the chaffing is not on my side, and that I am really anxious to have matters clearly understood, I beg leave to submit the following facts to your judgment:—

" When I challenged him in Manchester, for £100 a-side, he pretended to treat my offer with contempt (though he had never, but in one instance, fought for more), and named £500 as the least stake, a sum three times greater than any for which he had contended. But though he was afterwards shamed into agreeing for £300 a-side, yet he calculated on my inability to raise so much; and, to prevent my doing so, he and his friends, besides throwing other obstacles in my way, contrived to induce the gentleman who agreed to put down the whole sum for me to withdraw his patronage, so that it was with the utmost difficulty I raised the battle money.

" As to the battle, it is needless to repeat that I have good reasons to complain of the treatment I experienced. Every unprejudiced witness will bear me out in this, and my friends are so satisfied with my conduct, that they are ready to back me against Spring for £500, on a stage, which they think the only way of guarding against a repetition of unfair treatment. But when Spring finds me thus supported, he raises his demand to £1,000, on the ground that I challenged him to fight for any sum from £300 to £1,000. My words were, that I would fight him for from £300 to £500, or for £1,000, if I were backed, and I do not deny them; for if I had £100,000 I would confidently stake it. But £500 is a sum between £300 and £1,000; and if I could get backed for £1,000, I should rejoice at it, as it would at once do away with this excuse of Spring. I think, however, that it will not tell much for his credit, if he continues to reject the £500, which I can command, and £50 of which I am ready to lay down at Belcher's, to make the match, any time he thinks proper. I believe nine out of ten in the sporting world will agree that Spring cannot honourably refuse this proposal, were it only to meet the complaint of foul play, which I am justified in making with regard to the former battle.

" But he also pledged himself, when he received the championship, to imitate the donor's conduct. Then why not redeem his pledge, or resign the gift ?

" He says that he does not wish to enter the ring again. This is mere shuffling. He ought not to hold a situation for which he has no taste : he cannot, in justice, have the honour without the danger. If he will not fight, then let him resign the championship to one that will—to a man who will not want to make a sinecure of the title, and will always be ready to fight for a stake of £500.

" Permit me again to repeat that I am ready to make a match to fight Spring for £500 a-side, within a hundred miles of London, on a stage* similar to the one on which Cribb and Molineaux fought. Sparring exhibitions I cannot attend till I set-to for my friend Reynolds, on the 17th of March.

" I am, gentlemen, your very obedient servant,

"JOHN LANGAN.

" *Castle Tavern, Holborn, February 26.*"

Letter from Langan.

Later the same evening Spring and Cribb were guests of honour at the Castle Tavern where tables were laid for fifty-two gentlemen Langan turned up for a short while to witness the posting of the final instalment of the £1,000 stake, which was then handed to the President of the Daffy Club. The fight was a definite. Most of the blunt went on Spring to win at odds of four to one.

28

Tom Spring, the Bucolic 'Beau Geste'

That Spring was now firmly established in the public perception as a folk hero is illustrated by this tale. It was a freezing winter's night in busy, impersonal London. A coach was about to depart for Birmingham. Clinging to the doorhandle was a poor woman, windswept and desperate. Holding on to her was a pale and sickly baby. Tom Spring, immaculately dressed and muffled against the chill wind, observed the poor woman's plight. He opened the carriage door and asked politely, 'Is there any room in there for a lady and a baby?' There was no reply. Removing his cloak and top hat, the pugilist asked again but this time with a little steel in his voice. 'My name is Tom Spring. Is there any room inside for the lady and her baby?' At once the door sprang open and the lady and child were quickly accommodated in the carriage.

While he waited for the rematch Spring boxed exhibitions against anyone who fancied a bloody nose from the Champion of All England. On 24 March 1824 he returned to Hereford to spar with a local non-entity. The 'battle' was later commemorated by the limited production of a porcelain jug bearing a picture of a roped ring and two circling fighters being watched by a crowd. It bore the inscription 'Spring, Champion of Great Britain and Thomas Smith of Hereford'.

For the return with Langan, Spring was taken by Cribb to a familiar haunt in Surrey to prepare. The champion's training was interrupted by a mild throat infection, but Spring quickly recovered. When asked to predict the result he replied that victory was a 'tolerable certainty'.

The venue originally suggested for the historic battle was Manchester. Warwick Racecourse was also considered, if only because a business-man had offered the boxers a bonus of £125 each if they agreed to fight there. However, the magistrates intervened at the eleventh hour, causing a swift change to a place situated 'in a south-easterly direction not quite seventy miles from London'. It turned out to be Birdham Bridge, near Chichester, selected because the landlord of the Swan inn, a Mr Hewlings, offered the champion a £200 sweetener and a spacious suite of rooms after the fight. The alteration threw the Fancy into disarray as they frantically turned their vehicles around. The long train of galloping, running, walking, panting humanity on the roads to Chichester presented a sight not seen before or since.

At the very last minute a message came from Warwickshire saying that all was now in order, the Magistrate had been 'squared' and the fight could go on there. This too-tardy offer 'met its merited fate' and the Fancy inexorably headed for the new venue. Langan, however, had failed to get news of the switch to Chichester and 'under the direction of his backers had taken his departure to a place near the intended field of honour.'

* * * * * * * *

The ring was built on Monday morning 7 June 1824 'in a ploughed field belonging to a venerable lady on the other side of fourscore'. It was carefully constructed to avoid the disordered mêlée both fight-ers endured in their first encounter. The wood was planed and great care was taken to ensure that all the ringposts were well rounded. According to Henry Downes Miles:

> The progress of the work attracted the curiosity and excited aston-ishment of the Yokels, to whom such preparations had something awful in their appearance, and they could scarcely persuade them-selves that, instead of a stage for reaping pugilistic honours, it was not a scaffold for the execution of a criminal.

The location, three miles from Chichester, was ideal. It was surrounded by water, with just one entrance that could be easily policed. Local farm-ers, 'informed of the high gratification awaiting them', volunteered their wagons to form the outer ring and before long fifty-three wagons were arranged in a considerable circle.

As fight fans thronged to see if Spring could best the Irishman a second time, every coach that set out from the capital in a south-easterly direction was crammed, despite the operators doubling their fares in avaricious anticipation. A few hardy Corinthians set off on Sunday on horseback, and on Monday the roads filled with vehicles of every description. The pedestrians who had set out to walk through the night to Warwickshire were worse off. Many of Langan's Irish supporters failed to get to Chichester in time.

The small Sussex town braced itself as thousands of noisy fans milled around aimlessly, pouring in and out of the inns, jeering and cheering, teasing the girls and grinning in windows. To the relief of the citizens the 'quality' also turned up. 'Post chaises, and carriages and four, began to pour into the town, and by the respectable appearance of their inmates, a more favourable opinion, if not of the taste, of the rank of the supporters of the prize ring was formed.' The Dukes of Beaufort and Rutland, the Marquis of Worcester, Lords Yarmouth, Uxbridge, Fife, Lowther, Gwydyr, Deerhurst and Loftus, Sir Bellingham Graham, Colonel Berkeley and Squire Osbaldson all arrived in style and were shown to the best rooms in town.

Of less noble lineage but similar excitement value was the dramatic arrival of the square-shouldered behemoths of the prize ring: Oliver, Martin, Harmer, Shelton, Burn, Randall, Painter and Scroggins. The fighters, some old and grizzled, heavily decamped from their coaches and with quiet dignity joined in the bustle of the pre-match prepara-tions. The sports writers of the day harried the old pugs for conten-tious quotes, but 'when pressed for their comments on the coming battle, each in his turn called forth some shrewd remark.' John Gully arrived in state to seek out his old friend Cribb.

'Every inn was crowded to an overflow, and scarce a bed which could be had for money remained without an occupant.' The asking price for a decent room was a guinea 'but in many cases even this sum was not sufficient to secure comfortable quarters – and not a few remained up the whole night.' Some noisily headed for the fight venue, selecting ditches to sleep in. Rumour had it that as Langan was trapped in Warwick, the fight was off. A counter rumour had it that Spring's backers had bribed the Irishman with the promise of at least £100 – win, lose or draw – as long as he got to Chichester on time.

It was with some relief that the fight promoters heard that Langan's carriage was seen passing through Guildford. He was accompanied by Colonel O'Neil and Tom Belcher. Spring was also on the road, quite close to the town. A crowd gathered in expectation. *Pugilistica* reported:

> At half past seven an open barouche and four was seen driving down the main street, and in a few minutes it was drawn up to the door of the Swan Inn. Spring who was accompanied by Cribb and some of his friends was instantly recognised, and received with three cheers. The Champion seemed in excellent health and spirits, and appeared grateful for these marks of favour. Apartments having being engaged for him in the house, he immediately alighted, and an immense crowd was soon collected in front of the inn, to catch a glimpse of his person.

Langan and his party, weary from the agonisingly slow journey from Warwick, were conducted to the Dolphin Inn. It was hardly appropriate preparation for a long, bare-knuckle slog with the best fighter in England. While Spring, after a light training session with Cribb, enjoyed a hot bath and a good dinner in fine apartments, Langan had endured an unnecessary journey of almost 200 miles. Even so, the Irish boxer 'was in high spirits, laughed heartily, and looked extremely well'. Perhaps he felt his fortunes would be different this time.

29

Spring's Last Fight

By half past eleven the fight-bound crowd, catching a glimpse of the grandstand Jack Martin had 'borrowed' from Epsom Racecourse, quickened their step. Many avoided a drawbridge erected to control the crowd, taking advantage of the normal confusion of the big day to slip in for free. A large number climbed between the ropes to try out the ring, just 'to say they had been there', although 'none appeared to envy Spring and Langan, whose bones were so soon to come in contact with its surface.'

A pound per head was charged for a seat in the grandstand, which soon filled up. Seats in straw-filled wagons at five shillings a head also disappeared. The attendance was considerably lower than expected, however, at an estimated 12,000 – a third of the number that showed up at Worcester for the first match. The disparity was due entirely to the last-minute change of venue. Several coach drivers were aggrieved to have to abandon hundreds of potential fares in Warwick.

At noon a man came with a bucket of lime to chalk the ring. The crowd booed good-naturedly. The workman smiled and waved his wet brush. Cries of 'Bravo, Spring!' and 'Good man, Langan' rang out in the warm air. Then Cribb and Painter, with Belcher and O'Neil, climbed onto the stage to check the arrangements. Josh Hudson lurked ringside waiting to offer his services to Langan. The old fighters smiled at the reception they received and withdrew to make way for the principal actors.

Jackson made his usual imperious entrance accompanied by Lord Uxbridge, Colonel Berkeley and 'several other gentlemen of respectability'. They all agreed they 'had never witnessed a better formed ring, or a more orderly assemblage.' The bag containing the stake money was passed to Jackson but he declined to take it. Instead the monies were entrusted to the safe hands of Brooks and Co., bankers of Chancery Lane. The two umpires and the referee took up battle stations in a purpose-built box near the corner of the ring, where they could get a clear – and safe – view of the milling combatants.

Jackson signalled the two men to be brought to the ring. Spring, who met with the thunderous applause he was now so accustomed to, threw his hat into the ring with a confident flourish and as lithe as a tiger followed it. 'His manner was cool and collected, and although there was a smile of confidence on his countenance, still he did not manifest any unbecoming levity.' Langan bounced jovially into the ring and smiled and waved at the onlookers. The Irishman had made many friends and gained respect after his brave showing in the first fight. Spring joined in the applause at which point Langan walked up to him and said, 'Well, Tom, we'll see today who is the best man.' 'We will,' Tom said, clasping his rival's hand, 'and the best man will win the fight.' 'Right,' Langan said, 'I'm sure we'll both do our best.' The surly Cribb wasn't impressed by the fine words. 'Stop your chaffing and prepare for work,' the veteran grumbled.

Langan, while he waited for Spring to perform his toilette, looked around with great humour towards some of his friends, to whom he nodded. The sun beat down on his head and if persisted both men would 'almost be broiling under its influence'. The fighters came to scratch just after one. The crowd went quiet. Paddy O'Neil, a 'rough and unpolished mountaineer', was designated as Langan's bottle-holder. Belcher would play the more important role as his second, with assistance, if required, from Hudson. The John Bull fighter, on seeing Langan's naked back already reddening from the effects of the sun, shouted to Langan, 'Have you any cold cream Pat?' 'Divil a crame,' Langan said, 'but me mother's milk,' pointing to the brandy bottle. Irritated by accusations that Painter kneed Langan while he was on the ground in the first fight, Cribb and Painter made great play of putting on knee-caps, made of chamois leather and stuffed with wool.

When Spring threw off his outer garments 'he was a beautifully made man, with a handsome, intelligent face, and a grace and symmetry about his frame that no sculptor has ever surpassed in bronze or marble.' The fighters tossed for ends and Langan won, condemning Spring to box with the sun's glare in his eyes. Langan declared, 'we won the first notch', while Cribb tied Spring's colours to the upper rail of the stage.

Langan whipped off a black silk scarf he had tied around his neck and handed it to Belcher, who tied it over Spring's fogle. The scarf was given to Langan by a Mrs O'Brien, a mysterious admirer whom the Dubliner had met in an inn. The woman had initially offered him a green scarf, but Langan refused, saying, 'I am not important enough to make it a national affair… it is only to be decided which is the best man.' Impressed by the Irish charmer's modesty, Mrs O'Brien is reputed to have looked him in the eyes and said huskily: 'You are Irish. Colour is immaterial to a brave man. Glory is your only object. Go then, and conquer.' 'Sprinkle my eyes,' Hudson said as he fingered the silk scarf. 'That looks black.' 'Aye,' said Randall, another old champion sitting ringside with the celebrities and the nobles, 'somebody will look blue before it's over.' He then winked at Langan.

At thirteen stone and seven pounds, Spring 'never looked so big, nor so well, in any of his previous contests'. Spring's figure was 'indeed a manly display; cool, collected and wary, steady as a rock, and firm as one of the oaks of his native soil.' One gentleman sitting ringside exclaimed, 'There is something about the person of the champion, if not truly noble, yet manly and elegant.' However, Langan was not to be intimidated, as Downes Miles wrote; 'Notwithstanding the Norse God in front of him, Langan bunched his fists and seemed anxious for work.'

Low-sized and round-shouldered, the powerful Langan tipped the scales at just twelve stone four pounds. As in their first encounter, it was going to be science versus guts and brawn, with Spring backpeddling and grabbing then popping Langan with swift, damaging punches when he could. Tom Spring's defence was reputed to be the finest among the heavier men.

Before a punch was thrown the challenger opened his drawers and observed, 'See Tom, I have no belt about me.' This was a humorous reference to their first fight. 'Nor I neither, Jack' Spring said, pulling at his own drawers. There was good-natured applause and Cribb, entering into the spirit, 'laid hold of Tom Belcher's fist and Painter shook the bunch of fives at Paddy O'Neil'.

In the opening round Spring was poised, ready to defend. Langan came at him with his head down. This was a bizarre ploy to make Spring break his hands on the Irishman's skull. Langan's first punches hit fresh air as Spring stepped sideways and countering swiftly as he 'planted a tremendous battler on Langan's knowledge box'. Aroused, Langan tore into his foe and biffed and cudgelled, his crude blows coming from unorthodox angles. He yelled 'first blood', after seeing a crimson dribble from Spring's mouth. The referee disagreed. Cautiously, Spring pawed and patted away the blows, content it seemed, to let the visitor let off steam. Then determined to warn the Irishman not to take liberties, Spring 'disengaged his right sledgehammer and with the rapidity of lightning drove a smash into Langan's smeller' which had the Irishman's eyes not so much smiling as watering.

After a period of fairly even exchanges Spring floored Langan. While the Irishman sat on his rump Spring 'patted him on the back'. Langan already had a cut under one eye. The round lasted four minutes, with Spring already well on top.

As the men came to scratch for the second, the umpire called out – for the benefit of the ring-side gamblers who put money on such things – 'First blood from Langan, and Langan first down'. Money changed hands. The following round was even, with Langan pressing and Spring happy to counter when necessary. Langan upped the pace and made several furious attempts to grab Spring. One lunge caught the champion and, using his great strength, Langan succeeded in introducing the calm Englishman's face to the wet grass. Langan then flung himself on top of Spring, trying to knock the wind out of him. The round lasted three minutes and Langan's fans, of which there were a few, cheered and yelled.

In the third, Spring resumed his steady boxing and he made some expert stops as Langan piled in. Jackson was so impressed with Spring that he cried 'Beautiful' as the champion let fly with both hands. The speed and accuracy of his punches stopped Langan's charge and, as the Irishman reeled away bloody and bemused, Spring threw him to end the round. Spring was in charge but this could change. Langan was far from finished. Swallowing his own warm blood he attacked with even greater ferocity, boring in with his head. The Irishman's persistence paid off and he landed several good shots on Spring's face, one of which drew blood. 'Fight, Langan,' Belcher ordered. 'You have all the best of it.' However, many of Langan's blows were glancing. A period of wrestling followed, which Spring had the best of, and Langan went down.

As the fighters returned to their respective corners following this exchange, it was noticeable that 'the left hand of Spring was already going'. The familiar curse had struck the champion once again. 'They were soft and puffy, guaranteed to swell to a great size, becoming so tender that it was agony to hit with them.'

The fourth was even with both men landing blows and Langan wrestling Spring to the floor. In the next round, Spring landed left- and right-hand punches which, because 'Langan's snuff box was in the way', literally burst Langan's face open and caused him to lose blood in gobbets. The Irishman 'smiled and made play' then licked his lips, curled his bloodied hands into fists and plodded forward. Spring jabbed Langan but the Dubliner grabbed him and threw him. Spring's face was now a mask of blood but he was well on top and odds-on to retain his title.

Langan rushed across the ring at the beginning of the sixth, but the Herefordian 'grappled him like another Hercules and succeeded in planting a blow on his pole'. Both men fell. 'Spring jumped up and laughed', while Langan was leaking claret. In the seventh, Spring 'displayed all those tactics for which he is celebrated' and landed some beautifully clean shots to Langan's face, but the Irishman kept coming, flinging punches, pushing, shoving and grabbing. 'Keep up your head, Langan,' Cribb said. 'Fight first,' Belcher advised his charge, 'he can't hurt you.'

Langan's friends exhorted him to step up the pace as there were clear signs that Spring was tiring from the constant wrestling. Both men looked exhausted, but it was Spring who gained the impor- tant fall, triggering shouts of, 'It won't last long' and, 'Five to two on Spring'. The champion staggered to his corner and sat with a heavy sigh on Painter's knee.

Cribb refreshed his man with a few well-chosen curses, a quick leg massage and pushed him out for the next round. Belcher had difficulty getting his man to scratch. It was a short round, with Langan closing feebly and Spring easily throwing him. Langan got the worst of the ninth too. Spring 'planted a few nobbers' and Langan went down. There were optimistic cries of 'it's all up' from Spring's supporters, but

Langan kept coming until Spring threw him again. During a hectic tenth, Paddy O'Neil sang out, 'Give him a back fall, Jack, but don't hurt him.' Langan did just that.

Spring fell heavily in the twelfth and took an ugly knock against the lower rail of the stage. The next round was even. In the fourteenth, Spring looked weak, and Langan gained a second wind. The champion was forced to fight Langan's fight, 'pulling, hauling, grappling and catching'. By the fifteenth, Spring's left hand was 'swelled and puffed like a blister'. Ignoring the pain he caught Langan with a good punch as the Irishman was going down. The crowd cried 'Foul, foul' – Spring was clearly the better technician but Langan's untutored battling gained the neutral's respect, even if his antics did not please the more knowledgeable spectators. In the sixteenth, as both boxers lay on the ground, they laughed at each other and Langan good-humouredly tapped Spring on the breast – bringing cries of 'Bravo!' from the audience.

Spring began the seventeenth brightly with some superb boxing, but Langan caught him with an expertly executed cross-buttock 'which shook him terribly and his legs rebounded from the ground'. In the eighteenth, Langan pursued Spring and they both fell. In the nineteenth, Spring appeared to be all in, which deceived Langan – who was quickly dropped. In the following round Spring threw Langan with such force it looked as it was all over. Langan also went down in the twenty-first and the twenty-second. Spring, confident of victory, was smiling as he sat on Painter's knee. Langan was handed brandy and water by Belcher during the interval and returned to scratch 'as if nothing serious had happened', He flung a few punches but was thrown again in the twenty-third and the twenty-fourth.

In the twenty-seventh, Spring's hands were looking bloodied and broken. However, it was Langan who went down, without being hit, according to Spring's umpire, who advised Belcher:'Tell your man not to go down without a blow or I shall notice it.' Belcher ferociously challenged the aspersion. Langan was sent up to the umpire at the beginning of the twenty-eighth to say, 'Sir, I did not go down'. This apparent gamesmanship by the wily Belcher made Cribb so angry he called over to Langan, 'Why don't you come to the scratch? I want nothing but fair play.' To this, Belcher replied, 'Lick us fairly, and I shall be satisfied.' Cribb himself was accused in this round of shielding

Spring by getting in Langan's way as the Dubliner attempted to punish the champion. In the twenty-ninth Spring 'planted a heavy facer' on Langan which felled him. Cribb smiled and remarked 'That's a little one for us, I believe. Our hands are gone, are they?'

The exhausted Langan shipped tremendous punishment and was badly abused in the thirty-second, hitting his head so hard when he fell that the crowd thought it was all over. 'That's a finisher,' someone was heard to remark. In the thirty-third, 'Poor Langan came up with the heart of a lion but the frame of a lamb. He charged once again to grapple with Spring who avoided the charge and let the exhausted Langan topple over without a blow being struck.' Langan then wobbled back to his corner.

* * * * * * * *

As Spring had failed to stop Langan by the hour, all bets on that possible outcome were lost by the end of the thirty-fourth. Spring was in total command, but Langan was brave and persistent and Belcher was hoping the champion's hands would give out before Langan did. By the thirty-sixth, the humanitarians in the crowd were shouting for Langan to be taken away. Belcher and his helpers manhandled the battered and bloodied Irishman back to his corner and told him unconvincingly, 'You are not hurt yet, Jack. Spring's hands are too far gone to hurt you now.' The Irish champion 'surprised the coasting Spring with a few stiff blows' in the thirty-seventh but he was 'out-fought at all points' and went down at the end of it. He was spent and had only an obstinate gameness left. Langan stumbled and flailed ineffectually but still managed to dredge strength from somewhere to remain a constant nuisance.

When Langan went down again, stupefied, there were cries of 'take him away, Captain O'Neil'. To this, Belcher cruelly said, 'he's not hurt, he's as right as the day.' Langan came out again 'with a will, but although resolved to do or die, the latter seemed the more probable'. Langan collapsed. As he staggered forward again, he called out to Belcher through a mouthful of blood and teeth to 'keep the brandy cold'. As Langan rushed into Spring's arms, the champion let him down like a sleepy infant. Appreciating Spring's generosity, Langan patted Spring on the back as he made his way wearily back to his corner and the unsympathetic Belcher.

The great battle.

A fight that had start so brightly was slowly descending into a grim farce with both men waltzing around like two arthritic old ladies at a tea dance. Spring tried to vary his punches, switching from body to face and back, but they carried no authority and Langan stumbled through them like a man tormented by midges. His legs buckling, Langan was up and down like a puppet on a string. Every time Langan seized Spring, both men fell together. Cribb, on this occasion as he did on others, complained that Langan was 'holding Spring by the drawers'. It seemed as if neither man had trained properly for a long fight, although the weather was tropical and Langan's only aim was not to box Spring but to grab him and haul the elegant champion down to his own abysmal level. As a spectacle it was unedifying, but no one left the arena.

As the rounds wore on Spring tried to resume his clean hitting, but his damaged hands were bouncing off Langan's cranium and the blood was spouting through the champion's fingers. Langan tried to respond and even landed a few light blows, before Spring hit him with 'some chopping hits on the muzzle' and Langan went down again with the thirteen-and-a-half-stone Spring on top of him.

By the start of the forty-seventh Hudson called across to Belcher, and swore he would be lumbered (sent to gaol and clapped in irons) if he didn't pull Langan out of the fight. Belcher was having nothing of it. 'You don't frighten me' he said, 'my man is not done yet.' Meanwhile, Langan went down 'like a sack of sawdust' and more cries of 'take him away' came from the crowd. By the forty-ninth, Langan was almost blinded by bruises and blood but he was not going to quit – that was up to his second and Belcher was blind too. 'Make use of your hands' was all he could say. Langan promptly swung a crude haymaker. Spring stepped inside it and decked the Irishman with a short and lethal punch. Although Langan threw the odd punch he spent most of his time lying on the grass staring at a very narrow view of an azure Sussex sky.

Spring was very tired but he threw his challenger seemingly at will. However, he could not finish him off, which concerned Spring's backers. The hands that broke so easily had gone again. One-handed he had to fend off an awkward opponent who moved to the champion's left and threw his own left hand into Spring's face. Spring blinked but remained upright. There was no fighter better than Spring when it came down to patiently absorbing pain and discomfort. Spring boxed carefully, keeping out of trouble and throwing his man when he could.

By the fiftieth Belcher was still exhorting Langan to attack. Spring was very tired, but Langan's alleged superiority in throwing was proving to be mythical. Spring 'was always even with him and in most cases superior'. Langan's corner told their man to box. This the Irishman did to some extent and he landed several smart blows on Spring before the champion countered with a few swift right-handers of his own that made Langan back up.

There was a certain amount of levity in Spring's corner, with Cribb joking with his man – who was virtually unhurt except for his hands and a couple of weals and nicks on his face. And while Langan was as brave as a man can be in the circumstances, gamely battling on without complaint, the heavy falls he was now regularly sustaining were having a serious effect on his stamina. As Cribb looked across at Belcher working furiously in Langan's corner, he must have had a warm feeling that the fight would soon be over.

In the fifty-third, Langan caught the champion with a good shot, but Spring 'nobbed his brave adversary down'. 'Is there anything the matter with that hand? I should like to know,' Cribb teased. In the fifty-fourth, Langan came back from the dead to fling Spring on the ground. Jackson, who had seen them all in his time, was impressed by Langan's bottomless courage. 'He's an extraordinary fellow,' Jackson said, 'really a very good man.' In the fifty-sixth, Spring tried an upper-cut with devastating effect. Langan capsized 'like a log of wood'. Surely this was the end.

Langan got to his feet, took the half-minute respite to clear his head and came back biffing and snorting. There was a shock in the next round when Spring found himself on the floor. He had again tripped over Langan's outstretched leg. The crowd roared, 'Well done, Langan.' This gave Belcher reason for hope. 'We are not going to give in yet,' he said, 'We will give you as much as we can.'

At the end of the fifty-eighth round, with Langan being helped to his corner, the spectators thought it must be over. In the next Langan grappled with Spring, 'who now looked quite fresh' and he punched the Irishman. Langan fell flat on his back 'with dreadful violence'. This time surely Belcher would step in. But no, he allowed his man out again. By the sixtieth, ringsiders were amazed when Langan got Spring on the floor again. 'You can guess how pleasant a tumble on those planks, with a twelve-stone man on top of you, must have been under a broiling June sun.' 'It's not so safe for the champion,' Little Jack Randall said: 'I never saw such a fellow (as Langan), he'll fight for a week.'

Glazed plaque of Spring and Langan.

In the sixty-fourth, Langan went down from the merest touch, but Spring's hands were in such a mess he could not bunch them to hit with any power. Both men were showing signs of punishment, fatigue and blood loss. Round sixty-six was astonishing. Langan tussled with Spring and, grabbing hold of him, used all his remaining strength to gain the upper hand. The two men smeared with blood and dirt fought a bare-gummed, snorting battle for supremacy before Spring, with an eye-balling grunt, gradually forced his man to his knees. In the next round Langan fell without receiving a punch. In spite of cries of 'Shame, take him away', Belcher closed his mind to the mob and pushed Langan out again. In this round and in the next he was thrown heavily.

The macabre farce continued with Belcher taunting Langan by repeating to the crumpled Irishman the derogatory remarks of the crowd. 'Do you hear what they say, Jack?' Belcher hissed into Langan's ear. 'I will not be taken away,' Langan whispered, 'I can win it yet.'

By the seventieth Spring, in an effort to have the fight stopped, beat Langan severely, flooring him heavily in the process. There was still no surrender from Belcher. The sympathy of the entire crowd was with the stupidly heroic Langan and they were astonished the fight was allowed to continue into the seventy-first. Cries of 'shame' drew Captain O'Neil to the umpire's chair. 'I have left the man in Belcher's care,' he said, adding that as Langan had £200 of his own money on the fight, he did not like to interfere. Belcher for his part said his man was not beaten, and bringing him up to scratch cried, 'Fight! Fight, Langan!' Like an old Irish donkey fetlock-deep in a bottomless bog, Langan 'though perfectly stupefied, pricked up his ears on the word of command rushed up to Spring and was thrown heavily.'

Spring's backers wanted the fight stopped but Captain O'Neil, said that while 'he did not want for humanity' it was worth carrying on, considering the 'tumefied' state of Spring's hands. Langan came out for the seventy-second round. 'Fight, my dear boy; Spring can't hurt you,' Belcher ranted. Langan was battered by Spring until he collapsed. Surprise was expressed that Spring did not finish Langan, but the state of Spring's hands, both of which were now dreadfully swollen, sufficiently accounted for this deficiency. However, Spring 'wore his man down by his cool imperturbable manner. He fought with his head and legs more than with his fists, for his brain was always clear, his temper calm and his active pedestals ready to carry him quickly backwards or forwards as he wished.'

All those spectators watching from a distance saw was two grim silhouettes dancing their slow and dreadful waltz in silence. The boxers were immune to the birds singing in the summer trees and the bees buzzing the daisies by the fans' bare feet. It was a strange, slow day, the lachrymose tranquility only disturbed by a rude yell or the squishy thump of Spring's broken fist on Langan's tattered face. Langan came out for the seventy-third. The incensed Randall went up to the Irishman's corner and argued with Belcher to take the man out. 'Langan will not, Jack,' Belcher said. Spring, now with total control over his insanely brave opponent, 'fibbed his man and nobly laid him down gently'. As Langan sat 'almost senseless' on Paddy O'Neil's knee during the half-minute rest before round seventy-five, Cribb and Painter walked over to his corner. 'So help me,' the old champion said, 'Langan, you are as brave a man as has stepped in leather but you have not a shadow of a chance, so don't be gaumond to come again.' 'You can't win,' Painter said, 'it may prove dangerous.' 'Leave me alone,' Langan whispered, 'I will fight.' His back and sides were a mass of bruises from perpetual throws on the hard wooden stage. Spring could have thrown him with tremendous force every time but he had shown remarkable restraint.

Cribb, concerned that Spring's humanity might in some way lose him the fight, said: 'Give no chance away now, you must finish the battle.' Spring continued to pull his punches and guided his brave but almost senseless foe to the floor again. Remarkably, Langan stumbled forth for the seventy-sixth. Spring's fairness and humanity towards a thoroughly confused and beaten man was loudly applauded. At last the umpire stepped in, overruled Belcher and declared that it was cruel to go further. Belcher reluctantly gave in. The fight, one of the most brutal and pointless in the history of the bare-knuckle game, lasted one hour and forty-eight minutes. When Spring went over to the jaded, cut and bleeding Langan, the Irishman opened his battered eyes to ask, 'Is the battle over?' 'Yes,' Belcher snapped. 'Then I've lost,' Langan said. Spring's victory was 'hailed with loud acclaimation by his friends who at the same time could not withhold their pity for his game antagonist. For skill, coolness, circumspection, scientific stopping and determined bravery, he never had his equal.' Such a triumph was not without a cost. Spring's face was blackened by blows and his hands were swollen 'to the size of large apple dumplings'. William Sant, his backer who climbed into the ring with Jackson, said to Spring: 'I have never saw such bad hands in any battle. If you fight again I will never speak to you.' 'Sir, I never will fight again,' Spring said. He was to prove as good as his word.

30

The Aftermath

It had been the fairest of fights. Belcher said he did not stop the contest because his wanted Langan's fellow countrymen to know he gave the Irish Champion every possible chance to win. *Boxiana* thought Spring, 'who had improved since the fight at Worcester' had 'vindicated his right to the Championship' and had 'taken the conceit most effectively' out of Langan. The champion 'had done all he said he would – redeemed every pledge, and in his hard-earned victory displayed equal manliness and humanity'.

Spring, who had won over £1,000 in stake money in his last three contests, as well as substantial sums on bets, was taken by carriage to the Swan Hotel, Chichester. On the way 'he was received by the shouts of the populace all along the road; ladies waving their handkerchiefs at the windows as he passed along. He was immediately put to bed, bled, and a warm bath prepared for him. In spite of his injuries he was cheerful, and quite collected.'

Langan meanwhile was holding court at the Dolphin. He admitted he lost the battle fairly but said: 'I have travelled two hundred and sixty miles within the last two days. I was feverish, and on the road instead of my bed on Saturday night; I wanted to rest.' He admitted he deliberately fought with his head down to encourage Spring to hit him on the nob and ruin his delicate hands. Egan said, 'while Langan has unquestionably proved himself as brave a man as ever entered the ring, he is no fighter; he does not use his hands with anything like effect.'

After a good sleep, Spring felt well enough to receive Colonel O'Neil and Belcher at his bedside. Painter, Sant and Cribb were also present. Spring inquired after Langan and was told by Belcher he was doing well. All except Spring, who remained in bed, went over to the Dolphin to visit the Irishman. Langan lay in bed with cuts on his face and both eyes closed. Sant asked, 'Well, Langan, how do you do? Do you know me? You can't see me. I am Spring's backer but nevertheless your friend.' Langan said he was obliged and that Spring was 'a smart, clever fellow and he wished him well'. After a long rest, Spring came down for dinner dressed in a white waistcoat, dark blue coat, black evening breeches and white silk stockings. Apart from his wrapped hands and his puffed face he seemed strong and in good humour.

The champion arose early next morning to visit Langan. Although his eyes were rheumy slits, the Irishman shook his head and attempted a smile. The two men talked in a friendly fashion until 'upon taking his departure the champion shook Langan by the hand, leaving ten pounds in it'. The following morning Spring, Cribb, Painter and Sant, seated in their smart barouche, left the yard at the back of the Swan and headed for London. There were cheered off by a crowd waiting for them in the sun. Spring waved a bandaged hand.

On arrival in London, Spring bought a solid silver snuffbox, had it engraved 'to W. Sant, Esquire, as a small token of gratitude for the many favours received from him by his obedient servant Thos. Winter Spring, June 8th, 1824'. On Wednesday 16 June 1824, the *Hereford Journal* reported: 'The city of Hereford received the welcome intelligence of the victory obtained by our countryman Spring with every demonstration of joy and satisfaction.'

31

Spring Celebrates at the Fives Court

When Spring arrived at the Fives Court on the Friday night for Jack Randall's benefit, he was received with loud cheering. His face still showed signs of the fierce battle. His left hand was still puffed and his right was in a sling. He jumped into the ring and waved the crowd silent. He again praised Langan's courage and said his left hand 'gave way very early' and his right went in round thirty-six. He also severely cut his elbow when he hit one of the ring posts as he fell. He gave Langan credit for his ability to stop punches with his face, and his ability to throw punches from afar, as well as his gameness and his durability.

Langan failed to turn up for Spring's final speech as champion, due, it was said, to his inability to get up in time. Langan was now more popular than ever and 'several offers awaited him when he was disposed for another shy'. However, Langan slipped quietly back to Ireland before returning to run a pub in Liverpool where every Irish harvester got two days' free lodging with plenty of porridge, potatoes and beer, a night-cap of poteen and a straw bed for the night, as long as he left his sickle or shillelagh outside the door.

Spring returned thanks for the numerous favours he had received at all times, and begged leave to inform the crowd he had left the ring for good, but trusted that by his good conduct he should still hold an intercourse with the sporting world, and as his behaviour merited he only wished for their support. The champion then bowed and left the stage amid thunders of applause. As Spring's old friend Tom Shelton climbed down from the ring he went to Spring and said, 'Both your eyes are black. You ought not have let him do that.' 'I couldn't help it,' Spring said with a laugh. 'Why you ain't half licked,' Shelton cracked. 'I've had twice as much as I wanted', replied Spring.

* * * * * * * *

Langan and Spring eventually met to spar at the Fives Court, reliving that memorable afternoon in both their lives. They received a boisterous welcome. Wearing gloves to protect his fragile hands, Spring had the best of that too. At the conclusion of the assault, both men were again greeted with cheers.

Spring, assisted by Cribb, also made a guest appearance as second to Pea-Green Hayne's fighter Edward Baldwin, 'White-headed Bob', when the Ludlow man fought the teenager Ned Neale at Viginia Water in Surrey on 19 October 1824. Ward was handling the bottle for the 'Streatham Youth'. The bout was well supported by the gentry. Having at last landed the title for his boy, Cribb was in fine wisecracking form in the opposite corner. Spring told Baldwin 'to lead off with his left and it would be alright', but Neale was too good for Spring's charge and he outgunned the older man over forty gruelling rounds.

* * * * * * * *

The bellicose Hudson finally got the title fight he desperately wanted when he was matched with Tom Cannon, 'The Great Gun of Windsor'. Unfortunately, the chance came too late for the ebullient Cockney. The fight was staged in pouring rain on a slippery wooden stage at Warwick on 23 November 1824. Hudson thought little of Cannon and was so certain of achieving his life's ambition to become the Bare-knuckle Champion of England that he did no serious training and appeared in the ring to laughter. Fat hung from him like suet from an abattoir hook and his face was florid from drink. Although Hudson was in no condition to fight, he could always sell tickets with his braggadocio. The large crowd got poor value when the novice Cannon knocked out the Falstaffian Londoner in twenty minutes and claimed a title once held by the likes of Jackson, Cribb, Gully, 'Hen' Pearce, Jem Belcher and Spring.

Cannon lost to the favourite, Jem Ward, the following year on a scalding July day at Warwick in ten minutes, despite having the combined wisdom of Tom Spring and Tom Cribb in his corner. Oliver and Randall helped Ward. A large number of the patrician class attended, including Squire 'Pea Green' Hayne (who backed Ward) and George 'Old Squire' Osbaldeston ('the finest all round sportsman of his own, or any other age, whose fame was world-wide'). In a pressure cooker atmosphere, the thirty-five-year-old Cannon was well beaten. After a thrashing in the tenth he was spouting blood and grovelling on the floor. Spring tried an old trick of blowing brandy up Cannon's nose. It didn't work. Cannon tottered for a moment, then fell to the boards unconscious.

Ward, a capable and skilful fighter, if a mite prone to take a dive if the money was right, set his sights on a fight with Spring, a tiff having taken place between them. Spring, whose weight had ballooned, said he had no intention of re-entering the prize ring. The amiable Cannon, one of the weakest of champions, became a close friend of Spring and the two of them attended many a fight together. Cannon was a swan watcher for the Corporation before, being 'poor, ill and depressed', he blew his brains out on 11 July 1858, leaving an attentive widow in narrow circumstances. Jem Burn, whose pub, the Queen's Head in Haymarket, was second only to Tom Spring's Castle Tavern as a favourite haunt for sportsmen, raised money to 'alleviate Mrs Cannon's forlorn condition'.

Ward fought the elderly and once proud Jack Carter, who hadn't earned a penny in the ring since he was whipped by Spring nine years before. Ward was thirty to one to win. When the humiliating fracas reached the seventeenth, the timekeepers, none other than Tom Spring and Peter Crawley, entered the ring and begged Carter to give in. He refused and 'was hit flush in the face' before falling to the deck like a tumbling chimney in a storm. Curtis and Sampson, Carter's seconds, made the decision for him. The crowd cheered the old man's gameness. As he left the ring, Carter was offered a small bag of coins (amounting to £5 3s 6d), which had been collected beforehand for the loser. Pigheaded to the end, Carter refused the money.

Spring at the Booth Hall, Hereford

With money in the bank and his reputation assured, Tom Spring cut himself off from London to return with Elizabeth to live in Herefordshire. There would be no more training, no more pounding roads and commons, no more of that rare feeling of total fitness and invincibility. Spring was drawn to innkeeping, although the background and experience of most pugilists was not usually the best preparation for tavern keeping.

On 13 November 1824, Spring took out a £400 mortgage on the Booth Hall, a freehold establishment in the centre of Hereford. It was a prosperous city at the time, with 'many public buildings that do credit to the city'. It boasted four churches, including the extremely impressive cathedral, the new county hall, the county jail and house of correction built in 1797 and 'well adapted for the purpose for which it was intended' and the infirmary built in 1776 'containing every requisite to further the ease, interest and happiness of those whom Providence has visited in such a way as to constrain them, to seek shelter, assistant etc. within its walls'. There was a lunatic asylum built to house twenty people and a 60ft obelisk with a bust of Admiral Lord Nelson, in whose honour it was erected. The city also possessed a covered market and a 'great number of very superior shops, stocked with every article desirable for domestic comfort'.

The adult population of Hereford in the 1820s consisted of 4,096 males and 4,994 females. The London, Oxford, Gloucester, Worcester and North and West of England mails arrived daily. There was a strong professional class as well as the usual bakers, basket-makers, cobblers, booksellers, chair-makers, grocers, ironmongers, cutlers, curriers, maltsters, woollen drapers, rope-makers, hosiers, pistol-makers, coach builders, tallow chandlers, pawnbrokers, millwrights, tanners, saddlers, plasterers, and milliners. Unfortunately for Tom, there were over fifty pubs.

* * * * * * * *

The ancient Booth Hall was handsome, with substantial timberwork and floorboards that had been polished by the feet of thousands. It had several ghosts when Spring acquired it, the building dating from 1392. The hall above the bars and snugs below it was (and still is) magnificently medieval. Guild meetings were held there and goods crafted from local wool and leather were displayed and sold on the premises.

The Booth Hall (drawing by Peter Manders).

It is fitting that Spring, a man fond of cockfighting, should take over a pub with a history of the sport. In 1686, one Thomas Parry, a painter, recalled, 'He was at the Cockpitt att Peter Seaborne's house called the Booth Hall seeing cockfitting.' Spring, a national hero, was a welcome addition to the multiplicity of landlords who owned or managed the dives, sheebeens, beer houses, cider dens, inns and hotels of the town. The Booth Hall was just thirty-six yards from the main thoroughfare, from which it was approached by a dark passage. The entrance was about twenty yards from East Street. It had stabling for several horses.

As well as trading on his fame, Tom and Elizabeth offered clean bed and board, good food, wines and an atmosphere of conviviality. The Fownhope Carrier – the daily coach and four – stopped right outside Spring's front door. For a while at least, Tom and Elizabeth were glad to be home among their own kind. The Booth Hall was an intimate place and Spring's clientele were good but simple men, hearty and generous but weighed down by the trivial cares and woes of the mediocre. Their conversation, inevitably humdrum, soon began to pall.

Tom had got used to the spark provided by the Cruikshanks, Egan, Hazlitt, 'Gentleman' John Jackson, Cribb and the other old pros. He missed the fighting talk, the characters, the gentlemen, the conmen and the bookies. Tom had plenty of time to read the *Hereford Journal* and would stand at the front door in his apron and watch the sun glinting off the spire of St Peter's. Soon Tom Spring the ex-Champion of All England was part of the furniture. Friends stopped coming in to book meals and shake his hand. Perhaps he became less genial. He soon learned one cannot depend on friends for a living. Tom would eagerly look forward to the summer when prizefighters on their sparring tours would drop in to see their old friend. He listened to stories of London, the Fancy, the backers and the excitement.

Spring Meets 'Big' Brown

On 26 May 1825, Spring went to London to take his last bow at the Fives Club as English Bare-knuckle Champion. It had been a brief reign but he was ready to retire. He watched the boxing, sparred with Edward 'White-headed Bob' Baldwin, then rose to speak. In taking his leave Spring 'impressed upon his brother pugilists the importance of integrity. He said it was the key-stone to their success and without it they would find it impossible to preserve the respect or support of their patrons.' With Spring's retirement, bareknuckle boxing slipped into decline.

Vincent Dowling, on 2 October 1825, reflected on 'the end of support for boxing by the upper classes', who, he said, 'had ceased to grant either the light of their countenances, or the aid of their purses towards the encouragement of the Ring. When honour and fame cease to influence the combatants a system of low gambling is substituted.' With a few exceptions that is exactly what happened.

* * * * * * * *

Determined to remain in touch with boxing, Spring began looking around for a fighter to manage. He got wind of Thomas 'Big' Brown, 'a good-looking gentleman farmer sort of man' from nearby Bridgnorth who stood 6ft 1in in height, and 'was a solid fifteen stone of bone and muscle'. Spring crossed the border into Shropshire to take a closer look at the giant. The fact that Brown was thirty-one years of age and unknown except for minor feats of athleticism in local events did not ring alarm bells. Spring returned to Hereford favourably impressed. He said Brown was 'fit to fight anything that ever trod upon shoe-leather'.

Spring contacted Cribb with a view to launching Brown in London. Cribb took a look at Brown, and advised Spring to launch the big farmer quietly. The tactic aroused suspicion in some quarters. Shelton, now well past his prime, was chosen as Brown's first opponent. The match was made at £100-a-side. Even the pub chosen to sign the contacts, The Ship in Great Turnstile, Lincoln's Inn Fields, was not a sporting-crib. Surprisingly, Pierce Egan, a good friend, was not told about the fight. As a result of this, Tom Brown's battle ran a very good chance of not being reported at all and the boxer might have gone down to oblivion. In fact the fight was deliberately staged in the shadow of a big promotion featuring the Jem Ward-Tom Cannon fight which all the scribes, including Pierce Egan, were covering.

Brown's career was launched at Plumbe Park, six miles from Stony Stratford on 12 July 1825. The attendance was not numerous, nor was it desired by Brown's backers. Those of the Fancy who bothered to make the trip thought Shelton would win easily because 'of the old 'un's tried game and capabilities' and the fact that Brown was 'unknown to fame' except for his 'Shropshire and Worcestershire conquests over stalwart yokels'. Spring, however, 'had gone further out on a limb to report Brown's qualities to the swells'. Unmoved, the ringside turf accountants made Shelton a five to four favourite to win.

Shelton turned up in Stoney Stratford and was put up at the Cock. Brown arrived with Spring that afternoon and they stayed at the same hostelry. Hudson and Peter Crawley arrived from London to act as Shelton's seconds. Spectators were impressed by the huge, unmarked and handsome Brown, who looked fit and powerful while the scarred and haggard Shelton, who was conceding over three stones in weight, and about four inches in height, looked a wrinkled pygmy by comparison. The betting swung to Brown among 'the rurals' while the clever money remained with Shelton, the crafty old campaigner who boasted, 'A countryman lick me? Lick me, indeed! I'll be carried out of the ring first!'

Cribb and Spring arrived in stately fashion with the massive Brown. Hudson, as usual, chivvied Spring. Shelton flung his hat into the ring with Brown's, only to see it skim out the other side – a bad omen according to at least one spectator. As the two men stood at scratch the difference in size and condition was embarrassing. 'Brown looked like Hercules while Shelton's face was thin – his neck did not appear to possess that strength which characterises a fighting man – and his legs had gone to grass. But his heart was in the right place and in spite of the ravages of time he thought of nothing but winning.'

* * * * * * * *

Brown dropped the veteran with his first punch, a tame-looking swat. Spring claimed first blood, which was hotly refuted by Hudson. In the second, Brown again lumbered forward and toyed with the scraggy Shelton, stopping his weak blows and cuffing him in return. Shelton reached up like a boy trying to reach sweets on a high shelf and swung futilely. Brown simply waded in and dropped him again. The 'chawbacons' were in their element and rooted noisily for the countryman. In the third, Shelton tried everything he knew but he could not make any impression on the slow-moving mountain of flesh in front of him.

Brown clipped Shelton 'on the canister weighty enough to put his upper works in confusion'. The genial farmer then stopped to admire his handiwork instead of clubbing Shelton insensible, allowing the old pro to launch a vicious attack which 'tapped Brown's claret'. 'Well done Tom', cried Hudson, 'you have made the young one a member of the Vintner's Company. Go and draw his cork again.' It is fitting that Hudson should apply a vinous connotation, as he trained on 'Messrs Sherry, Blackstrap, Eau de Vie, Daffy, and Heavy Wet'. Brown closed on Shelton and wrapping his big arms around his grizzled opponent, pulled him to the floor.

In the next round Brown's ox-like strength made it impossible for Shelton to escape his awkward lunges and he soon had the older man gasping for breath. Brown pinned Shelton on the ropes then let him go without punishment. Such restraint had been so typical of Spring in his pomp, and it went down well with the crowd. In the next round, Brown was boxing quite prettily. Popping out a jab here, a hook there, and making the desperate Shelton miss. A report said: 'It was now clear that the countryman was nothing like a novice, and also that he had been under good tuition.'

In the sixth, Shelton seemed to have broken his right hand. Oliver, an old opponent and friend of both Shelton and Spring, and who was peering in from the crowd 'was full of anxiety for the fate of poor Shelton'. Oliver's anxiety may also have to do with the fact that he had backed the 'Ould One' to win at five to four. Brown ended the round by pummelling Shelton through the ropes. An overexcited Spring shouted at Hudson. 'A countryman do you call him? He stands a good chance to be Champion!'

In the eighth, the crafty old Shelton hit Brown with a terrific back-hander in the mouth which all but knocked the big farmer senseless. The blow had Shelton's fans yelling 'Master Brown does not like it!' The ninth was sensational, the usually mild-mannered Spring becoming embroiled in a shameful punch-up with the tempestuous Hudson. Brown had been boxing well, the ageing Shelton was looking bedraggled and beaten. A pointless battle seemed to be heading towards its conclusion when suddenly there was uproar. As Brown attacked, Shelton retreated until he had his back to the ropes.

Somehow the confused old fighter got his head entangled between the upper and middle strands. Hudson rushed to his aid. Spring, somewhat out of character (although he was a manager now with a vested interest), tore across the ring and pushed Hudson out of the way. Hudson pushed back and to everyone's amazement Spring flashed a right cross that caught Hudson in the face. Hudson roared his outrage and, bunching his fists, went for the former champion, catching him under the left eye. A scramble ensued: Spring and Josh were both down. As they engaged in their unseemly private tussle, Brown, keeping his head, caught Shelton and decked him. Oliver rushed to the veteran's aid and wanted to take on Brown. Young Gas leapt into the ring and put his mitts up too. Meanwhile old Cribb, like a big old wise tortoise, stood with his arms on the ropes waiting with the bottle and the orange ready for Brown to return to his corner.

The fight resumed with Brown well on top and Shelton doing his brave best not to concede too early. It went on until the fourteenth, with Shelton all but out on his feet. Brown sent him to the floor where his head made such violent contact and 'bounded like a ball'. The crowd begged for the fight to be stopped. Shamefully, Shelton was sent out for the fifteenth, although in no condition to defend himself. As he stood wavering, his foot to scratch, Brown measured the old man and hit him point-blank in the face with all his strength. Shelton hit the floor spark out. It was a savage ending.

As he lay wriggling on the cold damp grass, Shelton came to and foolishly tried to get up to fight on. Hudson stopped him. Afterwards Shelton said he was ashamed of himself to be beaten in such a short time. *Pugilistica* said of the contest, 'Shelton was not disgraced by the defeat. He showed himself a brave man and never flinched from his opponent.' He was 'overmatched by strength and youth but he found it out too late'.

As for Spring's potential champion, the verdict was that 'Brown fought better than expected. For a big man he was extremely active on his legs, stopped well, hit hard and did not want for courage or science.' Spring was so enthusiastic as a result of his man's victory over a spent force that he offered to back Brown against anyone for £500-a-side. Shelton, after various attempts at murder and suicide, killed himself by swallowing prussic acid in the Ship Hotel, Bishopsgate. He was forty-three years old.

****

In a letter in the Weekly Despatch, dated 1 March 1826, Brown challenged Jem Ward for £300- to £500-a-side. On Tuesday 28 March 1826 at the Tennis Court in London, in front of a thousand spectators – which included most of the boxing alumni of the time who had come to see Spring spar with his protégé – Brown repeated his taunts.

It was a boisterous occasion with fighters jumping into the ring between sparring exhibitions to badmouth potential opponents, fling out colourful challenges and have counter challenges flung back in their faces. It was all part of the entertainment at benefits. If the aged fighter or the young buck had a few shots of Dally beforehand, all the better. Phil Sampson, a roughneck in the style of the Gas, taunted Brown and offered to fight him for £100-a-side. 'If that didn't suit Mr Brown he would set to with him there and then for a bellyful.' This crack drew laughter and applause. Spring said it was not worth his man's while boxing for a mere £100.

Jem Ward was incensed by Brown's temerity in coming up from the sticks to throw out challenges to his betters. Ward declared himself ready to fight Brown for £300 and offered to put down a deposit immediately. At this, Tom Spring mounted the stage to a flattering reception. He said he was in business, and it would require at least a month's training under his tutelage to get Brown in shape and if his man won the battle the 'expenses would be greater than the gain'.

As for facing Sampson at this point in his career, it was out of the question. Spring reiterated that while Brown was under his management, he would not let him do wrong to his friends and backers. Sampson came forward angrily again to repeat his challenge. Sampson won the day as 'the oratory of the ex-Champion was lost in a roar of applause and disapprobation'. Amid the calls for Samson and Brown to fight and the beating of pewter pots on oak tables and the general unruly hubbub, Spring, who was more used to adulation, must have wondered if management was such a good idea after all.

Sampson milked the audience shamelessly. 'The thing spoke for itself,' he said, 'it was too plain; Spring did not like to let the cat out of the bag. He would not let Brown set to with him because it would tell tales. It would show Brown's talents, and Spring was determined to keep Brown all to himself.' Sampson said the fight should go on and let the Fancy 'form a judgement as to the laying out of their money'. They were yells of approval for Sampson. Someone shouted 'Spring is not such a flat as to show off Brown; it would betray want of judgement, and not the caution of a sporting man'.

Even although it was painful for Spring to have his professional judgement so openly and rudely questioned, he took the insults as stoically as he had taken punishment in the ring. Then Jem Ward rushed onto the stage flashing a fifty pound note, saying he would post it immediately towards making a match for £300 with any man in England. 'Go to it Jem,' the crowd bayed, 'you can beat any chawbacon, let him be as big as a Goliath'. Brown sat glumly listening to the abuse he and his manager were taking. Spring reclaimed the stage to impetuously state he would make a match that night at Cribb's for Brown to box Ward in August. In making this statement, Spring was reacting to the crowd instead of doing the best thing for his fighter. Pitting the limited Brown against the talented Ward would be a mismatch, not the act of a good and thoughtful manager.

When Spring took the stage again he was stripped with the gloves on for a sparring session with Brown, which had been advertised as

part of the evening's entertainment. Sampson, the unpleasant oppor-
tunist, also climbed into the ring stripped for action. Grabbing a pair
of mufflers he danced around the ring as if prepared to fight. Spring
refused to allow Brown to spar with the Brummagem Youth. Sampson
goaded Brown. There was uproar; the Fancy wanted action. Spring
threw his hands in the air and left the ring feeling bruised and fed
up.

Spring returned to the ring, probably on Cribb's advice, to try to
retrieve something of his reputation as a sportsman. He begged silence
to plead for his man. As Brown's manager he said it was his duty to
look out for him. He would not let Sampson use the occasion to
advertise himself. It wasn't that he or Brown were afraid of Sampson,
far from it; the day would come when he would let his man box
the Brummie, but it would be on his terms and for the right purse.
Certainly not now, especially 'on the account of the anger displayed
by Sampson'. At this, there was 'a mixture of applause and hisses' and
cries for Sampson.

Spring must have ruminated on the good old days when a past
champion was entitled to the respect of lesser mortals. The mob had
taken over and it was not an attractive prospect. 'Brown, gentlemen,'
Spring said, 'is here, ready to set to if you wish it.' There were cries of
'Bravo' from Spring's friends. Brown, meanwhile, threw off his over-
coat and, looking massive in breeches, he ascended the stage to a
mixed reception.

Although Spring did his best to make Brown look good, avoiding the big man's telegraphed punches and tying him up in clinches
with ease, he only succeeded in exposing the Bridgnorth man as a
no-hoper. 'He is of no use,' one commentator remarked. 'What an
imposter,' another said, 'the money would be a gift to Ward. Brown
would do nothing in the hands of Peter Crawley either.' One lone
voice spoke up for Brown. 'He can beat anyone on the list,' he argued.
'He is a rare punisher with the right hand, one of his blows would
floor an ox.' The general impression though, was that the set-to with
Spring did not give satisfaction, and the public verdict was that Brown
was nothing but a strong countryman – although certainly a hard
hitter with his right hand.

Panting a little, Brown thanked the audience and repeated his challenge
to fight 'any man in England for £500-a-side and would accommodate

Mr Sampson for £300-a-side'. Sampson, clearly resenting the backing Brown was getting from Spring, said had the same interest shown in his career he would not just want to box for the stake money but 'for the whole of the money taken at the doors in addition'. Spring left with Brown feeling pretty fed up.

At a sporting dinner later at Cribb's, when Spring was attempting to relaunch Brown, Ward and Sampson turned up like a couple of hyenas stalking a wounded beast. It was obvious they both wanted to fight Brown after seeing him spar with Spring. Ward was first to put down a stake, saying he would fight Brown for the £500-a-side. As he had not yet seen his backers he offered to seal the deal with £10. The Fancy were unimpressed. Ward said he could get his hands on a further £50, which he would hand over at Sampson's benefit on the following Monday. A gentleman backer offered to facilitate the fight between Ward and Brown. Spring was asked to concede choice of venue to Ward for £100, as he did not want to fight too far from London. It seemed as if Ward's resolve was weakening.

The aggressive Sampson was still running up and down like a rottweiler on the loose ready to sink his fangs into any available ankle. 'Giving way to a spirit of hostility altogether misplaced', he repeatedly offered to fight Brown within a month for £100. Brown declined. The enraged and frustrated Sampson then offered to fight Brown for £10 in a room that night. Spring refused. His dander up, Brown said he would fight Sampson next morning 'for love'. Brown's friends, who were sick to the teeth with Sampson, cheered loudly. But Sampson was after easy money and he stuck to his original offer to fight Brown for £100. This not being accepted, he retired, no doubt feeling a little like a man who had misplaced a winning lottery ticket. Spring returned to Hereford, probably relieved to be back behind the bar of the Booth Hall.

* * * * * * * *

A few days later a bedraggled clutch of strangers wandered into the Booth Hall. They were said to be Irish navvies, tough, garrulous men, out to avenge Langan's loss to Spring. They supped, ate, belched and banged the wooden table. Tom watched them carefully. When he presented his bill, what happened next is the stuff of legends. A local newspaper of 1825 reported the following:

> Six fellows who had been selling silk handkerchief in Hereford took a fancy to the Booth Hall Tavern, drew largely on the land-lord's store, but when Spring pressed his just demand he was met with insolence and abuse. The constable was sent for, but refused to attend. Spring ushered his pregnant wife upstairs, donned his fighting gear and presented himself at the bar in his fighting pose. At once he was attacked by the six. Perhaps in his best days he never displayed such science, coolness, and courage as he displayed on this occasion. Right and left his every blow told on the sconces of his cowardly assailants and on one occasion they were all down on the floor together. In less than 20 minutes they were completely brought to a standstill and the Champion acknowledged victor. They were all stout fellows at least 13 stones each.

The temptation for Spring to get back into training and take on Ward and Sampson the same night with one hand tied behind his back must have been strong. On 13 December 1825 Elizabeth Spring presented Tom with an early Christmas present, a boy named Thomas William.

Life went on, with Elizabeth running the pub while Tom gallivan-ted around the country watching fights, training Brown, or acting as second, bottle holder, referee or timekeeper. He was as pleased as a dog with two tails when the great Pierce Egan booked himself into the Booth Hall one night. Egan was stakeholder for the fight between Young Gas Bissell and Robinson to be staged somewhere in Herefordshire. A report stated that:

> Several of the London ring have already gone down there and the muster of the metropolitan fancy will be inconsiderable. Tom Spring's Booth Hall, Hereford, is the headquarters, and the spirit of the Ring there seems to be kept up in the true old English style. By intelligence received yesterday, it appears that there is reason to fear that the mag-istrate's of the county of Hereford will interfere to prevent the sport taking place in their bailiwick. If so, a move must take place, and, in all probability, Radnorshire or Monmouthshire will be chosen.

As the commentator had feared, the home county of the recent champion had no time for bare-knuckle pugilism. The fight was staged on 23 January 1827 at a wintry Monmouth Gap. On the eve of the fight, Egan sat with his cronies in front of a blazing log fire at the Booth Hall, ate a good meal, drank Tom's wine and afterwards presided over a convivial meeting. Elizabeth was pregnant again. Spring left her and the toddler to travel to London where the Fancy had arranged a benefit for the past champion at the Fives Court. Spring was ecstatically received and he sparred several lively rounds with 'White-headed Bob'. Baby John was born on 17 September 1827.

On Christmas Eve, 1827, Tom paid his brother Joseph, a butcher in Fownhope, 'the sum of five shillings of lawful money' and the 'rent of one pepper corn' to lease Slough Orchard for one year, a piece measuring one acre, two roods and three perches.

On Christmas Day, flush from the sale of the Booth Hall in Hereford, Tom bought the land outright for £80. On his death the property passed to Tom's son, Thomas William Winter, who sold it to Thomas Price, a lawyer from Mordiford, for £71. Spring's estranged wife Elizabeth surfaced to countersign the sale particulars and agrees to forgo any claims on the property on payment of the sum of £10.

34

Tom Takes The Castle

After less than two years in his native county, Tom Spring, restless and still unfulfilled, uprooted his wife and their two children and once more headed south to take over the famous boxing crib, the Castle Tavern, Holborn. It was to be their last move. This time there would be no going back.

In spite of the decline in bare-knuckle fighting, the Castle was still the spiritual home of the boxing and the fans who gathered there (and who were still known as the Fancy). Egan's rhyme exemplified the spirit of these hardy supporters of prizefighting:

You lads of the Fancy, who wish to impart
The tokens of friendship and soundless of heart,
To Belcher's repair, at the Castle so strong,
Where he'll serve you all well, and you'll hear a good song.
The company's cheerful, the Sporting's the go-
Though milling's the theme, you'll not meet a foe;
But each in good humour, enjoying his pipe,
With tales of the fancy – and knowledge of life!
Then let us be merry,
While drinking our sherry,
For friendship and harmony can't last too long –
Be still our endeavour
That nothing shall sever
The Lads of the Fancy at the Castle so strong!

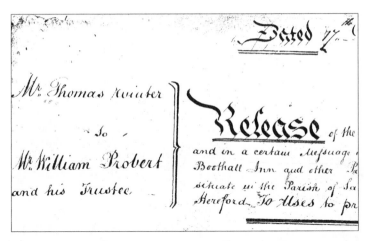

Release from Booth Hall contract.

The Castle Tavern was opened as a Sporting House in about 1810 by Bob Gregson, who called it 'Bob's Chop House'. Gregson was an imposing figure, weighing 15 stones 6 pounds and standing at 6ft 1½ins. It was said of him that 'In the course of a long day's walk in the Metropolis, or during the continuance of a week in London, a finer or better proportioned athletic man could not be met with.' Gregson possessed a 'a constitution truly robust, with a vivacious eye calculated to dazzle every spectator with its importance'. He was 'a good-natured fellow, extremely liberal in his conduct', with 'good intellectual faculties' and 'nothing supercilious to be found in his manner'. He was 'always fashionably dressed, and in the common phrase of the day, had a good deal to say for himself'.

Under this paragon's management, the Castle Tavern quickly became the mecca for fighters, their trainers and managers. Gregson introduced a Mine Host's parlour: this was a snuggery behind the bar – a sanctum sanctorum to the Fancy – where commoners never attempted to intrude upon the company where champagne of the best quality was tossed off like water; Madeira, claret, hock, and other choice wines were handed about with the utmost sang-froid; where 'persons of some consequence' could share in 'the sporting mirth, harmony and good fellowship'.

Tom's Parlour.

> His house is known to all the milling train,
> He gives them liquor, and relieves their pain.

Gregson fancied himself as a bit of a poet, but his style was dismissed by Egan, who said, 'Gregson does not possess the terseness and originality of Dryden or the musical cadence and correctness of Pope.' Gregson ended up in prison for the non-payment of debts. Hearing of the once jovial host's miserable decline, Lord Byron, who admired Gregson as a fighter and a man, paid up and had him released.

Tom Belcher, 'one the most accomplished boxer and sparrers of the day', succeeded Gregson. Belcher who 'nobly contended for victory in thirteen battles', had 'all the rooms retouched by the painter; elegance and cleanliness, backed by civility became the order of the day. A prime stock of liquors and wines were laid in to command the attention of the public.' Belcher removed the rougher elements and the Castle prospered once again. Portraits of many of the leading pugilists were hung on the walls. Among them were likenesses of Cribb, Jem Belcher, Molyneaux, Gregson, Jackson, Gully, Randall, Turner, Painter, Tom Owen and Scroggins, Deaf Burke and Dutch Sam. Every inch of the nicotine-stained walls was covered with a variety of other subjects, including Trusty – the famous rat catcher given to Tom Belcher by the sporting Lord Camelford. Trusty was to became 'the champion of the canine race, in fifty battles'.

Chaunting was as popular as karaoke is now. Arthur Mullard looka-likes with thick necks, flat noses and missing teeth clutched song sheets and bellowed discordantly through rusty teeth, their beer mugs aloft. A few broken old fighters who were allowed to perch on a long table called 'the ring', doffed their caps to gentlemen as they arrived. The lucky ones pocketed the odd sixpence. During Tom Belcher's sojourn at the Castle, the hard-drinking Daffy Club was instigated by James Soares, 'a great lover of harmony, yet no person fonder of making mischief'. Members of the Daffy Club were encouraged to be 'always in spirits'. Out-and-out drunkenness was not tolerated, however, as members amused the gathering with their sparkling wit and playful satire. *Bell's Life* tells of 'two itinerant gin-sellers' who drank jars of gin then smashed the empties over each others heads and 'concluded by crying most woefully over the fragments of their bottles and the bumps on their pericraniums'.

Belcher remained in charge for fourteen years before retiring to a cottage on Finchley Common, living at his ease like a man of fortune with his dog and his gun. Egan said, 'Tom skimmed the cream off the Fancy' and Belcher agreed. 'My friends may flatter me about my fine fighting,' he boasted, 'but blow my dickey, of all the hits I ever made in my life, none of them were to be compared with the hit I made at the Castle.'

Belcher had wrung the Castle Tavern dry by the time Spring assumed the threadbare mantle of custodian of what had once been the high altar to pugilism. Egan said that after Belcher 'the show had gone by'. The Castle Tavern was run down and faded. But Tom Spring, Egan observed 'who had not only been losing his time amongst his countrymen at the Booth Hall but, what was worse, his hard-earned money, was determined to have another shy at London and no man from his general conduct and deportment was considered so eligible in every point of view to succeed Tom Belcher.'

****

Following the astute Belcher was never going to be a bed of roses for the modest Spring. A few of the Fancy returned to take a look at the recently retired champion. The first thing they noticed upon entering the bar was a long table covered with a white cloth and glistening with Tom's silver trophies. The huge Hereford and Manchester cups, 'snuff-boxes, silver-topped canes, pencil cases, and other prizes' Tom had been awarded by backers and friends.

'While the Castle is correctly termed a fighting house', Egan wrote, 'fighting is expressly forbidden in it by the landlord Tom Spring. "Words", Spring lectured, "cost nothing; indeed they are little more than wind; and you may make use of as many as you like to support your argument; but blows are not only painful and sometimes dangerous, but very often prove expensive: therefore, you may talk about fighting as much as you please to promote milling, but not a blow shall pass in my presence. However, if you are determined to have a mill, and inclined to 'show off' in it, I advise you to get a ring made a few miles from Town, where you will have plenty of scope for your exertions, and fair play into the bargain."'

Under Spring's management, ordinary punters replaced the glittering peacocks who once frequented the Castle. Old fighters were particularly welcome and as some of them were so scruffy, smelly, gap-toothed and incoherent they put off the smarter clients. The novelty of Spring's much-publicised encounters with Langan attracted 'those persons who have never visited such houses, [and] in general feel anxious to take a peep at the resort of the Fancy'. Visitors might still find themselves sitting next to a lord but more likely it would be 'poor Jack Scroggins, a gentlemanly sort of man who generally pays a visit every night to his old friend Tom Spring who is a friend in reality to poor Jack. When the grog is not too much abroad Scroggins is full of humour and he contrives to keep the visitors alive by swopping his milling anecdotes for a tumbler of blue ruin.' Another old pro in straightened circumstances who made the Castle fireside his own was Jack Firby – 'Young Ruffian' who once fought the great Jem Belcher, but now was 'so reduced in appearance as to be little better than a mere walking skeleton, almost sans eyes, sans taste, sans blunt, and sans everything, depending on visitors not unmindful of his former efforts in the prize ring to contribute their mites to alleviate his distressed state.'

Tom Owen, a regular and the 'Sage of the East', liked to chaunt, raising his glass to old times and old faces from the past. Daniel Mendoza, the once great scientific Jewish fighter was occasionally seen at the Castle during Spring's tenure. Another regular was Jack 'Frosty-faced' Fogo, a walking encyclopaedia of prizefighting lore, who after Gregson's demise assumed the uncontested title as poet-laureate of the prize ring and even published a small volume of verse. A few distinguished visitors, Ministers of Parliament and the like, still made it to the Castle to sit incognito and quietly enjoy the craic.

'The company,' Egan said, could be viewed as 'rather promiscuous; therefore anything like a set of routine faces are not to be met with every evening as fixtures to the apartment; and it is this particular change of visitors that gives fresh life to the scene. The order at all times is excellent; and which good conduct renders the Castle Tavern a desirable place to pass away a dull or leisure hour, which otherwise might hang very heavily on a person's hands.' Egan went on to add, surprisingly, that as landlord Spring was 'more of a Sinner than a Saint', and, while the Castle Tavern was 'not exactly the 'Paradise' of the Fancy, it wasn't "Hell" either'. Egan concluded that Spring was 'nothing but a good man'. Under Tom's stewardship, Friday night was designated free and easy night at the Castle, when the grog flowed freely and customers were apt to stand up and sing. The appearance of the landlord was always very much in favour. Spring had a manly dignity about his person that was prepossessing. His behaviour was at all times civil and he was attentive to his customers. As Egan said, 'Tom contributes himself frequently towards the harmony of the evening, and is also considered a very fair chanter, and is a favourite with several of the professionals connected with the theatre; who at times were not backward in giving him a turn.'

Vincent Dowling, editor of *Bell's Life* in London – 'tall and gentlemanly looking with spectacles on' – was a great admirer of Spring and was often seen there drinking his claret and quite relaxed in such mixed company. Spring admired 'Dowling's independence, and his fair and manly support towards the men of the ring', adding, 'I wish I could say the as much for many other persons connected with the press!' Egan also spent many evenings at the Castle and 'derived considerable pleasure and information from the various classes of society with whom he mixed. 'You may meet poets on the look-out for a hero,' Egan said, 'artists for subjects; and boxers for customers. Young surgeons you may likewise meet who will cut you up in an argument, if they cannot in any other way.'

Egan's nights at the Castle Tavern with Spring at the helm caused him not 'the slightest regret' – on the contrary, they got him out of his garret where he might have been 'poking the ashes of his scanty grate and finding fault with the follies of society'. Instead he joined in the warm company of 'some of the roughest sons of Nature' and occasionally he had to sympathise with some broken soul as he watched a tear of sorrow stealing down a sandpapered cheek. Egan 'felt the strong grasp of friendship' with tough, beetle-browed individuals who were 'forbidding on the outside but with a heart melting within'. He would 'again and again witness charity bestowed, where the bestower of the mite had scarcely blunt enough left in their pockets to purchase a breakfast the next morning.' 'Such,' he concluded, 'are some of the advantages of mixing with society.' No fair-minded person, Egan asserted, could say 'I was sorry that I was last night at Tom Spring's'.

It was while at the Castle that Spring met Dan Donnelly for the last time. The Duke of Clarence was visiting at the time. Tom, concerned the unpredictable Irish heavyweight might commit a faux pas in front of the nobleman, gave Dan a quick lesson in etiquette. 'Listen Dan,' he said, 'when you address the Duke you must begin by saying Your Grace'. When an opportunity arose, Dan turned to the Duke and with head bowed said, 'For what I am about to receive, O Lord, please make me truly thankful. Amen.' The Duke smiled and slipped Donnelly a guinea. When Dan went to the bar to order a drink, Spring rounded on him for so blatantly begging in his pub. Dan shuffled uncomfortably. 'Sorry Tom, but you told me to say me grace.'

Not long after, the charming but undisciplined Donnelly, struggling with the effects of alcoholism and the disease he contracted 'in the promiscuousness of his amours' died in Dublin. *The Sporting*

Magazine said the route to the graveyard 'was covered with a moving mass of rags and wretchedness'. In a city with fifty breweries, twenty-five distilleries, two thousand pubs, three hundred taverns, and twelve hundred brandy shops, Sir Dan was assured of an appropriate send-off.

35

'Big' Brown Thrashed by Sampson

Tom Spring continued his interest in the career of 'Big' Brown. The gentleman farmer had finally given in to Phil Sampson's outrageous insults and accepted a match with the Brummagem Youth. The absence of wealthy backers meant the fighters had to do most of their own promoting. With Sampson in full cry tickets quickly disappeared. The press latched on to the fight. One paper asserted that 'The London Fancy must blush at the Brums taking the lead in so important a match'.

Brown was meeting a real pugilist, not a runner or a high jumper. Sampson, for all his vulgar verbosity, could fight like a tiger. They met on Tuesday 8 April 1828 in a ring built in front of the grandstand at Wolverhampton Racecourse. Spring recruited Richmond to help him in Brown's corner. Dick Curtis acted with Harry Holt for Sampson. Due to magisterial intervention the fight was switched to Bishop's Wood in Shropshire, 'a lofty eminence commanding an extensive and delightful prospect'. As a venue it was inadequate for a contest that proved to be the biggest draw since Spring fought Langan in Worcester. Upwards of 25,000 fans attended with at least 15,000 unable to see the twenty-four foot ring. As befitted an ex-champion, Tom Spring arrived in some style and he and Brown cut a dash in Brown's landau, which was drawn by four fine horses and decorated on the panels with the sign of Brown's inn at Bridgnorth – a hand holding a bottle. Both fighters stayed at the Bradford Arms. Brown, in his country gentleman's costume of blue coat, white cord breeches, and top boots, arrived leaning on Spring's arm and received a loud welcome. Sampson appeared wearing his trademark pantomime grimace. When Brown, offered his hand by way of greeting, Sampson turned away with an angry scowl.

The fight got under way, with the fifteen-stone Brown a surprising favourite at two to one. The Bridgnorth novice tottered forward, swung and missed. Sampson settled into a rhythm and skilfully outboxed and outfought the bigger man, catching him with hard straight punches.

* * * * * * * *

Spring was his usual quiet self in Brown's corner (at a time when a little aggressive vocal encouragement might have galvanised the amiable Brown). In the second round Brown stood in the middle of the ring looking remarkably like a gatepost; Richmond yelled at him, 'Don't stand there to be punished'. In the third, Spring made the mistake of pulling Brown to his corner when the big farmer was about to unload. The more professional Sampson was having it all his own way.

In the fifth Sampson planted a heavy blow on Brown's left eye and sneered, 'You Champion of England? Well there's a small taste for your Championship.' Covered in claret and thoroughly bemused, Brown crashed into a ring post. He managed to grab Sampson a few times but by the ninth, 'the left ogle of Brown was almost in darkness, and one of his listeners, and his nasal organ, was much swelled and out of shape'. By the eleventh the ring collapsed with mayhem ensuing. Both men were still striving to hit each other rather than the dozens of fans who had entered the ring though the broken posts and were pushing and shoving. Such boxing as was possible was all coming from Sampson and Brown began to look as if one of his prize Hereford bulls had trodden on his face.

In the seventeenth, as Spring struggled to move the battered Brown up to scratch, he noticed Sampson had already crossed the line. Spring put himself between his man and the advancing Sampson who considered Spring to be in the wrong and gave the esteemed former champion a sharp blow to the face. Sampson then rushed past the affronted ex-champion 'and suddenly floored the Bridgnorth hero like a shot'. Spring could have clobbered the insolent Brummie but instead he drew 'the admiration of the spectators, and showed his desire that the battle should be fought out fairly'.

Sampson's illegal blow finished Brown. Now the fight was entirely Sampson's as he belaboured the farmer's breadbasket with vicious body shots and didn't leave his head unattended either. Brown was dragged backed to his corner, water was dashed in his torn face, then hapless, bleeding, and soundless he was made to lap up further punishment.

The Shropshire man was barely able to move by the forty-second and stood wobbling, an easy target until the fight was stopped. Afterwards it was discovered that Brown's shoulder had been dislocated from as early as the fourth. After a rest, and the use of several towels to mop up his blood, the big farmer was able to stagger to his carriage, assisted by Spring and Richmond. The beating the big man received reflected no glory on Spring, who like many a Brown admirer had probably lost money on the result.

Sampson exulted in his victory and the local pubs did a brisk trade as his garrulous fans drank his health. As for Brown, the demise of the big Shropshire farmer had the whole county, as well as the adjoining Herefordshire, in mourning as they expected much more of him.

Under the patronage of Mr Beardsworth, Sampson rode in a splendid carriage drawn by eight horses. The entourage paraded through the streets of the victor's native Birmingham with the relatively unmarked Sampson smiling broadly and waving like an emperor to his cheering subjects. When they reached the inn owned by former fighter Arthur Matthewson, 'every room in Arthur's crib was crowded to excess, and the anxiety of the persons in the street to gain admittance, to get a peep at the conqueror of 'Big Brown' defied description'.

Brown's defeat 'had the effect of an occultation of a star of the first magnitude'. Determined to put the managerial error behind him, Spring began the search for a new opponent. If Brown was to be taken as a serious contender he had to start winning.

Sampson wanted more of Brown and he began a fierce tirade against both Brown and his manager to try to goad them into a lucrative rematch. The Brummie's language, never temperate, became even for him inflamed as one scurrilous diatribe followed another. Spring used his friendship with Vincent George Dowling, editor of *Bell's Life*, to respond with a flurry of letters repeating that Brown's loss to Sampson was entirely down to the fact the amiable farmer dislocated a shoulder in the fourth round making it quite impossible for him to 'ward off Sampson's nobbers'.

Spring was also indignant at the disrespectful way Sampson attacked him in the seventeenth. He criticised the 'ruffianism' of Sampson's friends and threatened to make a comeback to put the upstart Brummie in his place, offering Sampson £200-a-side, giving his motivation as being that 'it is not my principle to submit to a blow without wishing, like a man, to return it'. In a reply that was 'full of boasting, bombast and scurrility', Sampson questioned Spring's courage and impugned the Herefordian's spotless reputation by suggesting Spring was afraid to fight Jem Ward. Spring, he said, had made his name beating stale old men like Oliver and Painter. Spring leapt into print again. Sampson came back and both men stuffed the columns of the *Despatch*, Pierce Egan's short-lived weekly, *Life in London*, and *Bell's Life*. When Sampson boasted in all company how he would serve the 'old woman', that did it. That evening, with his hackles still upright, Spring dipped his quill in vitriol and replied:

Dear Sir,

Sampson accuses me of acting wrong in the ring, but he forgets to say in what respect. I defy him or any other person to say I did wrong. He also says I wanted to bring it to a wrangle. If that had been my object, I had a very good chance when he struck – not once nor twice, but thrice; had I returned the blows, it must have put a stop to the fight. I think Mr. Editor, I have answered quite enough of Mr. Sampson's scurrilous language; but when he speaks of chastising me I pity his weakness, and would have him take care that chastisement does not fall upon himself; for the first time I meet him, I will put the toe of my boot against his seat – not of honour Mr. Editor, he has none about him – but where his sense of feelings may be readily reached.

I hope Mr. Editor, you will pardon me for taking up so much room in your valuable paper, but unless Mr. Sampson chooses to come forward with his money I shall not condescend to take the least notice of anything he may say after this.

I am, Sir, your obliged,
THOMAS WINTER SPRING.
April 24th, 1828.

Pugilistica reported, 'All this gasconading, so foreign to Spring's char-acter, came to a most lame and impotent conclusion. Sampson could not get backed and the affair fell through.'

36

Spring Elected Chairman of the Fair Play Club

Even lifelong supporters were becoming sickened and disillusioned by the depths into which prizefighting had sunk. As early as 1828, just a year after Tom Spring retired, in a speech he delivered at the Tennis Court on Friday 20 May, Vincent Dowling referred to 'misconduct of some members of the Prize Ring... and those, who by temptation, had led them to abandon every principle of honesty, and render pugilism rather a source of fraudulent speculation than of fair and manly competition'. Clearly something had to be done to clean up the sport. After the decline of the influential Pugilist Club, an organisation 'originally composed of noblemen and gentlemen', and the retirement of Gentleman John Jackson, it was felt necessary to form a new organisation to represent the boxers.

While he awaited developments, Spring was engaged in seconding Alec Reid, the 'Chelsea Snob' in his return fight with Bishop 'Smuggler' Sharpe at St Albans on 15 July 1828. Spring was assisted by the garrulous Ned 'Lively Kid' Stockman. Sharpe had Josh Hudson and Dick Curtis offering the knee and peeling the oranges. The Snob helped himself to odds of six to four, putting down his last four sovereigns. Bishop looked the stronger contender, but rumour had it he was observed at a canvas tavern downing the 'real thing in copious quantities'.

Reid, whose father was a Chelsea Pensioner, started promisingly, cagily avoiding Sharpe's 'dangerous left-hand lunge by which he had before been robbed of victory when it was within his grasp'. After the initial skirmish, both men bled. In the second, Bishop attacked purposefully and had the Snob tasting dirt. Reid fought purposefully in the third, catching Bishop with a sharp shot in the mouth that floored him. Spring was further encouraged in the seventh when his man peppered Bishop with smart combinations, flooring him again. Shouts of 'It's all your own, Reid' sprang from the crowd.

In the nineteenth, as 'Bishop rushed in open-handed, in wild style. Alec drew back, poising himself on his hind leg. Sharpe followed, and as usual, napped it left and right, and was floored.' Sharpe landed plenty on the Snob's face and his eye and mouth were very swollen.

The gutsy Bishop was down in almost every round and it was no surprise when in the ninety-first he was knocked out. Reid was so exhausted it was several minutes before Spring could take him from the ring. As he left, Sharpe was still lying on the ground unconscious.

Reid changed his name to Jack O'Brien for his last fight near Chipping Camden against Jack Perkins the 'Oxford Pet' and recruited Young Dutch Sam and Dick Curtis as his seconds. As Snob was on bail 'for being present at a mill near London', Spring, a respectable pillar of the pugilistic scene, could hardly be seen to aid a felon. Instead, armed with a bullwhip, he 'was resolutely keeping order with John Gully, Phil Sampson, Tom Gaynor and several of the old school'. Hundreds of Oxford University undergraduates, who had given the slip to their 'bulldogs' and 'proctors' attended the demonstration of craniology and the practical essay on bumps which Messrs Reid and Perkins had prepared for their edification. Reid eventually won what was reported as 'one of the best and fairest mills on record'.

* * * * * * * *

At a public meeting held at the Castle Tavern on 25 September 1828, the Fair Play Club was formed. Tom Spring was unanimously elected its first treasurer. Egan was present to record the events of the evening, which were included in the final volume of *Boxiana*. A list of rules were drawn up to include the supervision of fights, both 'to preserve peace and order in the outer ring' and 'to ensure fair play to the combatants'. Spring, as agent and treasurer to the club, was 'empowered to employ pugilists at the fights, at the rate of half-a-guinea per man, according to the distance from London, assuming the battle money exceeded

£25' although 'Mr. Spring shall at no time employ any part of the funds without the authority of the Committee'.

The pugilists under Spring's control would use 'no more force than was necessary' to make sure no unauthorised person got within six yards of the ring during a fight. Meetings were to be held, 'in rotation, at the houses of those licensed victuallers who are pugilists and subscribers to this club'. As well as Spring's Castle Tavern, other inns participating were Alex Reid's Lowndes Arms, Jem Burn's Rising Sun and Alex Keene's Three Tuns. However, in spite of the efforts of the committee, the FPC never achieved the authority it needed to deal with the sport's problems in the late 1820s.

37

Farces and Dodgy Dealings

Inevitably as boxing slowly sunk below the parapet of quasi respectability, Spring, as an obsessive fan and facilitator, was sucked into the morass. As a prominent member of the Fair Play Committee he must accept some responsibility for a very doubtful match the FPC sanctioned in 1828. Jack Carter, a former opponent of Spring's, but now a weather-beaten thirty-eight-year-old, was languishing in prison for allegedly stealing £5 from a passenger on the London to Oxford coach. When he came out of gaol broke and unemployed, a blind eye was turned to his circumstances, Carter being matched with the tough up-and-coming Jem Ward. On stripping, Ward was in fine condition 'while Carter partook a little too much of civic importance'.

Spring was recruited as timekeeper, assisted by Peter 'Young Rumpsteak' Crawley. It was a public execution. Ward battered the overweight and out-of-condition Carter, who had not fought since his battle with Spring in 1819. He cut Carter's lip, threw him heavily on the grass, drew blood, blackened his eyes and generally duffed up the old has-been. The stupidly game Carter refused to lie down, even though he had earned his pieces of silver several times over. By the end of the eighth round, Carter was quoted as thirty to one to win. Finally in the seventeenth, with Carter hanging on by a thread and refusing to exit the ring, Spring and Crawley pleaded with him to retire. Carter shook his old head like a tormented bull and was floored again. Even the referee couldn't not persuade him it was useless to carry on: 'There's nought the matter with me,' Carter blurted through torn lips. At last Spring convinced the old warrior to give in – 'a decision that was met with general approval'.

★ ★ ★ ★ ★ ★ ★ ★

In the autumn of 1828, Spring had the misfortune to be asked to second the veteran Jack Martin, a publican, in his comeback fight. Martin's opponent was the twenty-one-year-old starlet, Samuel Evans, better known as 'Young Dutch Sam' whom the older man had taunted. Martin had once been good, with wins over Scroggins, Hudson, Sampson and Turner, but he was now a ragged thirty-three-year-old who had neither fought nor trained for several years. The pairing made the Fancy prick up their ears, and some who had not been to a fight for a long time eagerly put 4 November 1828, Knowle Hill, Berkshire, in their diaries.

Martin, living proof there was no fool like an old fool, told all his friends to back him. He was a certainty he said, omitting to mention a recent and severe illness from which he had not recovered. His friends, many of them wealthy gentlemen, piled on the cash. Both men lied about their weight, Sam claiming to be lighter than he was, the emaciated Martin claiming he was heavier than he looked.

On the morning of the fight the sun shone and the over the roads hung a dusty cloud as vehicles, horses and walkers all headed towards Virginia Water. Cribb was there to claim a good vantage point and he was surrounded by old pugs dying to see Martin chastise the cocky youngster. By noon there were over 10,000 quietly assembled.

Sam appeared looking pale and slightly puzzled at the size of the crowd. He was assisted by Dick Curtis and Jem Ward. Martin made his entrance with a confident smile, accompanied by Spring and Crawley. He was received with loud cheers. When Young Sam peeled, his body was lithe and honed, without a blemish. Martin looked like a corpse by comparison with leech bites on his pale skin, 'his breasts showing marks of recent blisters' and his ribs sticking out. A breathless silence prevailed as they men stood to the mark and the seconds retired to their corners.

Spring having lost the toss, the elderly Martin faced the blazing midday sun. He pawed and squinted only to be flattened by the cobra-like speed, well-oiled reflexes and sharp hitting of the youngster. When Martin got up he was cut, bemused and bleeding with one eye closed.

The Fancy were so incredulous they didn't even bother to try to hedge their bets. It was all over, they could see that. After Spring had patched him up, Martin decided to attack, but the young man was so slippery and his counters were quick and wounding. Sam stood like a well fed tomcat over a terrified mouse. Martin shuffled around with one eye horribly bulging with trapped blood, trying to think of something new. But every pathetic move he tried was squashed by youth and speed, savagery and confidence. Sam smiled at the old man's desperation.

Before the fifth round began, Spring called for a lancet to let the blood from Martin's right eye. There was none. Spring tried a blunt penknife without success. Martin rushed in blindly only to be thrown with force. In the sixth Sam measured the veteran and cracked him a fantastic shot to the face which dropped the innkeeper in a heap of old blue-veined flesh at his feet.

By the seventh 'it was Bushey Park to a Lark's sod'. Martin was down and ill used. Spring picked him up like a run over dog. Instead of accepting his man was totally and utterly outclassed and in mortal danger if the young man was allowed to work him over again, Spring refused to accept Martin's surrender and shamefully tried to persuade him to get up for a few more rounds. Martin refused and Spring reluctantly gave in for him. Martin staggered to his corner, sat on Spring's knee and vomited. The verdict among the hardnosed gentry was that Martin had fallen to 'below mediocrity'. They had given of their time and money when they could have been in their country seats watching their gardeners tend their geraniums.

Martin said he was surprised by Sam's aggression. Sam confirmed it was the brilliant Dick Curtis, the engaging 'Pet of the Fancy' who advised him to depart from his usual cautious style and tackle Martin head on to see what he was made of. After the fight Martin refused to shake Sam's hand. He complied when Sam gave him a tenner.

While the victor 'dressed on the ground and appeared as if nothing had happened', Martin trudged off to the Castle Tavern to drown his sorrows with Tom Spring's grog. He then travelled to Godalming were he 'was much depressed and refused to see anyone who called'. Flash Sam, meanwhile, pristine and unmarked, was cheered to the beams at Cribb's pub in Panton Street, where he collected his £100 stake.

* * * * * * * *

Spring seconded the ugly Jack Perkins, the 'Oxford Pet' in his fight with the unbeaten 'King' Dick Curtis, 'Pet of the Fancy'. Curtis, who was universally admired for his 'skill, neatness, finish, straight and swift hitting' was conceding over a stone in weight and was suffering from gout. He agreed to fight Perkins after some innocent chaffing 'produced an ill feeling' between the two men. Such was Curtis's reputation he was clear favourite to win. He was a scientific ball of speed and explosive hitting, but he was five years older at twenty-five and was a bit of a party animal who never went home 'until the gas was turned off'. Could Curtis prevail against a bigger man who also had something of a reputation? With his record on the line, Curtis trained enthusiastically. Those in the know 'considered it next to treason to harbour a thought of his defeat'.

The location was in the Parish Meadow at Hurley Bottom, Berks, thirty-four miles from London and too close to the Thames for comfort. It was described as being 'in summer no doubt a delightful spot but in the winter season far from eligible'. Several of the vehicles transporting the snobs got stuck fast. Curtis arrived resplendent in his bright orange favours accompanied by the ever-busy Josh Hudson and 'Young Dutch' Sam. Perkins looked just as smart in his crimson colours with Tom Spring and Harry Holt.

Upon stripping Perkins had a rustic hardness about him. His hair was patchy from ringworm as a child and he looked angular and square. He was the taller of the two by a couple of inches and was well muscled with a face that was criss-crossed with scars – 'convincing proof he had engaged in battles of no trifling character'. Curtis looked delicate by comparison but showed superior blood with his fair skin and upright build. His body showed 'that beautiful symmetry of for which he was so distinguished, and which would have formed the perfect model for the sculptor'. The bookies made him favourite at six to four but a few seasoned old-timers sitting close to the action whispered among themselves that Curtis was overmatched.

In front of a crowd of around 5,000 the two men came to scratch. The big-punching Perkins planted a rum one between Curtis's chaffer and sneezer, causing the excited Spring to holler 'First blood! We shall win it.' But the round ended with Perkins on his back on the grass. He was down again in the next but by dint of his own clumsiness rather than the Pet's firepower. In the next, the awkward Perkins fell out of the ring in his eagerness. Curtis was making him miss by quickly switching his feet and subtle movements of his head. It was a joy to watch. Perkins was made to miss again in the next and dropped by a punch. Curtis was cruising, but by the fifth he was showing signs of damage. In the seventh Hudson was compelled to give him brandy and water; he was catching the Oxonian but his punches lacked zip and were having little effect on Perkins' iron carcass.

Then the roof fell in on Curtis. The unmarked Perkins finally caught up with the weaving, retreating, dancing master in the eighth and flattened him to the delight of the gentlemen in the crowd who were 'almost out of their senses with joy'. In the ninth Curtis, his dander finally up, went on the attack. As Spring had wisely counselled, Perkins went down to end the round. Curtis went to his corner covered in blood and in some distress.

The eleventh round proved to be the last. Curtis went all out but walked into a hard nut who stood flatfooted firing hand grenades. Curtis crumpled under Perkin's raw power and went down in a heap. Hudson tried all he knew but Curtis was out cold. Perkins jumped out of the ring and ran around yelling. Spring had to haul him back for the official verdict. Curtis was taken to Maidenhead in bad shape after a fight that had lasted barely twenty-three minutes.

Perkins dressed and 'little the worse for his engagement, beyond a cut over his left eye and a little puffiness in his mouth and nose' was overjoyed. A few of Curtis's cantankerous backers claimed the fight was fixed. The ring-wormed winner lost to Harry Jones in the same ring on 17 January 1832 and retired after three short years in the ring.

* * * * * * * *

Spring became unintentionally embroiled in the shameful double dealings of the corruptible Jem Ward, Champion of England. After he had easily defeated Jack Carter, Ward was challenged by Simon Byrne, the Irish Champion. Their first match was cancelled due to a dispute over stage versus ring. A second match was mooted at the Castle Tavern. Accusations and counter accusations were made and deposits forfeited. The Irish called Ward a coward. That did it. Another day was fixed, with the apoplectic Ward promising to 'burst Byrne like a mealy potato'. Ward's supporters did not expect the fight to get beyond the first round.

On 10 March 1829, all highways, green lanes and rutted bohereens led to the Cricket Ground at Leicester. The elite of the Fancy, and the most distinguished amateurs thronged the streets. The Melton Mowbray hunt, in their flashy scarlet, dashed through, lending 'a sporting feature to the assemblage'. No one wanted to place a bet on Byrne. Ward was massively odds on to destroy the Celt in minutes.

Byrne rolled up in good time with Tom Spring on his arm and Tom Reynolds assisting. Ward made his entrance at the opposite end of the ground, arriving in a coach and four with his connections. He was immediately conducted to the house of a gentleman which backed onto the ground. As the spectators filed into the ground and took their places Ward was spotted chatting and plotting. He then disappeared into a privy in the garden with Peter Crawley his second 'who seemed to keep a steady eye on his motions'. The magistrates then appeared and ordered Tom Oliver, in his new role as Commissary of the Ring, to up stakes and move his ring. Everyone toddled to Humberston, ten miles away.

Crawley emerged from the privy to request a meeting with the organisers. Spring was invited as stakeholder. Crawley said Ward was unfit to fight. The news was received with blank stares and slack jaws – *Pugilistica* reported: 'Had a thunder-bolt burst among the auditors it could not have produced more astonishment or dismay than this declaration.' Crawley said Ward had passed a pint of blood on his last visit to the lavatory. No one believed him. Ward was summoned and damningly blurted that he was promised no money to lose the fight. Muttering that 'he could not win and would not lose', Ward left the room. It seems certain elements among the heavy gambling fraternity had backed Ward to lose, while the honest punters had put their bobs on him to win. Violence would have been the only outcome.

The promoters were now in a very embarrassing fix. Downes Miles noted that there were 'twelve or fourteen thousand persons of all degrees already assembled, including at least two thousand horsemen. All of whom were ignorant of Ward's conduct and were anxiously awaiting his arrival.' History does not relate which poor fellow had to make the cancellation speech – perhaps it was Spring, as maybe only he could have got away with it alive!

On his return to London, Ward was pilloried and stripped of his title. His backers deserted him, as did the hordes of trusting East Enders who loved him. Tom Spring's toothless Fair Play Club expunged his name from their lists.

* * * * * * * *

Spring, assisted by Harry Holt, was in Ned 'The Streatham Youth' Neale's corner when he boxed 'Young Dutch' Sam, the twenty-two-year-old stylist in Ludlow on 7 April, 1829. The town paid £100 to get the fight, which was poorly supported because of its distance from London. Neale wasn't in the best of shape when he arrived tired after a long coach journey. Sam, however, was 'in tip top condition and as sleek and active as a young deer'. Sam was looked after by Dick Curtis and Phil Sampson.

The ring was erected on the top of a hill in Ludford Park, just a hundred yards from the Herefordshire border. The farmers who 'behaved like trumps on this occasion, and were heart and hand in favour of the game' lent their wagons and haywains.

On Tuesday morning after a brisk walk, the fighters 'laid in a few strata of mutton chops and other belly furniture, after which they submitted to the titivation of their respective barbers who turned them out blooming as a couple of primroses'. Neale stripped a little on the lean side, but he seemed cheerful and ready to 'take a bellyful' to win. Sam looked the trained athlete, bright-eyed and alert.

Both boxed defensively at the start with plenty of pretty stops and skilful parrying. It was a contest for the purist. As they warmed up the action was became fast and violent with both men landing good clean hits. By the eighth both showed signs of facial damage. Sam had the upper hand by he twentieth but Neale 'game as a pebble' proudly toughed it out and closed on the dancing Sam and hit him hard and often. Neale's tenacity was breaking the young man's heart and there were signs the Youth was running out of gas: his jaw was slack and he was bleeding from the mouth.

By the fortieth Sam had gained a second wind and, planting his feet, he shot out fast straight punches which Neale could do nothing but ship. Spring was still hopeful his man could wear down the younger man. It was a great fight, with both men taking fierce punishment without flinching. Sam was the better boxer, but he was finding Neale a right handful. It was a joy for Spring to see his man battle with pride and grit after the dreadful Martin debacle against the same opponent.

The war raged on for round after round with both men concentrating so much on head shots their hands were sore and their nobs were like giant strawberries. Neale was getting the worse of it through the sixtieth and by the seventieth he was fighting from memory with Spring guiding him to the line. Finally in the seventy-eighth, with both men as weak as kittens, the Streatham Youth was nailed by a tremendous punch in the face. He tottered and fell, pouring blood and half blinded. It was admitted on all hands that a better fight had not been witnessed for many years. Sam had to be helped to his carriage. The golden boy was taken away by his high-born friends, having among his admirers several noble and aristocratic backers.

A quick return was planned but Sam had a dispute with the law and was bound over. It was a while before all hands could agree, but 18 January 1831 was nailed down. The location was Bumpstead in Essex. Spring and Tom Oliver were in Neale's Corner, Dick Curtis and Harry Holt in Sam's. The fight was well supported. Neale was in superb trim with Sam also in fine condition.

It was another epic battle, with both men taking and giving enormous punishment. Neale fought with speed and courage but the youngster danced and hit brilliantly, mixing his shots to head and body, moving smoothly out of trouble and going on the attack with purpose, destroying Neale's confidence with superb switch hitting. By the fourteenth Ned was in bad shape and distilling claret from many points. Sam caught him with a combination of swift lefts and rights on the face which proved to be the finisher. It didn't help when, slippery with gore, Neale fell off Spring's knee and landed on his head. The ring was broken into by invading back-slappers eager to congratulate Sam, and it was a long while before poor Neale could be taken to his carriage.

Neale, who 'had received enough to satisfy an ordinary glutton', was 'dreadfully mortified' at the result. He had trained like a Trojan and fought his heart out but Sam was just too quick to the punch, and his ability to duck below some vicious Neale hooks proved the result was no fluke. All sides were happy. Even those who lost money on Neale could not deny that it was blunt well spent. Sam was hailed by his noble friends as a young phenomenon, the best boxer at his weight in the country.

After a brilliant career, Sam became an erratic publican. A sensible wife who loved him could not save this spoilt child from himself. The once dashing young fighter occasionally exhibited his skill with the gloves on at the sets-to of the Pugilistic Association, which Tom Spring promoted at Westminster Baths. But the young man who once linked arms with aristocrats went into decline. 'Spitting blood and reduced to a shadow' he sadly died on 4 November 1843 at just thirty-six years of age.

The ring-worn Neale meanwhile, a brave man who shipped so much punishment from the brilliant young Sam, was also heading for the trapdoor. He had one more contest against Thomas Gaynor on 15 March 1831 for £300 to £200 in Staines. It was a fight too many. Spring was as usual on Neale's side, aided and abetted by Neale's former opponent, but now pal, 'Young Dutch' Sam. Neale was 'never better in his life' and Gaynor, now a publican, but not a big drinker, was supposed to have been well past his prime. Harry Holt and Ned Stockman acted for Gaynor. On paper it looked a welcome farewell present for Neale and a tidy betting coup for his faithful second, Tom Spring. Neale was a stone heavier and in the pink. Better still, at twenty-seven he was five years younger than his opponent, and he had beaten the semi-retired Gaynor previously.

The first round lasted an incredible forty-five minutes. Gaynor, who was 'as pale as a parsnip', had a 'mouse' over one eye and Neale smacked him hard on the 'ivories'. By the fourth Spring was shouting 'First blood for Neale'. In this round it was noticed that Stockman had plastered Gaynor's neck with grease to make him hard to throw. It developed into an even tussle, with both men scoring heavily. Neale raised his game as the rounds wore on and was definitely in charge and looked the stronger of the two. By the twenty-third Spring's money looked safe. Then the fight began to slip away. Neale was heavily thrown in the twenty-sixth, which seemed to take plenty out of him. 'Pro-di-gi-ous,' exclaimed 'Frosty Faced' Fogo at ringside.

In the thirty-fifth, as Neale stood dreaming at the scratch, Gaynor rushed from his corner and floored him. Gaynor was now galvanised and in the forty-fifth he gave Neale a pasting from which he did not recover. The Youth sat on Spring's knee, looking out to the world. When time was shouted Neale's head fell back Sam shook the battered fighter but the Streatham Youth out cold. It was the last time either man fought. Neale, who was mine host at the Rose and Crown in Norwood, died in November 1846 aged forty-one and was buried at West Norwood Cemetery. His friend Tom Spring would lie beside him ten years later.

On the following Thursday, Gaynor took a benefit at the Hanover Assembly Rooms, Long Acre. Tom Spring and Oliver and Young Sam were among those who put on the mittens. On Friday all the participants were invited to a dinner at Gaynor's pub, the Queen's Head, Bow Street. Gaynor died three years later from a chronic complaint of several years standing.

* * * * * * * *

Simon Byrne meanwhile, Spring's big Irish heavyweight, went to The Tennis Court on St Patrick's Day 1830 and in 'high spirits and excellent humour' he publicly challenged the rehabilitated Ward, who immediately accepted. All parties turned up at Tom Spring's crib the night after to settle the preliminaries. Ward and Byrne 'shook hands, took a drop together to make things right, after which it was agreed that Jem and Simon should have their grand turn-up four months afterwards' for £200-a-side. Ward was anxious to come in from the cold and once again be embraced as a bona fide member of the pugilistic brotherhood. Some of the old pugs felt Ward had said his penance and should be absolved.

Byrne fought Sandy M'Kay, an event that had disastrous consequences. Byrne killed his unfortunate opponent and was arrested. There were more unsavoury dealings regarding forfeits and cancellations before Byrne was cleared of the killing. After being 'duly feasted and dinner'd by the sporting world', he signed again to fight Ward. The match did come off this time, with all parties turning up on St Patrick's Day 1831 at Tom Spring's pub to sign contracts.

The venue chosen was Warwick. Both boxers were fat and grossly out of condition. Ward went to Liverpool to train and Byrne to Ireland after a stint with Ned Neale at Norwood. When Byrne returned from Ireland he looked as if he had done all his training in a pub. The week before the fight Byrne was all blubber, at least a stone overweight. Clearly Spring had played little or no part in his preparation. Ward came down from Liverpool looking sleek, determined to retrieve his lost reputation.

In a last-minute effort to lose weight Byrne stewed in a Turkish bath which did him no good at all. He was now weak and fat. On the Sunday he was drenched to the skin in a heavy shower without his coat and caught a cold while Ward remained indoors relaxed and warm. Warwick was swarming with fight fans eager to see the disgraced but hugely talented Ward murder the Irish upstart. The beaks stepped in, calling on Spring, who was in attendance on Byrne, to tell him the fight could not take place in the precincts of the town. Oliver, with his loyal helper 'Frosty Faced' Fogo riding shotgun, galloped off to check out the surrounding area. He selected a field at Willeycut in Stratford-on-Avon and began assembling the ring.

Soon a good crowd arrived and a considerable sum was collected at the gate. Every cart and haywain in the vicinity was commandeered. This meant that by the time Byrne was ready to make the journey from Warwick to the ring Spring had to hire a mourning coach – which was understandingly looked upon by the superstitious as an ill omen. To what further depths could the great former champion sink? Here was a man respected by the cream of the country squirearchy arriving for a title fight with a seriously unfit fighter in a hearse! To make matters worse, rain fell from the sky in buckets, soaking the poor 'toddlers' as they grimly splashed and slushed their way from Warwick and elsewhere.

At five minutes past one the two protagonists entered the ring. The contrast in their appearance was marked. While Ward looked tough, manly, upright and with a clear eye, Byrne looked like an old washerwoman whose best set of sheets had been swept downstream. Although he had shed nearly three stones, Ward looked mean and menacing. As for the indolent Byrne, he stood with a smarmy smile while 'the fat hung in loose collops over his drawers'. What an embarrassment for Spring.

The fight went as expected with Ward doing the hitting and Byrne doing the falling. By the third Byrne had bottled it. Ward's fans began shouting racist abuse at Byrne. The Irish in the crowd took exception and yelled encouragement to Byrne who looked at them with a bloodstained grin and said, 'It don't bother me.' Dick Curtis, Spring's elegant friend who was helping in Byrne's corner, said, 'He'll stand it.' Byrne did and actually managed to club Ward to the ground in the seventh.

Ward was unmarked, but the crowd were growing impatient at his insouciance. Some began to cheer Byrne's every clumsy, lily-livered, pot-bellied move. As the rounds ground on Ward was the stronger of the two but Byrne was slugging it out with him and he occasionally landed a decent blow. Spring kept him going with oranges and soothing words of encouragement, hoping Ward's stamina would suddenly trickle out like water from a radiator. It didn't and the East Ender did not have a mark on him as he stepped up for the thirtieth. It was all Ward now and he was dancing around hitting Byrne everywhere and at will. The Irishman's face resembled that of a boy who been caught stealing jam. He was thoroughly messed up and dog-tired. It came as no surprise when Spring pulled him out in the thirty-third. Such was Ward's nefarious reputation, a few armchair critics from the safety of their London clubs asserted that Byrne had taken a dive.

At a benefit for Reuben Marten at the Tennis Court, Windmill Street, London, Spring was invited to present the championship belt to Ward. Ward immediately retired to try his hand at running a pub. He managed a brace in Liverpool, before returning to do the same in a succession of cribs in London. The wily conman showed an artistic streak and had several canvasses hung. Indeed, Downes Miles said 'had Ward devoted himself to the study and practice of painting in his earlier years he would doubtless have attained eminence'.

Poor roly-poly Byrne died savagely and pointlessly in the ring two years later, killed by new champion 'Deaf' Burke after one of the most protracted and brutal of championship fights. In his corner that fateful day were Jem Ward and Tom Spring, who must share some of the blame by not taking their man out when he was still alive. Ward revealed the petty side of his nature by refusing to hand over his championship belt to the winner. Burke was later arrested for the killing but he was 'acquitted on the evidence of a medical man, who declared that Byrne's death was as much due to his own exertions'.

Jemmy Catnatch 'the famous catchpenny publisher of Seven Dials' penned an obituary in verse and had it distributed by his 'gruff-voiced hawkers'. This is part of the poem:

On Thursday, May the 30th day, Brave Simon took the ring,
Back'd by Jem Ward the champion, likewise by gallant Spring,
To fight Burke for two hundred pounds, a man of courage bold,
To stop reports that with Ward the battle he had sold.
(Chorus)
Mourn! Erin mourn, your loss deplore; poor Simon's dead and gone.
An hero laid in his grave as ever the sun rose on…

Spring was involved in another unsavoury incident when he was managing John Davis, 'The Manchester Black'. Spring arranged for Davis to fight Ned Savage, a cabriolet driver and a very odd individual. Savage was a tough, game middleweight, and a good boxer when in the mood – but he was not averse to the odd nefarious dealing if it enhanced his financial position. Spring had his man ready at Kitt's End, Barnet on 9 June 1829 but Savage, feigning an injury, refused to come to scratch. It was suggested that he had fallen out with his backer and Davis was entitled to the stakes. Spring persuaded the Fair Play Club to 'exclude Savage from all benefits and protections of the Club, recommending pugilists not to spar with, nor suffer themselves to be matched with him, and enjoining the public to discountenance him as a pugilist.' It had no absolutely no effect. Six months later Savage was matched with Jack Gow, 'a promising young tyro'. Gow thrashed Savage but said later that Savage had offered to throw the fight.

A young, upright boxer called Harry Woods, fired by Tom Spring's reputation for skill, modesty and fair play, made his debut under the nickname 'Young Spring'. As all he had was Tom's name and none of the Fownhope man's skill, the optimistic sprog was soon forgotten.

* * * * * * * *

Spring now began to spend more time behind the bar at The Castle. One day Tom had a visit from John Clare, the Nature Poet. Unlike the suave Byron, Clare was diminutive, inarticulate, neurotic and plebeian, 'embarrassed by a consciousness of his rustic clothes and manners'. He had 'renounced the odours of the open field' to visit London and call on Coleridge, Lamb, De Quincey, and Hazlitt.

Clare was obsessed with bare-knuckle fighters, and with three fighters in particular – Little Jack Randall 'the Nonpareil', Harry 'Sailor Boy' Jones and Tom Spring. All these men were stylish boxers with the lithe skills, elegance and speed of thought and fist to beat up and humiliate the sort of tough bullies Clare was terrified of. The poet travelled around the capital with the wide-eyed enthusiasm of a country schoolboy. He visited the Fives Court and ventured into one or more of the Fancy's habitats and spoke with his fistic idols. He visited the Castle Tavern and Jack Randall's Hole in the Wall and was so fixated by the experience he couldn't pass either pub alone for fear of being drawn into its brutal magic.

Clare was particularly fond of Bristol-born, Harry 'Sailor Boy' Jones – a very useful fighter who beat Barney Aaron and Jack Perkins. Jones was married on 28 June 1824, forgetting he had another match with one Jem Aldridge on the same day. 'Not seeing how he could let honourably put off either his bride or his challenger, he met both.' After the marriage ceremony Jones left his new wife with a friend, raced over to Pentonville, beat Aldridge in twelve minutes, pocketed a fiver before returning to his wife 'for an evening of fun and merriment before the throwing of the stocking O!'

Spring, helped by 'Paddington' Jones, worked the Sailor Boy's corner when he boxed Dick Hill at Bagthorpe Common in June 1831. The gifted Jones won in sixty-nine rounds but died soon after at the tragically early age of twenty-eight. Haunted by insecurity, poverty and lack of recognition, John Clare's mind disintegrated and he was incarcerated in a private asylum. In solitude the little man, grinning gummily, danced around his cell flinging uppercut jabs at the padded walls, dribbling and crying, 'I'm Tom Spring!'

38

Brown Beats the Butcher

After a long-running and very public feud, Spring bumped into Sampson in Merryweather's booth after the racing at Epsom. The two men swopped insults until Spring could take no more and he challenged the 'Brummagem Youth' there and then to put up or shut up. Sampson continued deriding the ex-champion, who suddenly flung off his coat and demanded instant satisfaction. Without bothering to shed his outer garments, Sampson flew at Spring, both hands pumping. They were separated by some burly gamblers in the huge crowd, but the two men engaged again and – to the delight and amazement of racegoers – two of the finest fighters in the country fought four sharp rounds.

Fighting like a terrier in the cramped confines of the booth, Sampson was getting the best because Spring required room to show off his fine fighting. A few of Sampson's friends joined in and Spring was shamefully punched and kicked. The bruised and gasping former champion invited Sampson outside to make a proper fight of it on the grass. The Brummagen Youth declined.

The next evening Sampson presented himself at the Castle Tavern and declared himself ready to fight Spring for £300-a-side, halfway between London and Bridgnorth. Spring accepted the very next day at Tom Cannon's benefit at the Tennis Court and arranged to meet Sampson at Harry Holt's to make the necessary arrangements. However, the Brummy button-maker backed off, telling Spring 'he was rather fresh' and 'declared he had no animosity towards him'.

Spring demanded an apology for the blows he received. Sampson stared at his feet for a moment and, after been persuaded by his friends expressed his regret. The good-natured Spring offered his hand, Sampson accepted it and 'over a cheerful glass it was agreed to bury the past in oblivion'.

Spring turned his attention to finding a fighter for Brown. After the debacle against Sampson it would have to be someone not too strong, not too skilled or not too fit. In other words, a bum. Spring chose a real pussycat, Isaac Dobell, a large beer-bellied man who – when he wasn't pretending to be a boxer – ran the Black Bull in Smithfield. The stakes were set at £300 for Brown against £250 for Dobell, because Spring was prepared to pay £50 for Brown to fight in his own backyard. Dobell, who weighed fifteen stones, most of which was taken up by what an observer called 'his understandings', had recently recorded back-to-back victories over Stephen Bailey, a London butcher. Dobell talked a good fight and was prepared to heavily back himself against Brown.

He trained in Middlesex under Harry Lancaster and took the 'Wonder' stagecoach from London to the fight location at Deux Hill Farm, Bridgnorth. On the way he stopped in Towcester and 'excited the wonder of the yokels by his wonderful bulk, and the amount of the stakes he declared confidence in winning'. By Monday, Dobell had made it to the Royal Oak at Bridgnorth to await his chance of fame. Brown, who had trained under Spring at Shipley, returned on Monday evening to Bridgnorth and booked into his brother's pub, the King's Head. Spring, Cribb, Ned Neale, Henry Holt, 'and several other celebrated men of the London PR' joined him there. Most of the smart money was going on Dobell to lick Spring's leaden-footed novice. When a rumour circulated that Dobell was feverish and unwell, Brown suddenly became favourite. Surely he could beat a sick, grossly overweight publican?

Then dinner was interrupted by another rumour that a local magistrate was about to serve a writ banning the fight. What followed next was pure pantomime. Early next morning Spring left the pub with Brown and headed for Deux Hill Farm, where he met with representatives of Fair Play Club who were already building a ring and surrounding it with empty wagons. The magistrate arrived and attempted to served a writ on Brown. Spring commandeered a postchaise, wrapped Brown in a blanket, stuffed his portly friend inside the coach and galloped off in the direction of the Severn Bridge, stopping just short of the toll house to drop off Brown. On receipt of an order from the toll-keeper to stop and be searched, Spring alighted with an innocent smile and opened the chaise door to allow the toll-keeper to see it was quite empty, except for a crumpled blanket in a corner. Brown meanwhile was clambering into a boat and rowing himself across the Severn. Spring picked him up from the opposite bank and doubled back to Deux Hill Farm, arriving to great cheers at half past twelve, in good time for the fight with Dobell (who was mysteriously restored to health).

A small crowd had assembled, among them the grinning Sampson who supported Dobell from the outset. Spring and Neale were in Brown's corner, Lancaster and Jem Burn in the big innkeeper's, with ex-pugilist Stockman 'The Lively Kid' as principal chaffer. Brown, whom Spring had put through the hoops for the return, 'seemed to have lost condition since his last fight and had an aged and worn appearance'. This was nothing compared to his opponent who with his distended stomach and round and portly body looked anything but an active boxer. It seemed Spring had picked the right man to get Brown back into the winner's enclosure. And so it proved.

The fight commenced with Brown trying something new. He began belittling his plump opponent, 'smiling through his arms' at the obese Londoner. Dobell, whose face bore the downhearted look of an unemployed gravedigger, shipped punishment as Brown went on the offensive. After plodding round his stationary foe like a hyena examining a dead elephant, Brown landed a tremendous smack on Dobell's nose which drew claret. Gamblers ringside shouted ten to one in Brown's favour. Almost certainly Spring had a few pounds on his man to win – Neale certainly did and was 'in high glee' at Brown's superiority. Dobell came up for the second trying his hardest to look mean. Brown, a fixed smile on his face, pasted Dobell with stiff jabs, rammed him with straight rights and then retreated. Dobell barrelled in, flinging punches in all directions, some of which hit the target. Brown responded with a fierce left hand that unzipped Dobell's eyebrow. Undeterred by the gushing stream that cascaded over his various chins and ran down his chest, Dobell rumbled forward and forced Brown to drop, ending the round.

The fight progressed with the dull thud of punches as the two fatties traded blows. Worryingly for Spring, Dobell began catching Brown with some good shots, although he was catching plenty too. Soon Dobell's 'dexter ogle had an ugly appearance but he fought bravely', occasionally inconveniencing Brown with his rumbustious assaults. The heavier hitting was mostly coming from Spring's man, who decked Dobell with 'a heavy slap on the right jaw amidst encouraging exclamations from Sampson'.

By the fourth Dobell was told by his corner to get inside. It was still all Brown, who easily dodged Dobell's intemperate rushes and 'caught the Bull's Head on the grinders and downed him again'. 'Bravo Brown,' his fans chorused, 'it's all your own! Take him away.' But in the fifth, instead of tamely capitulating, Dobell charged into Brown, hit him a few times and stood back to see the huge farmer collapse. Dobell's scattering of supporters, wound up by Sampson, cheered loudly. It was crisis time for Brown. His first knockdown came just when he seemed to have the fight won. Did he have the heart to repel the rejuvenated innkeeper? Could he emulate his famous manager and gain strength from adversity? Acting on advice from Spring, Brown boxed on the retreat, sticking out his log-like arms to keep the gluttonous Dobell at bay. It worked until Dobell rushed him and they both fell, with Brown smothering underneath Dobell's 'substantial understandings'. Spring must have been shaking his head in disbelief.

Brown boxed cagily to regain his momentum until the seventh, when another Dobell rush made the charming farmer seek the sanctuary of the grass without being hit. This did not please Dobell's fans who roared 'Fight fair!' Spring would have agreed. Brown seemed a little too keen to go down and his obsession with self-preservation began to antagonise both his own supporters and those rooting for Dobell.

After dominating the next round, Brown sunk to his knees again. It was a cowardly display. In the tenth it was the same, Brown jabbing and succeeding then going down for no reason. On receiving a blow on the back Brown cried 'Foul' but the umpires ignored it. It was a frustrating contest for trainers, judges and spectators. Brown slipped to the canvas in the tenth too, while Sampson and others showed their disgust with finger gestures. Brown was down again in the eleventh, but this time he was hauled down by Dobell, who was already sitting on the grass. It was an awful fight. In the next round after an exchange Brown caught Dobell and knocked him down. Stockman chaffed loudly, libelling the Bridgnorth giant. Brown, who seemed to have hurt his shoulder, was in no mood for insults. Dobell's corner urged their man forward but the innkeeper, in the act of landing a blow, was walloped by Brown, who then lay down.

Both fighters were now leaning on each other. Brown landed a terrific punch flush on Dobell's nob and watched as the big publican slowly measured his length on the muddy grass. However, he got up and gamely charged again in the fifteenth again. Brown floored him once more. The agitated Stockman kept chaffing but he wasn't the only one. The country boys behind Brown gave Dobell a hard time, even the older, more seasoned ring-boys indulged in disgusting and unsporting behaviour.

In the next round it was one-way traffic with Brown clobbering the dogged Dobell at will, while still being cursed and generally insulted by Stockman. At the end of the round Dobell's brother begged him to retire. As he rumbled in once more, Brown stood his ground and simply nailed Dobell in the mouth. The publican capsized like a shot stag, his eyes rolling. When he got up he reluctantly mumbled 'enough'. The fight had lasted only twenty minutes, but it had seemed like a year. It also showed that against an unskilled opponent Brown, with Spring's coaching, at times punched correctly and 'showed the superiority of length and science over strength'. Skill allied to his punching power could win Brown fights against moderate opposition. The trouble lay in the big man's frustrating lack of aggression. The handsome farmer seemed too nice to fight. 'At in-fighting neither man was clever or knew much about the correct way to throw an opponent,' a ringsider opined.

After the contest, Brown confessed that he 'was not in the best condition for the fight'. He also admitted that he was following Spring's advice in not getting to grips with the cumbersome Dobell in case he put out the injured shoulder. He was incensed by the fight-long chaffing and grabbed a whip to chastise Stockman before Spring calmly disarmed him.

Dobell returned to London convinced his defeat was due to a severe cold which meant he could not train properly. He immediately challenged Brown to a rematch at £200-a-side. Spring signed the contract but Brown discovered a knucklebone was broken in his right hand so the return was delayed. Negotiations reopened when Brown was declared fit but Dobell, on reflection, withdrew, not once but twice, each time forfeiting his £5 deposit.

The return was finally arranged for 24 November 1829 near Uckfield, Sussex, on the Crowborough Road. On the Monday morning Spring and Neale made the journey from Streatham in London to the Shelley Arms in Nutley. On the way they called in on Dobell and his seconds, Tom Shelton and Peter Crawley, who were staying at East Grinstead. 'All was in good humour, and each man seemed confident of the result of the approaching combat, no doubt booking himself as the victor.' But at the crack of dawn on a bitterly cold morning, just as Oliver and Fogo were supervising the clearing of the ground to erect a ring at Nutley, a call came from the Dobell camp saying they wanted the fight switched to Crowborough.

Officials, fans, ring builders and their labourers, no doubt collectively cursing Dobell and his clan, 'proceeded across the country, by a most villainous road, and at risk of being scattered like chaff before the wind, which blew like a perfect hurricane. While both fighters, accompanied by their managers and backers, galloped along the main roads in their warm and comfortably appointed chaises, the wind almost swept the convoy of carts hauling the timber for the ring floor and stakes, as well as ropes and straw and tools, off the road. They eventually arrived at the new venue only to find Dobell followers had already started to build the ring below a hill to give the spectators an uninterrupted view of the contest.'

Brown failed to arrive at the appointed hour. Even though the ring had still to be completed, Dobell's side rather optimistically claimed forfeit. Brown eventually appeared, but as both boxers waited for the fight to start, 'the storm raged with unabated fury and the crowd and the combatants were exposed to its utmost severity. The consequence was that hats and umbrellas were seen driving across the heath in all directions – their owners in full chase – while those who were preserved from these casualties were only secured by the aid of cord, straps, and handkerchiefs, which were so applied to resist the furious blast.'

When the fighters peeled for action the wind cut them to the bone. In Brown's corner were his manager Tom Spring and the rugged veteran Tom Oliver, with Neale assisting. In attendance for Dobell were

Peter Crawley and Tom Shelton, who was probably glad of the money. Dobell was 'lighter in weight and firmer in flesh, but still too much of the Bacchus to suit our notions of the milling hero' according to *Pugilistica*. Brown on the other hand was 'thin as a greyhound and his general appearance showed freshness and vigour'. He was two to one to win, with Dobell's friends gleefully snapping up those odds.

Following Spring's orders Brown stuck to his natural non-violent approach as the battle began. Dobell dropped his hands in exasperation as Brown prodded and pawed and waited for the London butcher to make the first move. Brown kept his guard up and ignored Dobell's posturing. Goaded by his friends to get to work, Dobell advanced, swatting as he went. He caught Brown on the cheek with a feathery blow but before he could withdraw Brown put him 'on his capacious base' with a swift punch correctly delivered to the innkeeper's frontispiece. Mercifully it finished a frustrating round that had lasted seventeen minutes.

In the second Dobell, spurred on by Shelton who yelled in his ear, 'Go in to him', rushed from his corner only to stop a brilliant right-left combination from Brown which caught the butcher in the mouth and nose almost simultaneously. It was great stuff from Brown and when Dobell hit the floor he got up with 'a purple stream distilling from his mouth and his proboscis'. The ringside bookies now were offering four to one against Dobell. In the third the normally peaceful Brown was so full of confidence he went on the attack and pulverised Dobell, smashing the fat butcher around the ring with a dazzling display of scientifically applied firepower. Where did this come from? Spring of course. His hard sparring with the amiable farmer was paying off. For the first time since he discovered Brown, Spring must have been feeling pleased and justified. If only the big man could retain this form he would surely be champion one day.

In a desperate attempt to stem the flood of violence projected at him Dobell threw a punch and broke his hand on the point of Brown's elbow. It would have made no difference. Brown was invincible. It was his day in the sun and, even with a gale howling around them, his fans were ecstatic. At the end of the round with Dobell at his feet, his head tangled in the bottom rope like a bear in a noose, Brown stepped back to allow Peter Crawley to assist the big fellow to his feet. The fight thrashed out of him, Dobell meekly gave in and left the ring pathetically clutching his broken hand. The fight lasted twenty-one minutes, including the seventeen wasted on the first round.

Dobell's concession aroused suspicion in Peter Crawley's mind. Could it have been a fix? Crawley's remarks gravely offended Spring. Crawley should have known his friend Spring would never be party to skulduggery. Secondly, because Brown had made giant strides with his boxing under Spring's skilful tutoring, Crawley subsequently regretted the aspersions he had unfairly cast on all concerned.

An exceedingly happy Brown returned with Spring to the Castle Inn. Dobell, defeated, damaged and broke, was forced to stay overnight in East Grinstead while his arm was set by a Mr Jones, assisted by two surgeons. His damaged limb in a sling, Dobell returned to the Black Bull on Wednesday night 'which instead of sparkling with illumination, looked as black as an undertaker's shop'. Such is the fate of the fighter.

During a rousing dinner at the Castle, Brown made a short speech. He raised his glass to thank Spring and his other backers and helpers, then to everyone's surprise, he announced his retirement from all claims to championship honours. Spring must have blinked, but he accepted that the 'Bridgnorth Bruiser' was the only person to decide. Brown had suffered great public humiliation and had been unfairly ridiculed by ruffians like Sampson and his Neanderthal followers. And yet he had the pride and purpose to train assiduously and he came back to win and proved his critics wrong. If only Spring had taken over as Brown's trainer when the big farmer was in his prime, harnessing the power of that right hand. Spring now severed all managerial connections with Brown, but they remained friends.

39

Brown Gets Even with Sampson

Brown's story had a satisfying ending. Two years later, ignoring the Bridgnorth man's claim to be among the retired, the boastful and persistent Sampson began a tirade through the newspapers, attacking, taunting and challenging the quietly spoken farmer to a return. At length, after nine months of chaffing, they both signed up to a fight on 19 September 1831. Sampson continued to quibble about the arrangements to try to get the last advantage. To seal the fight Brown's new connections had to pay the Brummie an extra £50, as well as conceding to him the choice of venue.

To the delight of Sampson's wily backer, a Mr Beardsworth, the fight was to be staged in Doncaster, Mr Beardsworth's home town. The exact location was to be the Town Moor but the authorities intimated their intention of interfering, so it was switched at the last minute to Pegbourn Leys, four miles away. The fight was scheduled for nine in the morning so as not to interfere with the day's racing.

A reasonable crowd was expected, due to the fact that it was race day and also because few prize fights were held in that part of the country. The choice of location illustrated how far prizefighting had plummeted as a gentleman's pastime. However, the locals rallied round and the mellow Monday morning saw that the 'thimble-riggers, prick-in-the-garter men, gypsies, and all the motley toddlers of a race meeting were gathered'. There was, however, a very poor sprinkling of the upper-crust patrons of the ring. There was also no Tom Spring in Brown's corner. Instead, the big man was seconded by 'Yorkshire'

Robinson and the old fighter, Tom Oliver. Sampson was attended by Jem Ward and Harry Holt. It was very much a provincial occasion, a far cry from the halcyon days of Byron and his friend 'Gentleman' John Jackson sitting ringside and the rows upon rows of titled men in their wigs and their finery spread out behind.

Brown was greeted with a slight murmur of applause while Sampson's mob raised their hats and hooted. Some taunted and threatened the big Shropshire man. When Brown advanced in a frank manner holding out his hand, the Brummie, eyeing Brown with a savage and defiant look, withheld his own hand and walked towards his seconds. Brown was now past forty years of age and looked it. Sampson was only thirty and had plenty of fight left in him and he entered the ring looking much more the trained pugilist. His 'attitude was graceful, indeed, elegant' while Brown's was 'constrained and stiff'.

Sampson lost the first when Brown threw the smaller man and fell on him with all the weight of a collapsing dry-stone wall. The second was more of the same with the usually aggressive Sampson being very careful of Brown's big right hand. Sampson found an opening at last and landed heavily on Brown's eye 'which instantly swelled with the force of the blow'.

When Brown attacked resolutely in the third, Sampson went down rather too quickly. In the fourth Brown, realising this was not the ferocious Sampson he boxed on the earlier occasion, began to put together a few good punches. One blow was a fair hit with the right straight on Sampson's left ear that floored him. Brown's fans were surprised.

Brown pressed and in the fifth he had a wonderful chance when he had Sampson on his knees but, 'in his anxiety to avoid any appearance of unfair advantage' waved the Brummie to his feet. Sampson paid him back by smashing a tremendous punch into Brown's right eye. Now both the farmer's eyes were damaged.

Then in the eighth Sampson suddenly 'exhibited signs of distress'. He was gasping for air and looking fatigued. Brown closed and using his massive weight advantage he threw Sampson. Sampson's friends had suddenly, and ominously, gone very quiet. Their man began the tenth with a huge lump on his forehead. Brown ended the round by hitting the inrushing Sampson with a smack with the back of his hand which felled the 'Brummagem Youth'. It was great stuff. Sampson could make no impression on the rejuvenated Brown. In the twelfth

Holt, one of Sampson's seconds, deliberately rolled into the ring and under the fallen Sampson to save direct contact with the ground.

The middle-aged farmer was not going to let his tormentor escape. His old legs, which had given away so easily in the first Sampson fight, were still strong. His throwing had also improved. In the next round the Shropshire giant picked up Sampson and flung him across the ring like a dead cat. In the next he treated Sampson to an expertly executed cross-buttock. As Sampson rose he looked 'queer and stiff'. His seething spectators smashed the outer ring and attempted to get to grips with Brown who, when trying to nail Sampson with a clumsy haymaker, missed and fell. Had the old man's wind given out? Was this the reviled Brummie's chance to turn defeat into victory?

No, it was not. Brown was moving sweetly and his big punches were landing on target – with appropriate sound effects. One in particular landed with pulverising force on Sampson's reddened face. How sweet it must have been for Brown to see the Brummie's nose explode and shower the ringsiders' immaculate shirts with claret.

In the twentieth Sampson's rowdies decided to take a hand. They smashed their way towards into ringside seats where 'several robberies were effected'. The cries and denunciations of Brown were furious. In the twenty-first Brown gleefully hammered Sampson with punch after sledgehammer punch until the shattered Brummie 'fell across the ropes where Brown hit him with four or five more blows, until he fell stupefied'. What would Spring have given to be in Brown's corner at that moment? But Sampson's thugs had seen enough. With a thunderous stream of oaths and the crashing of chairs and screams from the molested, they charged, one man 'pressed into the ring with a bottle in his hand'. Brown was struck. Enraged, the bleeding rustic battered Sampson into the dirt.

The Brummie was allowed a full three minutes to recover by a fearful official, who stopped the fight then fled to a Doncaster pub with a glass of whiskey in his shaking hand, having declared Brown the winner. Sampson's friends were not having that. They picked up their shattered hero and placed him wobbling at the scratch. Brown's seconds told their man to box on. Brown walked up to the befuddled Birmingham bully and flattened him. Sampson's fans leapt on Brown and hit him with a ring stake and kicked him in the eye as he lay on the ground.

To save his life, Mr Marshall, Clerk of the Course of Wolverhampton, ordered that Brown should be removed forcibly from the ring. Brown was immediately accused of deserting his post and the purse was withheld. Beardsworth, who 'skated on the very edge of honesty', said as Brown left the ring that he had given the money to Sampson. It appears that he was persuaded to do so by a large number of Sampson's fans who 'had hunted him up'. Brown left the ring penniless, while Sampson quickly disappeared with the cash and celebrated his untoward victory with his henchmen.

The big Shropshire farmer took Beardsworth to court at the Stafford Assizes the following March. The jury, under the direction of Mr Justice Littledale, gave the verdict to Brown. Beardsworth refused to pay on time and it was left to Brown's lawyer's to seize Beardsworth's horse at Ludlow as it lined up to race. Brown got his money and the horse won the race! Having secured justice, Brown retired to run a pub in his native town, where he earned the respect of his neighbours and customers. Tom Spring would have been proud of the big farmer.

40

The Middle Years

Spring kept in touch with boxing as an official, or sometimes merely as a spectator. Ridiculed by church leaders and small-minded politicians, prizefighting was all but out on its feet. A few old Corinthians still attended and past champions Spring, Cannon and Curtis were among a small gathering on 20 November 1832 who saw teenage sensation Owen Swift take on Londoner Jem Collins. Swift embarrassed Collins with his speed of foot and fast hands and he ended the fight with a knockout in the twenty-first round. Then, in true Terry Downes fashion, the dapper and unmarked Swift dressed quickly and watched the remaining bouts from a comfortable ringside seat. In 1835 laws were passed to ban bull and bear baiting, as well as Spring's own particular vice, cock-fighting.

By the middle of the 1830s, the epicentre of the fighting game had moved from London to the provinces, with fights staged in Birmingham, Bradford and Sheffield. Once important locations like Moulsey Hurst were now seldom used. Open spaces for recreational purposes were very much at a premium. By 1833, 'from the increased value of Property and extension of Public buildings, many inclosures of open spaces' had taken place, limiting access 'for exercise or amusement to the humbler classes'. 'The poor have no relaxation,' Joseph Kay said, 'but the alehouse and or the gin palace.'

The Castle had become a mausoleum of memories for nostalgic fight fans. In 1835 young Branwell Brontë came through the Castle doors while he was in London to join the Royal Academy Schools.

Tom Spring in middle age.

He immediately fell under the spell cast by the Castle and its ageing and famous landlord and the lad returned to Haworth broke, having deposited his blunt in Tom Spring's till.

Again, Spring continued his connection with the Fair Play Club but the organisation revealed its lack of teeth when the old champion sent an edict to Jem Ward in 1835 demanding he should defend his title or surrender it. Ward, as Tom Cribb would have done, thumbed his nose and said it was none of the Club's business. Lacking influential support and cash to help alleviate the plight of broken down old fighters living in squalid penury, the continuing existence of the Fair Play Club was a struggle from then on.

Spring joined a number of very distinguished old fighters, including Gully, Cribb, Crawley, Belcher 'Young Dutch' Sam and Curtis, at the Nick Ward versus 'Sambo' Sutton battle in a secluded paddock near Finchley in 1835. After starting in a sprightly fashion, and giving the lumbering Sutton something of a boxing lesson, Ward, the younger brother of the more talented Jem, at the first sight of his own blood quickly lost interest in the eleventh round and walked out of the ring. This did not impress the august gathering of old champions, but they were at least amused by the winner standing on his head and singing a song. He could also dance a hornpipe on his head and spar with his feet at the same time. There was, it seems, no end to Sutton's talents – but they did not including boxing ability.

An old rival of Spring's died the same year when Josh Hudson the 'John Bull Fighter', succumbed to 'the free life of a publican' at a comparatively youthful thirty-eight years of age on 8 October at the Flying Horse in Milton Street, Finsbury. Hudson's bickering with the sober-sided Spring not withstanding, he was a popular man among his fellow bruisers and the leading sports journalists of the day, especially Pierce Egan. Hudson was described by the writer as a rumbustious figure in many ways, who was 'fond of a mill' and irritating practical jokes but 'remarkably inoffensive' with 'a heart of gold'. Spring might have quibbled at that description.

With the departure of men like Hudson, a new temper of moral seriousness was invading society. Bare-knuckle fighting was becoming increasingly anachronistic. Egan was nearing the end of his brilliant journalistic career. It was a time for reflection, a last opportunity to weigh up and evaluate pugilism and its most memorable actors. In

1836 he wrote in *Every Gentleman's Manual*: 'Since the days of Cribb, Molineaux, Spring, Neat, Cooper, Hickman, Jem Ward, etc, the ring has not exhibited any big or great men, possessing anatomical beauty, with corresponding talents, so as to excite the attention of the public.' In 1837, Victoria ascended the throne 'to gaze over the nation in her austere, disapproving way'.

* * * * * * * *

Tom Spring continued backing his fancy and placing bets for others who didn't pay up when they lost, although he never managed to make the hostelry pay. Like most boxers, Spring was not a great businessman and at times only just managed to keep his head above water. He continued to attend fights with old friends, regardless of the quality of the fare on offer. With Cribb, Dick Curtis, Belcher, 'Deaf' Burke, Barney Aaron and Johnny Hannan, he was among a tiny crowd in a meadow near Finchley on Boxing Day 1838 to watch Jack Carter, a lightweight and no relation to the old heavyweight, fight Kendrick. Although a stone and a half heavier, Kendrick proved himself, according to *Bell's Life* in London on 30 December 1838, a 'regular muff', putting up 'an abject performance'. Kendrick was punched in the eye twice 'which brought about his prompt capitulation'.

In 1840 'Lord Chief Baron' Nicholson invited Spring to attend a meeting to establish a Benevolent Institution for decaying pugilists. Nicholson was there in place of the inconvenienced Dowling. 'Spring', Nicholson wrote, 'as is well known, was a man of peace, and no provocation, however annoying, would have led him into mill or melee. It would, indeed be a work of supererogation to say that he was an honourable man and a good fellow.' The meeting was held in The Castle and, being well attended by old fighters, got off to an unpromising start. Ned Neale, Dutch Sam and Owen Swift were enjoying a quiet drink and a chat when they were insulted by Enoch Price, a 'huge railway contractor from Warwickshire who'd had sufficient to make him ripe'. Spring, who had grown used to fighting men inflamed in drink and putting up their dukes, speedily got rid of the combatants, and order was restored.

In 1841, a weekly newspaper called *Tom Spring's Life in London & Sporting Chronicle* appeared. Published by W.M. Clark, a 'Wholesale

Dealer in Cheap Publications' it ran for three years. Its short life was an indication of the waning popularity of bare-knuckle boxing. The days of the big promotions, the great outdoor spectacles that attracted upwards of 30,000 fans (who travelled mighty distances, many with just enough blunt to gain admission and buy a pie and a jug of cider) were gone. Much of the panoramic colour, the laughter and the money-making had been drained from boxing. The self-important magistrates tearing around the country waving scraps of paper, the muddy fields, the fogles, the gentry in their splendid carriages and the packed, warm and raucous inns when all humanity blended were a thing of the past.

That Tom Spring accepted the slings and arrows of bare-knuckle boxing is illustrated by the Charles Hunt cartoon of the fight between Johnny Broome and Jack Hannan on a freezing January day in 1841. Tom is seen standing ringside with old warriors Tom Cribb, Peter Crawley, and the man who accidentally killed his friend Simon Byrne, 'Deaf' Burke. Vincent Dowling is shown sitting on the cold grass furiously scribbling an account of the fight. Many of the fights staged were minor dust-ups – matches made between novices for a tenner a side, which was still a sum many could not come up with. Spectators included 'the rouged and villainous countenance of the brothel-bully, the saloon girl's fancy-man, or the wary and well dressed figure of the swell pickpocket. These, with a few dirty-looking mechanics and butchers at a hob-nob, compose the present audience.'

Spring allowed the Castle to be used to drum up support for the rematch of William Perry (the 'Tipton Slasher') with Freeman, an American. The pub was half full and backers had difficulty raising the modest stakes required. Spring had attended the first fight between the two men when the police stepped in to wreck the contest. The bold captain of police added insult to injury by recruiting Oliver, the Commissary that day, and Spring to help clear the crowds. Boxing was on the ropes. Jackson had lost interest and was spending his time organising a benefit for the starving peasantry of Ireland. Spring accepted work as a second or trainer to anyone who would have him and was a familiar sight at ringside, now slightly portly but as pleasant and as accommodating as ever.

41

Spring Stages a Comeback for His 'Old Dad'

Tom Cribb, the great old champion and Spring's former trainer, manager, mentor and surrogate father, was in straightened circumstances. He was asked to hand in his licence at the Union Arms due to unpaid debts. The boxing legend was spending his time looking after a sick relative and living with one of his sons, a baker in High Street Woolwich. The Pugilistic Club staged a benefit for the all-time great at the National Baths in Westminster Road on 12 November 1840. Spring, at forty-five years old, struggled into his breeches to make a comeback to support his old friend. In the opposite corner stood the formidable Ben Caunt, the current champion.

If Caunt thought he would take it easy with the old timer he was in for a shock. Wearing gloves to protect those delicate hands, Spring shrugged off his robe to reveal a body that still looked hard and relatively fat-free. And when he took up his familiar stance the crowd yelled and clapped. The years were rolled back as Spring advanced on the champion, flicking out jabs and easily avoiding the Nottingham man's wild counters. While Caunt 'evinced a sad ignorance of the art' Spring, who boxed with 'an ease and mockery of effort' made the champion look 'anything but a well-scienced man'.

'Caunt, a hot headed fellow with a short fuse,' the report went, 'hits at random and has no idea of defence.' The exhibition over the crowd rattled the boards and yelled their approval as Spring, with hardly a bead of sweat on his forehead, took a bow. Spring later took to giving Caunt lessons and the two became friends. On the same bill Tom

Belcher, now a sprightly forty-seven-year-old, gave a dazzling display of jabbing, swaying and getting away. It was a great night for the veterans and it revealed the paucity of talent in the ring at that time.

At the end of July, Reuben Marten, a forty-two-year-old con-man, was training for a match against an Australian named Gorrick who fought under the pseudonym 'Bungaree'. One of Marten's seconds was to be Dick Curtis. On Saturday 6 August, as Tom Spring was crossing Finchley Common after visiting Tom Belcher, he saw Marten in the Bald Faced Stag in the company of three very unsavoury characters. Spring was certain they were plotting something. Sure enough, Marten threw the fight, going down without a hit and staying down after four-and-a-half minutes of comic inaction. Martin, who once managed a minor bruiser called Tom Hurley, defrauded every man he met, including the baker and the landlord whom he depended on for his daily sustenance. He refused to pay Curtis his second's fee but Spring invited his friend Curtis and the other out-of-pocket ring assistants to the Castle where a subscription was made on their behalf. Martin ended his days in poverty.

42

The Final Years

In 1842 Frederick Gale published a fascinating account of his visit to Tom Spring's back parlour. He was wandering the streets of the capital one cold February day when 'a name on a lamp close to Gray's Inn gateway' caught his eye. 'That name was Tom Spring. Could this really be the famous inn where the great Tom Spring was mine host? Could a man have really seen Tom Spring and then walk about afterwards as an ordinary citizen?' 'I pictured to myself,' Gale wrote, 'a prize-fighter as a ruffian who lived on nearly raw meat, knocked everyone down who contradicted him, and into his mouth went nothing but brandy. My curiosity overcoming my scruples I walked up the passage into the Castle, and found myself in a very comfortable bar, behind which stood a tall, broad-shouldered man, who looked a very well-to-do Baptist minister, minus the hypocritical smile which some of those gentlemen assume – an oily, unctuous, cold, untoasted-muffin expression.'

Gale continued, 'The man must have been nearly six feet high, if not quite, and boasted a pair of very broad shoulders. His hair was getting slightly grizzled, as were his whiskers, which were bushy, but I shall never forget his eyes. If I remember rightly, his eyes were rather far apart; and in speaking, a kind of frown, which was not an angry frown, seem to come over his face and wrinkled his forehead a little. His nose was disarranged from the acqualine somewhat, as most of the PR heroes experienced. He had a nice voice and a frank and open manner, which stamped him as one of nature's gentlemen. He was dressed in an evening black suit, though it was early in the afternoon – for he always dressed for dinner – and wore a white neckcloth, and a brooch with some hair in it in his shirt frill, and his boots were polished in a manner such as I never saw surpassed.'

'I stood looking at him in blank amazement, and I thought to myself, "Can this man be Tom Spring, the great prizefighter?" Spring looked at me, and said with a smile, "Well, young gentleman, what are you staring at?" My answer was, "Are you really Tom Spring?" "Well I was Tom Spring this morning," he said, "and I suppose I am now."' Gale ordered bread and cheese and a glass of stout. Spring 'summoned his niece from the back parlour, which opened out into the bar and placed my lunch on the counter. She was a widow of very considerable dimensions. A little curly-headed waiter, named Hickman, a relative of the celebrated Gasman, and a pot boy, Joe Phelps, brother to Brighton Bill, completed the establishment. It was a very quiet, orderly household.'

Gale became a regular at the Castle, lunching there most days and after a while he was invited to Tom's inner sanctum. 'But I never smoked a pipe in Spring's parlour,' he recalled. 'Smoking was not allowed in the daytime in the front bar, and never in the private parlour. The Castle Tavern was a quiet, cosy place, well removed from Holborn by a long passage, and there was a homely appearance about it all. There was generally a well-to-do cat snoozing in the sun, and a bird hanging up in his cage, which drew his own water with a little bucket and chain, and a thrush or blackbird singing, and frequently some flowers. In fact, nothing could be less like a prize-fighter's home. The Castle was a bona fide luncheon house.' Gale wrote that:

Bullet head ruffians… dressed in flash coats, with cheese-plate buttons adorned with fighting cocks and fancy devices and wearing fur caps, had no place in that bar. They might go in the taproom, if they did not get drunk or use bad language; though if they did, the way down the passage was speedily shown to them, and they would as soon have thought of insulting Tom Spring as a little parish clerk would of kicking the Archbishop of Canterbury. The old school, consisting of such men as Spring, Peter Crawley, Jem Ward, Jem Burn, Frank Redmond, and the like, had a position; having been backed by noblemen and gentlemen of the highest rank, they had acquired that natural good-breeding which is engendered by associating with people much above them in society.

Spring and Gale became firm friends. Gale, a nervous, unworldly young man in a teeming city 'with few friends and fewer opportunities to get out of his rooms' appreciated Spring's kindness to him. When he began to order brandy and water to appear flash, Spring gently guided him back to stout with the admonishment, 'Look here young gentleman, you will go to the dogs if you drink brandy and water at this time of day, and under twenty years of age, too.' Spring told Gale he never drank before dinner, and never had a glass of anything in the bar unless his niece was there to take the money.

Spring also lectured his young friend on the evils of card playing, which prompted Gale to write: 'I owe it to Tom Spring's advice that I hardly ever won or lost a sovereign at cards or in betting in my life.' When he challenged Spring about the old champion's own weakness for gambling Spring replied: 'You mind what the parson said – do as I say; don't do what I do.' Spring went on: 'When I used to fight I carried hundreds and thousands of other people's money; and when I had it, I used to put on some of my own; and what is bred in the bone must come out in the flesh. And then, I am very fond of a horse, and I do like to back a man too, when he is a good one.'

Spring revealed his thoughts about training and fighting. It was very important, he said to have a 'very cheerful trainer'. As for being a full-time fighter, Spring said 'having nothing to do and a good job in hand was very pleasant, particularly when you got over the stage when a man did not know what thirst was, and health and strength were coming every day; but the hard work was when you felt fit to fight twenty men, and the day was two or three weeks off; then I could see my trainer was fidgety, and I fancied that my backers might be fidgety too, and I would get suspicious, and would think they were keeping my friends away from me, or that too many people came to see me, and were writing about me in the papers; in fact it was a terrible time of trial and temper and patience; and when the time really did come, and I threw my hat into the ring, and saw my colours tied to the stakes, it seemed like taking a ton weight off my mind, and I would not have changed places with the King of England.'

Asked if he remembered his fights clearly, Spring said, 'Most of them, for, you see, when a man fights he sees nothing of the crowd round him, but his whole attention is on his opponent's face.' Recalling some of his fights, Spring said 'I can see now when I missed finishing a man off, or when I was open, and he never took advantage of it. Now about the pain. A heavy body blow or a bad fall must always tell, and hands will suffer; but the head blows weren't much at the time, when a man's in training and his blood's up, except, of course, behind the ear or parts like that, any more than a hard blow on the leg, which would make a man dance for a week in cold blood, hurts a cricketer hit by a ball in summer. You may depend on it that the greatest pain to a good man is to find he has lost, and that they have given in for him. A man feels down and done for. All his trouble is thrown away, and he fancies he may have lost his friends too; but if he happens to win, no matter how much he may have been punished, he feels fit to jump over the moon.'

Gale asked, 'What do you think of the Ring now. Is it better or worse?' Spring replied, 'There always were black sheep in the Ring, and now there are more black sheep than there were. They manage to get a fight or so, and call themselves fighting men, and set up low ginshops and make small matches, when "win, tie, or wrangle" seems to be the motto. Such men were pudding-faced ruffians who could not stand one in the face from a boy.' 'Mr Jackson,' Spring said, 'was trusted by the highest in the land to arrange what we called "Prize Battles" when I first began, and any fight with a lot of noblemen behind Mr Jackson was pretty sure to be square, and if a young man really could fight, and did not show the white feather, he might make his way, if he took care what company he went into; but if he was ever seen in company with blacklegs, he was marked. The worst of the Ring was that, when a man had a house (pub) and wanted to make money quickly, he would keep a kind of raree shop, and sell any poison to anyone who would come and drink it, and then he generally went into the trap himself, and drank himself out.'

'The grand secret,' Spring said 'was to keep a good name and keep your friends. Why, all kind of gentlemen come in here at Derby time or Cattle Show week, sometimes a lord, or a baronet, or old country gentlemen who saw me fight my early battles perhaps, many of them twenty years old older than I am – and they treat me like a man, and come for old acquaintance sake; but I don't care for your swaggering betting man, half gentlemen, half, or more than half, rogues. Some of the sporting publicans will let any of these fellows pat them on the back, and call them 'Bill' or 'Jack' or 'Tom', and think their sixpennyworth of brandy-and-water is a great consideration. I wouldn't give sixpence for the whole gang. This is my house, and I am landlord, and I choose my own company.'

Gale recounted the occasion Spring lost his temper with a drunken sailor who insulted his niece after she asked him politely to leave. The sailor responded with a 'dreadful oath and called her a horrible name'. Spring was furious, so mad his hair 'almost stood on end. He let fly at the sailor in words somewhat warmly. The soldier eyed Spring up and down and said if he had been a younger man he would have knocked him down; and began to take his belt off. Spring had seen enough. Like a flash he came from around the bar and he grabbed the sailor, dragged him to the door and booted him down the passage. He returned seconds later with his temper completely under control. 'That fellow fight?' he said, 'Why my niece could beat him.'

'Spring was a very industrious man,' Gale wrote, 'sometimes in a white smock-coat when he was arranging his cellar. He enjoyed life. He knew a good horse, or dog, or gamecock, and was a good judge of farming.' Gale met him at the Cattle Show once 'amongst the Herefordshire shorthorns' and marvelled at how 'his countrymen welcomed him. Top-booted, sturdy farmers and graziers and their daughters crowded round him. Spring's opinion, particularly as he was originally apprenticed to a butcher – was cordially asked for.'

Tom Spring and Frank Redmond were among the guests invited by a third party to the shoot on a fine estate in Hampshire. The landowner was horrified. He 'expected wholesale slaughter and every kind of poaching'. Imagine his surprise when he received a letter from Spring apologising for accidentally shooting a hen-pheasant (hens being sacred in January). In his letter Tom said 'he fined himself half a guinea for his mistake, and had it paid to the keeper'.

Gale recalls the sad day he read in the newspaper that Spring had lost his youngest son John from a sudden illness. He rushed to the Castle

Tavern and was told by 'Mrs B,' (Tom's niece), that the governor was sitting alone, and very bad indeed. Gale found Spring 'sobbing audibly, with tears running down his eyes as he was trimming a gamecock for Peter Crawley'.

43

'Gentleman John'
Jackson Dies

1845 was the year in which the great 'Gentleman John' Jackson died aged seventy-seven and was given a send-off fit for an emperor. Spring, meanwhile, his hair greying and his face lined, was among the roughs near Greenhithe trying to referee a riotous encounter between Joe Roe and Harry Broome. A thousand spectators showed up determined to fight among themselves, create mayhem and make it impossible for order to be kept and the boxers to exercise their trade. A huge force of police were unable to break up the riot.

Disgusted by the ugly proceedings, Spring left the ring and the fight was abandoned. One of his past rivals, Jack Carter, passed away in Thames Street, in his native Manchester, on 27 May 1844. The former shoemaker was fifty-five years old.

In the same year the connections of Ben Caunt and William 'Bendigo' Thompson turned up at the Castle Tavern to pay the final deposit for their forthcoming title fight. Both men looked superbly fit. Caunt had trained at Hatfield, the Marquis of Salisbury's country seat, supervised by his uncle, Ben Butler, and Jem Turner 'The D'Orsay of the Ring', with constant visits from Tom Spring. The fight ended in recrimination and abuse with Caunt losing in the ninety-third round.

In 1846, Cribb, then about sixty-eight years of age, hobbled over to the Castle to pay Spring a lengthy visit. Cribb occupied his usual chair by the fire. Gale was present and he heard the champion's accounts of his early fights and of his two great battles with Molyneaux. The old champion also talked of Spring's great fights with Langan and Spring poured him a liqueur glass of neat whisky from a keg which Langan had sent him 'as a token of respect and affection, and in memory of the fight'.

Cribb, buckled with age, agreed to spar with Tom Oliver simply to raise a few pounds for his benefit. A huge crowd attended. 'It was a tremendous crush,' Gale wrote, 'and of course the old man could not spar, but he just showed us the old guard with his right fist held a few inches off his face, and his left hand advanced a little before it, and a few inches higher. It is impossible to exaggerate the wonderful reception which he received from people of all classes.' Spring, 'looking like a gentleman, in his black trousers and close-fitting white jersey, was there to spar with anyone put before him, and there were a great number of very tough men there who sparred with a good deal of fire.'

Gale attended many benefits with Tom Spring. The two men were 'found at the Westminster Baths and elsewhere'. Benefits, once a good night out for the fan and a decent source of income, had become meagre, penny-pinching affairs. Many of the better-known fighters were reluctant to travel long distances to help out an old friend. Spring, it was said, 'despite his winnings in the ring and his other sources of income, always seemed short of money.' Henry Downes Miles suggested Spring was addicted to gambling. A measure of the public's affection for the feckless Herefordian was that a healthy £500 was raised for Spring in 1846.

****

On 17 March, St Patrick's Day, Spring heard the sad news that Jack Langan had died. The Irishman was only forty-seven years old. Langan 'a fine story teller, good singer and hard-working and friendly landlord of the St Patrick's house pub in Liverpool had salted away his money and didn't want for any material thing.' He often came to London to visit Spring at the Castle Tavern and chat to old friends from his fighting days. Langan was worth over £30,000 when he died. His adversary Tom Spring was still alive and recieving recognition.

'After an excellent dinner' at the Castle on Tuesday 19 May 1846, Vincent Dowling 'initiated proceedings by alluding to the pile of letters he had received on Spring's behalf. Every one of which bore testimony to the public and private worth of Spring, who was a man of unblemished integrity, benevolence of heart, urbanity of disposition, and unquestionable courage.' Dowling, who had watched Spring from the first hour they met could conscientiously say that in his opinion 'a more honest or a more high-principled man did not exist'. He only regretted that 'every pugilist in England could not be assembled in that room to witness the fruits of a career distinguished by these virtues, as it would afford them the best encouragement to persevere in the same course, and probably elicit similar marks of favour'.

Spring's final bauble was a noble tankard in silver, of the capacity of one gallon, or six bottles of wine, with a lining of 450 sovereigns – the balance of a subscription of over £500 raised by the ex-champion's friends. The tankard, which was executed by Messrs Hunt and Roskell, was a work of art, ornamented with chased bands of leaves of the British oak and English rose. The cover was surmounted by a bold acorn, the outer edge having in raised letters, 'The Spring Testimonial'. On the shield it bears the inscription:

Presented

By Public Subscription to

THOMAS WINTER SPRING

Ex-champion of England,

In Testimony of the Sincere Respect in which he is held

For his Pure and Honourable Conduct

During his Long and Unblemished Career

In Public and private Life.

1846

Dowling hoped 'that Spring might long live to see the trophy grace his table, in addition to his other cups, as a sterling respesentative of his merits, and of the sincere respect to which he had entitled himself'.

After a short pause Spring rose, almost overpowered by his feelings. He knew not, he said, how to express in words the overflowing sentiments of gratitude with which his heart was bursting. He could not persuade himself that he was 'any better than other men', but he hoped he 'did not give ground for shaking the confidence of his friends'. Spring could not sustain such self-possession and, placing his hand on the on the tankard with deep emotion, concluded by saying, 'I can only thank you, and all else I might say I must leave to your own hearts to imagine.' There were loud and continued cheers to this and William Sant, Spring's last backer, proposed the toast.

44

Cribb Dies and Spring Declines

Tom Cribb – once the nation's hero and the man who beat the black invader Molyneaux, the fighter who was eulogised and lionised by every bare-knuckle-fancying nob and yob in the kingdom – died, as so many old fighters do, poor and bemused. Cribb's declining years were disturbed by domestic troubles and severe pecuniary losses and he was obliged to give up the Union Arms to his creditors. The greatest bare-knuckle fighter of all time stole quietly away with the sour smell of poverty and dough in his nostrils above his son's bakery on 11 May 1848.

Spring visited the sick old man just before he died. Cribb lay grey-faced, his once vigorous life ebbing from him. At the sound of his 'boy's' voice Cribb suddenly sat bolt upright, bunched his lumpy old fists and flayed the air. 'The action's still there Tom,' he said, 'but the steam's gone.' The once-Herculean battler was forgotten by the fair-weather toffs who lived off his fame when he was tearing the fighting world asunder, but posterity would remember him. 'As a professor of his art he was matchless, and in his observance of fair play he was never excelled; he bore a character of unimpeachable integrity and unquestioned humanity.' A huge monument, designed by the same man who sculpted Jackson's tomb, was carved from a twenty-ton slab of Portland stone and was erected over his grave eight years later. It bore the legend: 'Respect the ashes of the brave'. Cribb had a massive funeral; the ordinary folk, who looked upon him as a national hero in the way they looked upon Nelson, turned out in great numbers to see the old man off.

Spring would soon follow his old mentor, for he was ailing in 1849 when he accompanied Gale to see Keen and Grant box. Located on the Surrey-Hampshire border the fight nearly did not take place when the farmer in whose field it was appeared demanding rent. Spring and Jem Burn offered him £3, but the rustic demanded £5. After a wrangle he got it. Just as the fight was about to commence, a fine hunter-chaser cleared a high hedge near the ring. All eyes, including Spring's, turned on the new arrival. The rider dismounted and announced he was a magistrate. He lit his cigar and dropped a hint that the constabulary would not be here for at least two hours, whereupon the crowd gave him three cheers. The magistrate, after enjoying the set-to, gave a guinea to the loser.

The same year another old friend, Pierce Egan, who wrote with a rattling gaiety, couldn't talk the sunken-eyed cove with the rusty scythe out of it and was compelled to obey the awful summons. Pierce was sorely missed by milling lovers everywhere, who gathered round their festive board uttering lamentations and no doubt raising glasses of Daffy in his name.

Vincent Dowling, sadly, was to soon experience the other, more brutal, side of boxing. The genial pensioner was refereeing a contest when he was coshed by a belligerent spectator. If it wasn't for Spring's quick reactions, Dowling might have been killed. The fight featured the undisciplined Tom Paddock, 'The Redditch Needle Pointer', who made something of a habit of fouling his opponents. When Dowling disqualified him for hitting his opponent when he was down, Paddock's friends advanced on the elderly and civilised man and began kicking him. Flinging punches at chins and bellies, Tom Spring, who was ringside, soon cleared the ring and helped Dowling to his feet. Sadly the once robust reporter never fully recovered from the effects of the injury and he died two years later. Dowling was avenged when Paddock eventually fought Bill Perry. He gave Perry a violent blow after a round was ended and was mercilessly stalked by the Tipton man who chopped, cornered, battered and belaboured him until 'his face resembled the inner organs of a bullock'.

* * * * * * * *

As Tom Spring declined in health and strength, young Tom Sayers was fighting for fivers and building up a reputation. Spring had taken on a young welterweight called Dan Collins to help around the Castle. The lad wanted to be a fighter. Collins was quick and sharp – a boxer rather than a bulldozer, just like young Thomas Winter when he came to London determined to make his name in the prize-ring. And just like Cribb, another old landlord and former champion, Tom took the lad in and gave him work washing glasses, waiting on tables and acting as curate behind the bar.

Spring, gasping a little, taught the young man a few cute moves. The lad improved and was soon ready to fight in public. When he heard Sayers was looking for an opponent, Spring put up Collins's name and the match was made at £25-a-side, at Edenbridge in Kent, on 22 October 1850. The two novices fought nine rounds before the police moved in to stop the fight, which was just as well for things were not going too well for Spring's boy. Collins, a report said, 'was very clever, and as game as they make them; but his pretty style was useless against Sayer's resolute, business-like way of going to work.'

Boxers, management, backers, seconds and ring makers, followed by a stream of chattering spectators, headed off to nearby Red Hill to continue the scrap. The two youths fought another thirty-nine rounds before darkness fell, forcing the referee to stop the fight. Both men were heavily punished, but Collins had much the larger share of wounds. The contest was declared a draw.

When his scars healed, Collins was anxious to have another crack at Sayers, the kid who was destined to become one of the greatest fighters of the bare knuckle era. The return was arranged for 29 April 1851. Tom Spring had but sixteen weeks to live, but there was to be no fairytale ending. On the contrary, it all ended tragically for Collins. Sayers had improved substantially, adding science to his big-hearted style. Collins hadn't and although he fought like a hero, he had to give in after forty-four rounds as his face was frightfully bruised and both eyes were nearly closed. That wasn't the worst of it. Collins, Spring's last young protégé 'went stone blind soon after the sponge was thrown up'.

Ten years after Spring's death, the same Sayers would come to Herefordshire as a renowned champion bedecked with numerous medals as the band played 'See the Conquering Hero'. Sayers, wearing his championship belt sparred three rounds with Mr Brown of Yarmouth, in a tent by the river at Ross, 'much to the satisfaction of the vast assembly'.

Tom Spring's monument.

Bill Perry, 'The Tipton Slasher', came up to London in 1851 to be under Tom Spring's tutelage for his forthcoming fight with Harry Broome. In love with the fight game up to the last minute, Spring was too ill to be of assistance. His condition gave cause for concern. His son, Thomas William, helped man the Castle pumps while his father lay dying upstairs. The tough and wiry Spring, who battled with broken hands against Langan, finally succumbed to a combination of dropsy and a lingering heart disease. On 20 August 1851, the year of the Great Exhibition in Hyde Park, when 'Britain was approaching her noon of Empire, when nearly one third of the earth's surface would be joyfully be incorporated in her imperial designs', Tom Spring died. He was fifty-six years of age. He had fought 393 rounds in the prize ring and 'for a considerable time been suffering under a severe indisposition until his case had been pronounced hopeless by his medical attendants'.

On Sunday 25 August, Tom's remains were followed to West Norwood cemetery by several mourning coaches, and other carriages. In the leading vehicle were his surviving son, Thomas William, Mr Price from Hereford (his solicitor and executor), a Mr Elbam from Piccadilly and Henry Downes Miles, author of the classic three-volume *Pugilistica*. Spring was interred in a low-numbered grave he had the foresight to have purchased previously. A monument was erected and inscribed 'Peace to his Manes'. 'Few men who have led a public life', Downes Miles wrote, 'have less reason to dread the last call of time.' A gaudy mock-Grecian obelisk, carved from porous bath stone, was erected above the grave. It bore a head purporting to be Spring's. At the foot of the object a lion slept with a lamb. The symbolism was obvious.

The *Hereford Times* of 23 August 1851 in their obituary referred to the 'worthy, manly, upright, mild, brave, urbane ex-champion'. The *Hereford Journal* of 27 August declared that he would be remembered as an 'upright, sterling, worthy, and brave man' who retired from the ring 'carrying with him an upstanding character having earned the confidence of his patrons and the respect of numerous friends'.

Pugilistica had said of his career that 'A new era in boxing arose about the period of Spring's appearance'. Egan, who saw them all, said, 'If Spring does not rank with the late Jem Belcher, a Cribb, or a Gully, he is well acquainted with boxing, and knows a little of everything about the points of milling towards victory.' Gale wrote, 'Tom Spring died, as he lived, respected.' No longer would old members of the Pugilistic Club and men of rank, give him a call, have a bottle of wine, and talk over old times. 'No one,' Gale said, 'ever heard him say an unkind word, or saw him sponge upon anyone, or do a shabby trick of any kind'. The clergyman who attended his deathbed wrote a letter in *Bell's Life* about Spring's last moments and told how he left life as he had lived – an honest Englishman. *Bell's Life* also reported that William Gladstone, while sitting to dinner with young Etonians, was asked by one, 'Can you tell us Sir who was the Champion of England in 1824?' 'Why Tom Spring of course,' the old gentleman replied.

Vincent Dowling died in 1852 and Spring's old friend, supporter, faithful bottle carrier and second, Ned Painter – the only man to lower Tom Spring's colours in the prize ring – died a year later. Painter was the same age as Spring, fifty-six.

****

What of Spring's position in the pantheon of bare-knuckle champions? Downes Miles insisted that for 'an artificial fighter' one with 'no natural hits belonging to him', Spring had 'overcome these defects of nature' and become a 'celebrated tactician'. 'Spring,' he said, 'without what are vulgarly called 'natural' capabilities for fighting, has become Champion of England.' The Herefordian 'was always cool and collected with good legs' and was 'the greatest master of the art of self defence. And if he could not hit hard, almost prevented others from hitting him at all.' In spite of his 'defects', Downes Miles placed Spring in the highest place on the boxing list.

Tom Spring's large frame occupied grave number 154, Square 61, and he could not be buried in a better place. Around him the ground was crammed with sporting heroes of one kind or another. There were several ancient cricketers, a footballer, a wrestler, a billiard player, a marksman and 'conjuror', a cyclist and acrobat, two athletes (both, bizarrely, knights of the realm), a brace of racing journalists, and several old fighters, including the Broome brothers Harry and John, and Tom's friend, Ned Neale, the 'Streatham Youth' whose blood he had mopped in battles in which poor Neale was allowed to take too much punishment. Now this brave young man who had gritted his teeth, gamely stood his ground and flat-footedly swung, was mouldering under a modest tomb next to the imposing pile on top of his idol and second, Tom Spring. A bookie rotted nearby. What conversations their ghosts must have had!

★ ★ ★ ★ ★ ★ ★ ★

The monument quickly deteriorated in the London smog but as a proof of the respect in which Spring's memory was held it was handsomely restored by public subscription, at considerable cost. The Duke of Beaufort was among the subscribers.

★ ★ ★ ★ ★ ★ ★ ★

George Borrow in *Lavengro*, published in 1851, reflected on the passing of the great days of prizefighting with the lament: 'for everything there is a time and a season. How does the glory pass from it. What a vigorous aspect pugilism wore at the time. Let no one sneer at the bruisers of England. I now see them upon the bowling green, the men of renown, amidst hundreds of people of no renown at all, who gaze upon them with timid wonder. Cribb, "perhaps the best man in England", Jem Belcher, "the most scientific pugilist that ever entered a ring", Shelton, "whose one blow would unsense a giant", little Jack Randall "the king of the lightweights", Ned Turner the Welshman, Bulldog Hudson, "Fearless" Scroggins, the Black Richmond, the most dangerous of blacks, even with a broken thigh. Purcell, who could never conquer till all seemed over with him and Tom Spring, a true species of English stuff, sharp as Winter, kind as Spring, unbought by yellow gold, the unvanquishable, the incorruptible. 'Tis Friday night, and nine by Holborn clock. There sits the yeoman at the end of his long room, surrounded by his friends: glasses are filled and a song is the cry, and a song is sung well suited to the place; it finds an echo in every heart – fists are clenched, arms are waved, and the portraits of the mighty milling men of yore, Broughton and Slack who adorn the walls appear to smile grim approbation. None better since the days of Spring in the British ring did stand. Can the rolls of English aristocracy exhibit names belonging to more noble more heroic men than those who were called respectively, Pearce, Cribb and Spring?'

45

Spring Dies Comfortably Off

Those who thought Spring an inveterate gambler were clearly mistaken when one examines the following document. The list includes two gentlemen availing themselves of Tom's excellent bed and breakfast.

In his will, which was shakily penned a matter of weeks before his death, Spring, in spite of all the hints about his excessive gambling and pathetic inability to look after his money, died a comparatively wealthy man. Like the cagey millionaires of his native county who dress in greasy rags, drive clapped-out Toyota pickups, and lean on knobbly sticks at the City market, Spring concealed his worth. He owned the Castle Tavern as well as land in Marden and Fownhope in Herefordshire. The bulk of his estate went to his surviving son, Thomas William Winter, who was twenty-six years old at the time and who seemed to be attempting to make a career for himself as a classical singer under the classical cognomen, Melchior. Upon receipt of his father's largesse, Thomas William seems to have disappeared off to Australia, taking some his father's more interesting memorabilia with him. And what became of Spring's wife Elizabeth, his partner in pugilism, pubs and mother to his two sons? There is no doubt they parted company some years before his death.

An article in the *Hereford Citizen* of Friday 24 September 1954 gives the tale an intriguing twist. It seems an old lady named Winter was picked up off the streets of London in the 1860s and taken to the beadle of Wapping parish, Mr Stocks, who applied to Mr Woolrych

1851 UK Census
Occupants of Dwelling

```
County and City Location:  Middlesex -A St Andrew Holborn
Dwelling Location: Page 11, Number 26
Address: HIGH HOLBORN 25

                         Position      Marital
Name                     in Family     Status   Age Sex
WINTER, THOMAS           HEAD          WIDR      56  M
WINTER, THOMAS           SON           U         26  M
EDGINGTON, CATHERINE     HOUSEKEEPER   U         40  F
BRIDGES, JOHN            WAITER        MAR       38  M
OSBORNE, SARAH           SERV          U         25  F
PRIOR, JOHN              POTMAN        U         18  M
FELKIN?, WILLIAM         VISITOR       MAR       38  M
RUSTON, RICHARD          VISITOR       MAR       38  M

More info on above names:

                                     Approximate
                                       Birth
Name                     Occupation    Year   Birth Place
WINTER, THOMAS           *LICENSED VICTU1795   TOWNHOPE @ HEF
WINTER, THOMAS                         1825    HEREFORD @ HEF
EDGINGTON, CATHERINE     HOUSEKEEPER   1811    ALNWICK @ NBL
BRIDGES, JOHN            WAITER        1813    WICKHAM MARKET @ SFK
OSBORNE, SARAH           GENERAL SERVANT1826   GARSBROOK? @ SFK
PRIOR, JOHN              POTMAN        1833    OXFORD @ OXF
FELKIN?, WILLIAM         STOCKING WEAVER1813   NOTTINGHAM @ NTT
RUSTON, RICHARD          COACH MAKER   1813    BYFORD @ HEF

Data above that did not fit in the allotted space is indicated
by the character * and is shown in full below:

* LICENSED VICTUALLER
```

1851 UK census occupants of Castle Tavern.

'to receive the legal examination of a poor woman who was in the garb of a pauper'. The woman had for some time been 'chargeable to the parish of St John, of Wapping, the County of Middlesex'. When questioned under oath she said her name was Winter and she was the wife of the late English Bare-knuckle Champion Tom Winter, whom she had married in St Peter's Church in Hereford in 1821 and who died in 1851. She said her legal settlement residence was above the bar at the Castle Tavern, 25 High Holborn. Mr Woolrych signed the necessary papers and the woman was forthwith removed to the workhouse of St Andrew's, Holborn, in September 1861.

I Thomas Winter of the Old Castle Tavern
Holborn in the County of Middlesex Licensed Victualler do hereby revoke
all Wills Codicils and other testamentary dispositions by me at any time
heretofore made and declare this to be my last Will and testament I desire
that all my just debts funeral and testamentary expenses shall be paid by
my executors hereinafter named I give and devise my messuage or dwell
ing house wherein I now reside called The Old Castle Tavern aforesaid
and also a piece of land called the Slough situate in Hawkers Lane in
the Parish of Fownhope in the County of Hereford and also a piece of
land situate at Wyatt in the Parish of Sutton Saint Nicholas in the
same County with the rights incomes and appurtenances to the said
messuage or dwellinghouse and pieces of land respectively [xx]
unto my son Thomas Williams Winter his heirs and assigns I give
and bequeath unto Vincent George Dowling Esquire as a mark of my
esteem the silver snuff box which was presented to me by Peter Henly
Esquire of Cheltenham [xx] I give and bequeath unto my friend Thomas
Hancock late of Bayswater the silver cup which was presented to me
by Mr Sant And I give and bequeath all my household goods and furniture
Stock in trade book debts plate subject to such two specific gifts [listed] herein
and *all other my personal estate* whatsoever and wheresoever unto
my said son Thomas Williams Winter his executors administrators and
assigns and it is my Will and I so therein require that the silver cups
presented to me by the Inhabitants of Manchester and Herefordshire and
the silver cup presented to me in London shall not be sold or parted with
but shall be preserved and kept by my said son and his descendants as
heirlooms in the family but nevertheless the said wish and request
shall not be construed to abridge or restrict the absolute property of my
said son or his descendants in the said silver cups And I appoint the said
Thomas Hancock and George Green of the Paymaster Generals Office
Particular *Executors* of this my Will and I authorize the acting
Executors or Executor for the time being of this my Will to satisfy any
debts claimed to be owing by me or my estate and any [?injuries?] to which
I or my estate may be alleged to be subject upon any evidence they or
he shall think proper and to accept any composition or security for any
debt and to allow such time for payment either with or without taking
security as to the said acting executors or executor shall seem fit and
also to compromise or submit to arbitration and settle all accounts and
matters belonging or relating to my estate and generally to all [xx] [xx]
[xx]
[xx] thereto as they or he shall deem expedient without being responsible
for any loss thereby occasioned In witness whereof I the said Thomas
Winter have to this my last Will and testament set my hand this twelfth
day of April one thousand eight hundred and fifty one --- *Thos Winter* ---
Signed and acknowledged by the said Thomas Winter as his Will in the
presence in presence at the same time and who in his presence and in the
presence of each other have hereunto subscribed our names as witnesses
Chas Price Green 6 Stone Buildings Lincolns Inn ---------Hen Winter
14 [?24?] Collier Place Camden Town
On the the 5th Novr 1851 Admon, with the Will annexed, of the Goods
chattels and rights of Thomas Winter late of the Old Castle Tavern Holborn
in the County of Middlesex Licensed Victualler deceased was granted to
Thomas William, in the Will written Williams, Winter the son and resi
duary Legatee named in the said Will having been first Sworn duly to
administer, Thomas Hancock and George Green the executors named in
the said Will having first renounced the probate and execution thereof
as on Acts of Court appears.

A formal copy of Tom Spring's will.

Where did Spring make his money? By all accounts he was not a great businessman, like Belcher before him. Most recorded comments about Spring's business acumen are negative. Perhaps he was not such a hayseed after all? As a stakeholder for many years he could have made money legitimately. Boxers used their fame to contact wealthy backers when an interesting match was in prospect. The backers, probably after a good night's entertainment, unquestioningly doled out the cash. The stakeholder then retained part of the money as commission.

When Nat Langham become mine host at the Cambrian Stores and Mitre in St Martin's Lane as a 'financier in affairs connected with the Prize Ring' his name stood high with everyone except the profes-sional pugilists, who rightly or wrongly, had an idea that 'whenever a match for, say £50-a-side, was made, Nat used to get at least three times that amount from the swells who patronised his house'. Apart from Jem Burn, Owen Swift, Peter Crawley and one or two more, they all did it.

46

Tom Spring, Forgotten and Remembered

Spring joined other luminaries in Hutchinson's *Herefordshire Biographies* published in 1891 but only after the compiler agonised as to whether it was appropriate to include a mere prizefighter with such important figures as Nell Gwynn. 'Some may possibly object,' Hutchinson wrote, 'to the inclusion of this "worthy" in these Biographies.' Hutchinson could not deny that Spring had 'attained to considerable distinction', even if it 'was not of the highest or most ennobling order'. However grudgingly, it was still a singular honour for the humbly born Fownhope man to be included with the likes of Roger of Hereford, the twelfth-century mathematician and astronomer, Roger Mortimer, the warrior and statesman (died 1330), Sir Richard Whittington, merchant and philanthropist (died 1423), Thomas Traherne, son of a shoemaker and author of Christian Ethicks, David Garrick, actor (died 1779), Richard Payne Knight, classical antiquarian (died 1838), Sir Uvedale Price, horticulturist and essayist (died 1829), James Cowles Prichard, physician and ethnologist (died 1848) and artist James, 'Jemmy the Sketcher' Wathen (died in 1828).

* * * * * * * *

Tom Spring was forgotten until 1951. A century after his death there was a sudden flurry of interest in the old champion. A Herefordshire policeman, Sergeant A.V. Lucas, formed the Tom Spring Memorial

Committee, the object being to to provide for the restoration of Spring's memorial in West Norwood. A second objective was to erect a rustic monument made from a cider mill with a suitably inscribed bronze plaque. Lucas, according to the *Hereford Times,* 'reverently, calmly and joyously' laid a wreath of laurels on the obliterated mound of stone that was once Spring's magnificent tomb, while a friend placed a sprig of oak leaves, and a spray of cider apples on Spring's grave on behalf of the Herefordshire Boxing Association. A bronze medallion made in Ross on Wye was affixed bearing the original inscription 'Sacred to the memory of Thomas Winter Spring, born at Fownhope, Herefordshire, 22nd of February, 1795 and died at the Castle Tavern, Holborn, 20th August, 1851.'

Lucas also helped raise a cider press memorial in Woolhope, a couple of miles from Spring's actual birthplace at Witchend in Fownhope. A plaque made from stone quarried from Capler Hill, an ancient site where Spring may have played as a lad, was inscribed:

INVICTAE FIDELITATIS PRAEMIUM

THOMAS WINTER

Born at Rudge End, Fownhope, Herefordshire, February 22nd, 1795, and Died at the Castle Tavern, Holborn, August 20th, 1851. Buried at West Norwood Cemetery, London. Erected by his countrymen of the land of cider, in token of their esteem for the manliness and science which in many severe contests in the pugilistic ring, under the name of

SPRING, CHAMPION OF ENGLAND 1823/24.

'Thou mighty master of the milling set
More potent far than any that have met
In P.C Ring; may Mars, who watches o'er,
The half-stripped votaries of the sawdust floor,
Protect thee still, and round thy laurels cling,
While Cribb, with iron lungs, shouts 'Go it, Spring!''
Boxiana, Vol. IV. 1824.

THE LIFE AND DEATH OF
THOMAS WINTER SPRING.

But boldly in the ring we could depend on Spring,
For honour and glory he would fight.

Poor Tom Spring was never bought, all his battles well he fought,
In is praise Old England would sing,
All classes far and near, so delightfully would cheer,
And their motto was Victory & Spring

We have left you all do know, Tipton caunt and Bendigo,
And numbers connected with the ring,
But search all o'er the land, you will never find a man,
To equal poor Thomas winter Spring

Britions will record his praise, whil in the tomb he lays.
And call him an honour to the ring.
A marble stone complete, shall be placed at head and feet,
Saying here lies poor Thomas winter Spring

In Holborn he did dwell and he was respected well,
And when his neighbours looked upon his bier,
There did many grieve full sore, saying alas he is no more,
And for Spring was shed many a tear.

But tom was doomed to go, and lay in the shades below,
And his leaving caused the ring, to deplore,
And honest britons say, in his grave be happy lays,
Alas ! Thomas Spring is no more.

Then lay down the belt so low, the gloves on his tombstone throw,
Thomas winter Spring, was an honour to the ring,
And he's travell'd to the shades below.

We once had a Champion, his name was Winter Spring.
A man both upright and kind,
By high and low esteemed he was loyal to his Queen,
So brave and so noble was his mind.

Chorus.

Then lay down the belt so low, the gloves on his tomb stone throw,
Thomes winter spring, was an honour to the ring,
And he's travelled to the shades below.

He boldly fought and beat Jack Langan Ward and Neate,
And all who opposed him in the ring,
There never was a man, who was born on Britain's land,
Could speak disrespectful of Spring.

He was born as you shall hear in famed Herefordshire,
Where all did the champion adore,
They presents him did give, and they wished him long to live,
But alas poor Spring is no more:

He did oppercsion hate, no advantage would he take,
He was allways manly and right,

T. Hodges, Printer, Toy and Marble Warehouse, 31, Dudley Street, Seven Dials.

In memoriam Tom Spring.

The Old Cider Mill Memorial at Woolhope, Herefordshire, dedicated to Tom Spring.

The unveiling, which took place on Saturday 21 August 1954 was an appropriately local affair, with a good deal of energy and goodwill extended to their dead hero by the men, women and children of Fownhope. After the unveiling a group of rustics in smock frocks raised their drinking horns and recited the one time famous slogan vociferated by Spring's supporters to encourage him on to victory: 'Spring and old cider! Spring for ever!' The Fownhope Floral Dance began at the crossroads by the church and lolloped through the village to great laughter and good humour.

In 1992 Spring was elected to the International Boxing Hall of Fame, taking his rightful place alongside his blood brothers Jack Johnson, Joe Louis, Rocky Marciano, Jack Dempsey, Joe Frazier and Muhammad Ali. On the 150th anniversary of his death Spring merited a footnote alongside President George Washington, philosopher Artur Schopenhauer, and film director Luis Bunuel in *The Times*. Some going for a butcher's boy from Fownhope.

Bibliography and Notes

Bare Fists, Bob Mee, Lodge Farm Books 1998

Bareknuckles, Denis Brailsford, Lutterworth Press 1988

Boxers and their Battles, Thornaby, R.A. Everett and Co. 1900

Boxiana, Pierce Egan, London the Folio Society, Edited by John Ford 1976

Boxing Companion, The, edited by Denzil Batchelor, Eyre and Spottiswood, 1964

Bucks and Bruisers, J.C. Reid, Routledge and Kegan Paul 1971

Cashel Byron's Profession, George Bernard Shaw, Constable and Co. Ltd. 1932 Edition

Clare, John, and the Picturesque Landscape, Timothy Brownlow, Clarendon Press, 1983

Cruikshank, George: His Life in London, Michael Wynn Jones Macmillan 1978

Cruikshank – Social Change in Graphic Satire, Alan Lane, Penguin Press, 1967

Dictionary of National Biography, edited by S. Lee, Smith Elder, 1909

Drawing in England, Lindsay Stainton and Christopher White

English Spy 1825⁄6, The, C. Malloy Westmacott, Bernard Blackmantle

Fancy, The, John Hamilton Reynolds, Garland Publishing Inc. New York and London, 1977 edition

Festival of Britain (1951) History of St Peter's Church, Hereford, By Charles Evans

Hereford Civic Trust Newsletter no. 50 Winter, 1992/3 for a word picture of the modern Booth Hall in Hereford

Gentleman Jim Corbett, Patrick Myler, Robson Books 1998

George IV 'The Grand Entertainment', Steven Parissen, John Murray, 2001

Great Prize Fight, The, Alan Lloyd, Cassell, 1977

Hazlitt, William Essays, Folio Society 1964 edition

Herefordshire Biographies, Hutchinson, editor, 1891

Herefordshire Field Name Survey, Woolhope Club, Archaeology Section

Hogarth to Cruickshank, Social Change in Graphic Satire, M. Dorothy George, Allan Lane Penguin Press, 1967

Illustrated History of Boxing, The, Harry Mullan, Hamlyn, 1990

In the Wind's Eye, Byron's Letters and Journals, edited by Leslie A. Marchand John Murray, 1975

Inns and Friendly Societies of Monmouth, E.T. Davies and K.E. Kissack, Mon. Ed. Trust 1981

Lavengro, George Borrow, Everyman, 1970 Edition

London Anthology, The, Hugh and Pauline Massingham, Phoenix House, 1950

Lord of the Ring, Peter Arnold and Bob Mee, Hamlyn 1998

Manly Art, The, Elliot J. Gorn, Robson Books 1989

Memoirs, The Life of Daniel Mendoza, edited by Paul Magriel. B.T. Batsford, 1951

Modern English Biography, Frederick Boase, 1965 edition

Muhammad Ali Ringside, Compiled and Edited by John Miller and Aaron Kenedi, 1999

Modern English Biographies, Frederick Boase, 1965

Noble Art, Tom Sawyer Unwin Hyman, 1989

Noble Art, The, Compiled by T.B. Shepherd, Hollis and Carter, 1950

Old Buffer, The, Frederick Gale, 1888

Pictorial History of Boxing, A, Sam Andre and Nat Fleischer Hamlyn 1998 edition

Pigot's Directory of Herefordshire, 1822/3

Popular Recreations in English Society, Robert W. Malcolmson 1700-1850, Cambridge University Press, 1973

Prizefighting, John Ford, David and Charles, 1971

Pubs of Hereford City, The, Ron Shoesmith, Logaston Press, 1998

Pugilistica Vol. II, Henry Downes Miles, Weldon and Co., 1880

Punches on the Page, David Rayvern Allen, Mainstream Publishing, 1998

Regency Rogue, Dan Donnelly and His Legend, Patrick Myler, The
    O'Brien Press, 1976

Road Travel and Transport in Gloucestershire, Nicholas Herbert, Alan Sutton
    and Gloucs. County Library, 1985

Rogue's Progress, Nicholson, Lord Chief Baron, Longman's 1965 edition

Rowlandson, John Hayes, Phaidon, 1972

Rowlandson Drawings, John Reilly, Paul Mellon Collection R.A.
    Exhibition, 1978

Rural Rides, William Cobbett, 1967 Edition, Penguin Press

St Peter's Church, Herefordshire, A Guide by Charles Evans and John
    Warren

Sound of History, The, Roy Palmer, Oxford University Press, 1988

Strange Encounters, James Brady, Hutchinsons, 1946

Sweet Science, The, A.J. Liebling, Grove Press, 1951

Thurtell-Hunt Murder Case, The, Albert Borowitz, Robson Books, 1988

Twenty and Out, Mickey Duff, Collins Willow, 1999

Up to Scratch, Tony Gee, Queen Anne Press 1998

What Do You Know About Boxing, W. Buchanan-Taylor and James Butler,
    Heath Cranton, 1947

Wedlock's the Devil, Byron's Letters and Journals, Volume 4 1814/15, John
    Murray

West Norwood Cemetery's Sportsmen, Bob Flanagan, Friends of West
    Norwood Cemetery

Wimbledon and Putney Commons, Alan Phillips, M.A. Wimbledon and
    Putney Commons Conservators

Worcester, the Book of, David Whitehead, Barracuda, 1976

Worcester's Hidden Past, Bill Gwilliam, Halfshire Books 1992

Worcester, A Pictorial History, Tim Bridges and Charles Mundy, Phillimore
    1996

Worcester, People and Places, Bill Gwilliam, Halfshire Books, 1993

DOCUMENTS

Baptisms and Burials, Hereford St Peter's Parish
Bird's Index, Hereford Journal, 1770-1821
Connop, Thomas, schoolmaster in Fownhope, 1802, L99/10
Fownhope Census, 1841
Fownhope Burials, 1813-1852
Fownhope Land Tax Returns
Fownhope Manor list of tenants etc. AB 47/1/9
Fownhope Parish Book-HRO AC 18/17

HEREFORD RECORD OFFICE:

AB 47/1/2 Fownhope Manor Court Rolls. NB Wych End on the 1841
Tithe Map, Print 1829, E 12/ IV/ 22744, Pamphlet 506, Spring at
Booth Hall, Letters, A95/V/W 74-76, Tom Spring's Trophy, K38/
F/S2, Lease of Booth Hall, AE79, Pamphlet 504, Photographs and
Article, Y24/1-4, County Presentation, A95/V/W/74-6, Trophy K38/
F/52, Pateshall's Collection, Box 54, 95/V/W/A/84/87/88, Winter
Spring, Thomas, signed Lithograph, 184.9
Pilley Collection 942.44 Hereford Country Library Reference Section
Last Will and Testament of Thomas Winter

NEWSPAPER AND MAGAZINE ARTICLES

Country Quest, April, 1970, 'Two Fisted Tom' by Jack Bartlett

Hereford Journal
12 July 1819, report of Spring matched with Neat for 100 guineas
10 January 1824 account of First Spring/ Langan fight and account of
Thurtell's Hanging
21 January 1824, Fives Court, Richmond Benefit, featuring Josh
Hudson
4 February 1824, Letter from Spring to Langan
7 February 1824, Spring and Langan arrive in London after their battle
in Worcester

9 June 1824, confusion re: location of second fight
16 June 1824 Second Langan fight, preview, Spring at Randall's Benefit
12 July 1819, Announcement of Match

Hereford Citizen and Bulletin
Friday, September, 1954, article on Spring's wife by Charles Evans
Field, The, 7/4/1960 Letter by Derek Evans, re 'Pottery Picture' of
    Spring/Langan fight (Newspaper Cuttings Book IV LC 942.44,
    Hereford Reference Library)
Field, The, 7/6/1960 Letter re: William Sant's snuffbox by his grandson
    (Newspaper Cuttings Book IV LC 942.44, Hereford Reference
    Library)
Hereford Snaps (Pilley Collection), drawing of cup presented to Spring

Hereford Times
30 January 1889, 'Recollections of Ross 60 years ago', letter to the
    editor by T. Sherwood Smith; 22 February 1919 (K38/F/52/62); 29
    May 1926, letter from John Preece. Articles on Spring: 20 July 1951,
    15 August 1951, 17 August 1951 and 24 August 1951, 28 August 1951,
    20 August 1954 (outline of Spring's career),7 October 1955 and 18
    November 1955 (on proposed restoration of Spring's Monument
    in West Norwood Cemetery); 28 February 1956, exhibition on
    Tom Spring in Hereford Library Entrance Hall; 7 October 1955,
    'Memorial Jug Found in Leominster' (See Newspapers Cuttings
    Book IV p.11); 'Farmer's Son Who Became Bare-Fist Champion of
    England,' article by Peter Walker; 'The Fownhope Carrier' 1860, a
    poem by M.M. (reprinted from *Hereford Times*).

Memorial at Fownhope unveiled 21 August 1954, (Scrapbook III, four
    photographs, LC 942.44, Hereford Reference Library)

WEBSITES & MULTIMEDIA

cyberboxingzone.com
familysearch.com
Pubsindex@pubsindex.freeserve.co.uk

THANKS TO:

Frank Keating for encouragement and cover picture; Brian Gange for additional research; Roy Palmer for boxing songs; Tony Davidson for photographs; Mark Aston, Librarian (Local Studies); Tony Jones for illustrations; Pam Burke for new information; Camden Library, for finding and photocopying relevant material; Hereford Record Library; Hereford Library, Reference Section; Ross Library; Worcestershire County Library; the Wright family in Hereford (who are related to the Winters and who still hold a family bible 'bought at Hereford July the first, 1775'); A.V. Lucas for his singular efforts to keep Spring's memory alive; Ken Pearce, Fownhope butcher, for tips on old-style butchering and James Howarth and his team for editorial assistance.